Teaching English As a Second Language:

An Annotated Bibliography

Garland Reference Library of the Humanities (Vol. 23)

Teaching English
As a Second Language:

An Annotated Bibliography

Compiled by

Wallace L. Goldstein

Garland Publishing, Inc., New York & London

1975

016.42824
G 624

Copyright © 1975

by Garland Publishing, Inc.

All Rights Reserved

Library of Congress Cataloging in Publication Data

Goldstein, Wallace L
    Teaching English as a second language.

    (Garland reference library of the humanities ; no. 23)
    Includes indexes.
    1. English language—Study and teaching—Foreign
students—Bibliography. I. Title.
Z5818.E5G64 ₍PE1128.A2₎ 016.428'007   75-17987
ISBN 0-8240-9991-5

Printed in the United States of America

Dedicated to my parents

Contents

Preface

This critical annotated Bibliography is intended for anyone teaching or preparing to teach English to people whose native language is not English. The Bibliography should also be helpful to administrators of English-as-a-second-language programs and to those people who have an interest in the teaching of English as a second language in the communities in which they live.

More attention is being paid to the need for ESL programs today than ever before. They not only function as separate programs but are also an integral part of widely expanding bilingual education programs. The reader can use this Bibliography to locate sources of information that discuss theories of second language learning, the techniques of teaching, ideas in developing curricula, the use of materials, and other topics related to the general subject.

The entries have been selected because they include helpful information about teaching English as a second language. The Bibliography sources are texts and guidebooks; reference materials; articles found in a variety of periodicals and anthologies; speeches and papers presented at conferences; city, state, and federal reports; graduate dissertations; and unpublished writings and speeches.

Most of the entries are those published after 1965 since several annotated bibliographies are available up to that date and because there have been so many changes in the approaches to teaching English as a second language since that time.

Entries with ED numbers are those that have been entered in the ERIC system and are available through the ERIC Document Reproduction Service.

All entries are divided into seventeen categories in order to help the user locate information easily. Since the category on

PREFACE

Methodology is so large, it is divided into two sections—A and B—merely for the convenience of the reader.

A key-word and an author index are included at the end of the Bibliography.

I am indebted to my colleague, Edward Powers, for his advice, and to the ESL teachers in the Greater Springfield area who helped to select many of the entries. I also owe thanks to Catherine Handy, assistant librarian at Westfield State College; to many other college librarians who generously offered me their assistance; and to Elizabeth Johnson, my typist. I am especially grateful to my wife Shirley for her important contributions and encouragement.

Wallace L. Goldstein

ADULT

1   Appleson, Marilyn and Barry Semple. English and Citizenship Programs
     for the Foreign Born: A Handbook for Teachers. Trenton, New Jersey:
     New Jersey State Dept. of Education. ED 066649.
          A guide for those teaching English language skills and citizen-
     ship to adults who are learning English as a second language.
     Suggestions are presented in using subject matter and methods.
     Some of the chapters are devoted to planning the curriculum,
     identifying problems in pronunciation, and instructional tech-
     niques. Lists of materials are included.

2   Bailey, Nathalie, Carolyn Madden, and Stephen D. Krashen. "Is there
     'Natural Sequence' in Adult Second Language Learning?" Language
     Learning, 24, 2 (1974), 234-243.
          The authors tested two hypotheses: 1) adults learning English
     as a second language will show agreement with each other in the
     relative difficulty of functors in English and 2) the adult rank-
     ings will be more similar to that of the child learning English
     as a second, rather than a first language. After testing 73
     adult subjects in 8 classes in ESL at Queens College, New York,
     the researchers found support for both hypotheses.

3   Baskoff, Florence. "A Writing Laboratory for Beginning Students of
     English." Journal of English as a Second Language, 3, 2 (1968),
     83-92.
          Since it was found that adult students taught by audio-lingual
     and structural methods were confined to writing only in brief sent-
     ences without knowing how to use many modifiers and function words
     properly, a writing program was developed for them. Each lesson
     contained a model composition, vocabulary lists, comprehension
     questions, an outline model, quizzes, and other aids. After meet-
     ing two hours a week for three semesters, students improved in
     many areas of writing and gained confidence.

4   "Building Communication Skills: Home-School Community." July 1, 1970
     to June 30, 1972. Florence-Firestone Project. Los Angeles, Calif.:
     Unified School District, 1972. ED 075689.
          Description of an ESL project for parents of Mexican-American
     students in the Florence-Firestone neighborhood of Los Angeles to
     create better dialogue between home, school, and community and
     permit parents to learn the language of the school. Morning and
     evening classes were offered in ESL for two academic years. Ex-
     cellent results were achieved. Parents understood the school
     system better, and attendance at school functions and parent and
     civic meetings increased.

5   Hanamia, Edith Almas Shahla. "Acquisition of English Structure: A
     Case Study of an Adult Native Speaker of Arabic in an English-
     Speaking Environment." Diss. Indiana Univ., 1974.
          A case study in English language acquisition of an adult native
     speaker of Arabic in an English-Speaking environment in order to
     determine how an adult proceeds to learn a new language, the methods
     used, the constraints under which the learner functions, and the

factors influencing development. The subject, receiving very little training, acquired the use of English in its early stages in a similar manner to that of a child learning his first language but at a slower rate. Overall similarities indicated that many of the same kinds of cognitive processes are utilized in adult and child language acquisition.

6   Mackey, Ilonka, Schmidt. English 1: A Basic Course for Adults. Rowley Mass.: Newbury House, 1974.
A practical book designed to teach adults the essential material required of them as new immigrants in English-speaking countr The text uses words and situations immediately needed by the students, and teaches an essential vocabulary of 475 content and structural words. Items that are learned at the beginning are re-used throughout. A Teacher's Manual detailing the oral work accompanies the book.

7   Martinez, Antonia, J. "An Analysis of the Present Status of the Teaching of English as a Second Language to Puerto Rican Adults in New York City." Diss. New York Univ., 1970.
An analysis and evaluation of the status of the teaching of English as a second language to Puerto Rican adults in New York City. The methods used in gathering data for assessment will be of more interest to people associated with adult ESL programs than the results. Thirty teachers were observed in the classroom and were rated with a Teacher Observation Checklist. In addition, all ESL textbooks were examined and rated according to a set of validated criteria.

8   Mattran, Kenneth Joseph. "A Study of Programs of English for Adult Speakers of Other Languages in Public Schools in the State of Michigan." Diss. Michigan State Univ., 1973.
This is a result of a survey conducted in the State of Michigan to obtain information useful to adult educators and other professionals in the field of English as a Second Language. Significant findings include the following: 1) Specific training in ESL teaching was not required; 2) The majority of ESL teachers had only minimal training in this field; 3) All responding teacher taught the subject on a part-time basis; 4) The Oral Approach and the Direct Method were most widely used.

9   Mullen, Dana. A Plan for Fluency First. Ottawa: Canadian Dept. of Regional Economic Expansion, 1971. ED 056565.
A report that offers information useful to teachers and administrators in ESL programs for adults. It describes the program for adults not literate in their own language with material close related to the individual's interests and experience. Working with disadvantaged adults in the northern prairie lands of Canada, teachers stressed the use of dialogue and also prepared language lessons to help students in reading and mathematics.

10 Navajo Adult Basic Education. Chinle, Arizona: Navajo Community
    College, 1971. ED 061492.
        There is some material in this report that is pertinent to
    teachers of adults who are learning English as a second lang-
    uage. The NABE (Navajo-Adult Basic Education) programs offered
    approximately 18 hours of classroom instruction each week by
    instructors and assistants who received special in-service
    training. The use of Navajo Community College's facilities and
    faculty serves as a model for similar programs that would profit
    from the utilization of community college resources.

11 Nixon, St. John. "Organizing an Advanced Course in Spoken English for
    Dutch Businessmen." The Modern Language Journal, 52, 5 (1968), 287-292.
        The methods used, the selection of participants, and the eval-
    uation of this course should provide valuable information to
    organizers and teachers of adult students of English as a second
    language. The course had to be an intensive one since the busi-
    nessmen were very busy and the subject matter had to be practical.
    Classes were held from 8:30 p.m.-10:00 p.m. for two-week periods.
    Lessons included structure drills, drills on audio-visual repeti-
    tion, pronunciation, dictation, discussion, and telephone exercises.
    The author found that the participants (35 to 60 years of age)
    considered writing more important than the speech training they
    were taking. General improvement was noted as the program pro-
    gressed.

12 Oskarsson, Mats. "Assessing the Relative Effectiveness of Two Methods
    of Teaching English to Adults." IRAL, 11, 3 (1973), 251-262.
        The primary purpose of this study was to investigate whether
    the audio-lingual or the cognitive theory provided the better
    basis for teaching English to adult students. Students from the
    elementary English groups participated in the experiment and took
    a general proficiency test before the lessons and an aptitude test
    following them. Each group received different training (audio-
    lingual or cognitive) covering the same material. It was found
    that adult learners acquired "grammatical competence in a foreign
    language better by a cognitive method" than by the audio-lingual.

13 Preston, Dennis R. "English as a Second Language in Adult Basic
    Education Programs." TESOL Quarterly, 5, 3 (1971), 181-196.
        A discussion of ESL instruction in adult basic education (ABE)
    programs, including some conflicts arising from the different
    methods of ESL and ABE teachers. The paper offers some solutions
    to problems posed by ESL-ABE classes including a recognition of
    the importance of student attendance rather than the hours of
    instruction offered. Those teachers claiming TESOL backgrounds
    can make contributions to ESL-ABE classes by sharing information
    and recognizing "differences among groups seeking English instruc-
    tion."

14   Regan, Timothy F. "ESOL and the Adult Learner." Paper given at the
        Third Annual TESOL Convention, Chicago, Illinois, March, 1969.
        ED 032517.
           Discusses the problem of disadvantaged adults in learning a
        second language. The writer maintains that the problem of ESOL
        instruction for adults is complicated by their native language
        vocabulary and the abstract concepts developed in their first
        language. He offers suggestions for avoiding the use of certain
        techniques that might work with children but are not appropriate
        for adults.

15   Robinson, Byrl Elmer. "Use of the Initial Teaching Alphabet in English
        as a Second Language. Classes for Spanish Speaking Adults." Diss.
        Univ. of California, Los Angeles, 1969.
           Data were obtained from an instructional program in five ESL
        classes for adults in the spring semester of 1967 in two East
        Los Angeles community adult schools to determine whether the
        use of the Initial Teaching Alphabet (ITA) would have a bene-
        ficial effect upon English language learning when used initially
        in adult education classes composed of students whose native
        tongue was Spanish. Results showed that through the use of
        selected ITA symbols pronunciation skills increased signifi-
        cantly at 0.001 level of confidence and that ITA symbols should
        be used in ESL classes for teaching selected vowel and consonant
        sounds.

16   Taylor, Barry P. "Toward a Theory of Language Acquisition." Language
        Learning, 24, 1 (1974), 23-35.
           The article attempts to refute the theory that the adult is
        less capable than the child of learning a second language and that
        adult second language acquisition is cognitively different from
        that of a child. The author points out that an adult's "more
        advanced cognitive maturity" enables him to cope with language
        abstractions even better than children. He contends that effec-
        tive social variables may be lacking in adults and therefore
        lessen their motivation, and considers "cognitive maturity, the
        native tongue, and psychological learning strategies" as other
        factors.

17   Teacher's Guide; Books 1-2-3. Washington, D.C.: Immigration and Natur-
        alization Service, 1971. ED 061515.
           A revised edition of a teaching guide comprised of three books
        that make up the "Becoming a Citizen Series" to prepare immigrant
        for life in the United States. Each book presents material at
        a different level of language accomplishment. Each book is
        accompanied by directions for presenting pre-reading preparation,
        the actual section to be studied, and subsequent related activi-
        ties.

Cross Reference

AUDIO-LINGUAL

18   Allen, Harold B., and Hadley A. Thomas. Oral English: Learning a Second
      Language. Oklahoma City: The Economy Co., 1968.
           A text that provides the teacher who has limited background in
      linguistics with some helpful aids in the Teacher's Edition. Empha-
      sis is on spoken English, and the book contains a pupil's picture
      book, language development cards, wall charts, and pocket chart.
      Lessons feature conversation and English language sound. The book
      is also recommended for use with children who speak nonstandard
      dialects of English.

19   Blackman, Clyde Thomas. "A Study Using a Structured Audio-Lingual
      Approach to the Teaching of English to Spanish-Speaking Kindergarten
      Pupils in Two Elementary Schools." Diss. Univ. of Houston, 1968.
           The results of this study showed that Spanish-speaking child-
      ren of the lower socioeconomic level, instructed in the Audio-
      Lingual Structural Approach to Language Development for Spanish-
      speaking kindergartners, as tested by the Kindergarten Evaluation
      of Learning Potential, achieved on higher levels of Creative
      Self-direction and of Associative Learning than those who were
      instructed in the regular kindergarten language program. The
      audio-lingual approach was therefore recommended as "a teaching
      strategy" for the classroom teacher.

20   Cook, V. J. "Some Types of Oral Structure Drills." Language Learning,
      18 (1968), 155-164.
           A description of the types of structure drills including four
      degrees of contextualization and basic operations: substitution,
      mutation, repetition, and addition. The contextualization drills
      are described as non-contextualized, semi-contextualized, context-
      ualization, and situational. The reader is offered specific
      examples in each category and can readily evaluate the use of
      each kind of drill.

15

21   Cosgrove, Desmond O. "Aural Comprehension Tests and How to Prepare
      Them." Modern English Journal, 1 (1970), 5-16.
            An aural comprehension test and the classroom teacher's eval-
      uation of a student's speech should supply enough evidence of
      the students's abilities in listening and speaking. Certain fac-
      tors should be considered, however, in developing an aural
      comprehension test on grammatical structure. Multiple choice
      tests, according to the author, with word completion or correct
      response should be considered as well as written answers to oral
      problems for students who can write well. Suggestions are offered
      in preparing, recording, and evaluating the test.

22   Day, Conley. "Pre-listening: Teaching toward Auditory Competence."
      Speech given at Fifth Annual TESOL Conference, New Orleans, La.,
      1971. ED 056576.
            Listening skills should be developed by language learners, and
      pre-listening skills, like pre-reading skills, should be taught.
      Once children learn basic listening skills they will be able to
      transfer their auditory abilities to other listening areas for
      better understanding of the language. The author divides pre-
      listening development into six different areas.

23   Freiheit, Beryle Rae. "Effectiveness of a Daily Auditory Training
      Program for Spanish-Speaking Children Learning English." Diss.
      United States International Univ., 1971.
            After they had studied material related to speech and ear train-
      ing and speed development based on sounds, children participated
      in an experiment. The children were from a self-contained ESL
      classroom with the experimental group participating in an ear-
      training program in order to evaluate such a program for Spanish-
      speaking children and develop auditory training materials and
      techniques. Statistical comparisons showed that the experimental
      group had significant decreases in articulation errors, but the
      control group showed significant increases in the number of errors
      as a result, daily auditory training programs were recommended for
      Spanish-speaking children.

24   Gefen, Raphael. "Sentence Patterns in the Light of Language Theories
      and Classroom Need." IRAL, 5, 4 (1967), 185-192.
            Gefen recommends the sentence pattern techniques of Hornby,
      Palmer, Fries, and Lado since they help the student to concen-
      trate on sentences rather than words in teaching English as a
      second language. He is critical of the use of transformations
      and intricate rules of phrase structure but recommends tagmemics
      since they will help students to familiarize themselves with sub-
      stitution and deletion. Audio-lingual practitioners haven't paid
      enough attention to contextualization and have neglected other
      language learning methods.

25 Hughes, John P. Linguistics and Language Teaching. New York: Random
    House, 1968.
        For the teacher or student who requires a background in linguis-
    tics as it relates to foreign language or second-language teaching,
    this book is very satisfactory. Hughes focuses mainly on aural-
    oral skills and provides a worthwhile introduction to the audio-
    lingual method of teaching language. He does not deal with writing
    or reading and concentrates mostly on the elementary level of
    language learning. The text can be used as a supplemental aid
    for the elementary school teacher.

26 James, Kenneth, and Lloyd Mullen. "English as She is Heard: Aural
    Difficulties Experienced by Foreign Learners." English Language
    Teaching Journal, 28, 1 (1973), 15-22.
        The authors explore the problem that students learning English
    as a second-language (at the University of Manchester, England)
    have in listening to speakers of English. Reasons for these aural
    difficulties are many: phonological interference, the difficulty
    of vowel reduction, juncture, the variety of accents, failure to
    predict sentence patterns through grammatical signals, and others.
    As a result of the study, the authors recommend that aural analysis
    should be taught in the ESL classroom.

27 Lum, John Bernard. An Effectiveness Study of English as a Second Lang-
    uage (ESL) and Chinese Bilingual Methods. Diss. Univ. of California,
    Berkeley, 1972.
        A comparison of Chinese bilingual and English-as-a-second-lang-
    uage approaches in teaching English to non-English-speaking Chinese
    students learning oral English, and an assessment of the use of
    Chinese in helping such students. In the ESL approach, Chinese is
    infrequently used, but in the bilingual approach the use of Chinese
    with other techniques is employed. Pertinent information is in-
    cluded at the end of the report.

28 McCallum, George P. Idiom Drills for Students of English as a Second
    Language. New York: Thomas Y. Crowell Co., 1970.
        Useful idioms were compiled to make up this series for inter-
    mediate and advanced foreign students of English. Students get
    repetitive practice since each lesson introduces five idioms that
    are followed by exercises and drills to demonstrate usage. Short
    readings that contain the idioms studied are also included.

29 Morley, Joan. H. Improving Aural Comprehension. Ann Arbor: The Univ.
    of Michigan Press, 1972.
        A text for upper level secondary students and adults who need
    to develop skill in aural comprehension and pronunciation. The
    lessons, which last from three minutes to fifteen minutes of lis-
    tening time, make it possible for students at various levels to
    use the text although they should have at least one course in
    English as background. Used as a supplement with texts that
    cover other language skills, the book can be very helpful. A
    student workbook and a teacher's book of readings comprise the
    text.

30   Nida, Eugene A. "Selective Listening," in Teaching English as a
     Second Language, Harold B. Allen and Russell N. Campbell, eds.
     New York: McGraw-Hill, 1972, 145-152.
          General principles of selective listening are presented and
     other suggestions are offered in order to improve techniques in
     teaching the auditory approach to learning a foreign language.
     The author discusses listening as a means of recognizing phone-
     tic features of a language, identifying vocabulary, and master-
     ing grammar.

31   Ott, Elizabeth Haynes. A Study of Fluency and Proficiency in Oral
     English of Spanish-Speaking School Beginners. Diss. Univ. of
     Texas, 1969.
          Disadvantaged Spanish-speaking elementary school pupils
     learning science in English were divided into two groups: one
     was taught by the oral-aural method; the other without oral-
     aural instruction. Results showed that instruction using
     non-aural-oral methods was as effective as instruction using
     oral-aural techniques in developing listening, vocabulary,
     grammar, and certain phonological skills. However, improve-
     ment in spoken English by the oral-aural group indicated a
     need for audio-lingual methods. Fifty-eight pupils were given a
     pre-test in September and a post-test in May.

32   Paulston, Christina Bratt. "Structural Pattern Drills: A Classi-
     fication," in Teaching English as a Second Language, Harold B.
     Allen and Russell N. Campbell, eds. New York: McGraw-Hill, 1972,
     129-138.
          Since the basic core of the audio-lingual method of teaching
     foreign languages is drills, the report is an important one
     since it analyzes their purposes and offers a division of drill
     classes: those that are mechanical, meaningful, and communica-
     tive. The author suggests that drills must be more than mechan-
     ical in order for the student to express his own opinion fluently
     in "appropriate situations."

33   Slager, William R., Project Director for NCTE. English for Today.
     New York: McGraw-Hill, Webster Division, 1973.
          A six-year audio-lingual program for teaching English as a
     second language to beginning students age 12 and over. The
     program contains a basic unifying theme for each level (Book
     One: At Home and at School) with drill materials, dialogues,
     and reading and writing exercises. Aids for the teacher are
     included. The program can be useful if taught by a well
     trained teacher who understands that flexibility is essential.

34   Streiff, Virginia. "Question Generation by First Grades: A Heuris-
     tic Model." Paper given at Conference on Child Language. Chicago,
     Illinois, 1971. ED 061807.
          A novel program called: "Listening" is designed to help child-
     ren learning English as a second language develop comprehension
     abilities that will enable them to understand not only what is
     said but what is implied.

35   Wingard, Peter. "Teaching Children to Listen." English Language
    Teaching, 21, 2 (1967), 178-180.
        The article stresses the need for developing children's listen-
ing skills and offers some simple but helpful suggestions to the
new teacher. The child should listen to only three or four sentences of a story at a time at first, and the material should be
carefully graded. Wingard does not believe that there is value
in listening to difficult passages that the non-native speaker
cannot understand. He states that the listening exercise is
pleasurable and easy when all units-- vocabulary and structure--
are familiar.

Cross Reference

18	Spoken English
21	Testing and Evaluation
27	Bilingual
29	Texts

AUDIO-VISUAL

36   Bordwell, Constance. "The Film and the ESL Program: To View or Not
    to View." Journal of English as a Second Language, 4, 1 (1969).
        Since visual aids are frequently used in ESL classes this paper
offers much food for thought for the classroom teacher. The
author states that the teacher should try to ascertain what
messages have the most appeal, how the aid can help students to
gain second-language skills, what criteria should be used in
selecting films, and whether the student is more interested in
the medium or in the message. Also included is a description
of an ESL program which indicated the film had a particularly
strong appeal to college fall-term overseas students.

37   Breitkreuz, Hartmut. "Picture Stories in English Language Teaching."
    English Language Teaching, 26, 2 (1972), 145-149.
        Although the use of picture stories as a device at the elemen-
tary and intermediate levels of ESL teaching can be stimulating,
the writer maintains that they should be integrated into the
actual lessons of the text rather than appear in margins or as
mere illustrations. Based on his own teaching experiences, Breitkreuz shows how the picture stories (a series of 3 to 9 pictures)
can be stimulating in forming dialogues, guiding composition and
language practice and acting out the story. An actual picture
story is presented and discussed.

38   Bruggemann, Christian, and Robert J. Elkins. "Comic Strips in the
    Teaching of English as a Foreign Language." Paper given at confer-
    ence on the Teaching of English. Kassel, West Germany, 1971.
        The authors consider the utilization of American comic strips
and cartoons in ESL classes, maintaining that they can provide
information about American life and that current comic strips
reflect social and cultural patterns. Criteria for using certain
comic strips and problems in their use are also discussed.

39   Delgado, Gilbert Louis. "A Study of Reading and Vocabulary Behavior
      Modifications on Non-English Speaking Children Through Educational
      Films Designed for Deaf Children." Diss. The Catholic Univ. of
      America, 1969.
           The researcher concluded that a series of educational motion
      picture films designed for hearing-impaired children can be
      effective when used with children from non-English speaking
      backgrounds. He also assumed that these materials used by a
      bilingual instructor trained in film instruction techniques would
      help these children make the transition to a "new educational and
      societal setting."

40   Farnsworth, Maryruth Bracy. "The Cassette Tape Recorder: A Bonus or
      a Bother in ESL Composition Correction." TESOL Quarterly, 8, 3 (1974)
      285-291.
           The tape cassette is being used more extensively in the ESL
      division of the Linguistic Department at Brigham Young University
      and the author recommends that the techniques be used in ESL pro-
      grams at other universities and adult education centers, and that
      results of its use be statistically validated "in the area of ESL
      composition correction." One student, in a written evaluation,
      stated that he liked the taped corrections because he felt more
      closely related to the teacher and that it was more personal.

41   Finocchiaro, Mary. "Making ESL Programs More Effective." Instructor,
      81, 6 (1972), 89-91.
           Some helpful practical suggestions are offered here for using
      visual materials in ESL classrooms. Finocchiaro shows how the
      classroom, the chalkboard, games and dramatics, real objects,
      and pictures can be used. The teacher, for example, can illus-
      trate the meanings of words and sentences by using the children's
      clothing, the furniture in the room, dishes, toys, magazines, etc.

42   Frazee, Naomi Burks. "An Experiment in Teaching English to Spanish-
      Speaking Beginners Through the Use of a Series of Original Pictures."
      Diss. Univ. of Houston, 1964.
           A study to determine how effectively Spanish-speaking beginners
      could learn English through pictures used as vicarious experiences.
      The investigation was carried on in four elementary schools in
      Houston, Texas. The Goodenough Draw-a-Man Test was given at the
      beginning of the year to children in experimental and control
      groups, and the Metropolitan Readiness Test was given at the end
      of the year. Analysis of the results showed that children in the
      experimental groups acquired a broader range of information, great-
      er understanding of sentence meaning and greater skill in visual
      perception. There was no significant difference in mental matur-
      ity of either group.

43   Gardner, Rosemary,and Carolyn Ingram. "The Yettem School Visual
      Literacy Project English as a Second Language." Paper presented
      at fourth annual TESOL Convention, San Francisco, 1970. ED 041257.

Maintaining that the traditional materials used in ESL teaching were inadequate, educators at the Yettem (California) School experimented with Mexican-American migrants who attended school part of each year in Mexico and part in California. The third and fourth graders were divided into control groups receiving traditional ESL instructions, and experimental groups who recorded experiences with cameras and told stories from which oral language drills and materials would be developed. Indications were that the use of cameras sparks enthusiasm, develops self-concepts, and increases communication skills.

44   Hall, V. P. "Applications of the Overhead Projector." English Language Teaching, 27, 2 (1973), 165-170.
      Five important applications of the OHP are presented without any kind of general introduction to the presentation of material. The author demonstrates how the projector can be used for oral practice to show relationships of people and things in a picture, and in the teaching of reading by associating sentences with these pictures. In addition, the projector can be used to introduce new words and introduce verb tenses. The author also shows how a sequence of slides can be used for oral and written compositions as the teacher asks questions and builds up the answers to form a story.

45   Hill, L. A. "For the Young Teacher-1. Blackboard Drawing." English Language Teaching, 21, 1 (1966), 60-62.
      This is the first part of a dual article on using the blackboard, the other written by Bernard Lott. Hill believes that the teacher of English or a foreign language creates many advantages when he learns how to draw pictures on the blackboard because pictures will enable him to present new words by bringing the objects into the classroom, testing the pupils' command of English words, testing their pronunciation, and giving pupils material for oral and written composition. For teachers who feel they have no artistic talent, Hill allays our fears by stating that simple pictures are preferable because children recognize them easily.

46   Ioannou, A., and A. S. Papadopoulos. English Now. New York: Longmans, Green, 1968.
      An audio-visual oral course in English as a second or foreign language covering a year's work for beginners in elementary or high schools or for students in need of remedial or review work. The material is graded. In the four-volume course are a picture book, a teacher's drill book, a reader, and a workbook. The course is accompanied by tapes. Although the course is an ambitious one, an imaginative teacher can make good use of selected material.

47   Kelley, Michael R. "English for Foreign Speakers - A Television Solution." Audiovisual Instruction, 17, 9 (1972), 25, 26, 28.
        Three local television networks in Washington, D. C. volunteered to present a series of 90 half-hour lessons on beginning, intermediate, and advanced levels of 30 lessons each for adults who wanted to learn English as a foreign language. Exercise booklets to accompany the levels were available at public libraries in Washington free to students. It was found that the lessons did introduce students to important English language elements and provided additional practice for those with some background in English.

48   Kreidler, Carol J. "Effective Use of Visual Aids in the ESL Classroom." TESOL Quarterly, 5, 1 (1971), 19-37.
        Simple visual aids can be very helpful in the earlier stages of teaching English as a second language. Aids should be unambiguous and clear and culturally recognizable. They can help create a situation outside the classroom and introduce unfamiliar cultural aspects. The author graphically illustrates the use of drawings and discusses the use of filmstrips, movies, the blackboard, the calendar, and even the bodily movements of the teacher The suggestions are practical and relevant.

49   Lee, W. R. "Audio-Visual Aids to the Learning of EFL for Vocational Purposes." 1972. (Speech). ED 061832.
        Visual aids can be helpful to students preparing for specific vocations by showing the actual work environment and circumstances in which language will be used. Recordings of people working in the vocation can offer examples of vocabulary and linguistic behavior. Students studying English as a second or foreign language need general language proficiency, but there are language characteristics that are allied with specific trades and vocation

50   Lee, W. R., and Helen Coppen. Simple Audio-Visual Aids to Foreign-Language Teaching. Fair Lawn, New Jersey: Oxford Univ. Press, 1964.
        A handbook for foreign and second language teaching that includes suggestions for making flannel boards, plastiboards, pictures, puppets, etc. It includes a listing of films and filmstrips.

51   Lott, Bernard. "For the Young Teacher-2. Blackboard Arrangement." English Language Teaching, 21, 1 (1966), 63-65.
        The second part of a dual article, the first of which was written by L. A. Hill. Lott suggests some ways in which the blackboard can be used most efficiently. He explains that the teacher should 1) use the central area and be sure that all items can be seen; 2) use enough space, and erase items already used; 3) list items in columns to the left and right of the central area; 4) and practice using the central area for diagrams and drawings. All of this may sound very simple, but blackboards are used frequently and they should be used most effectively.

52   Morley, H. Joan, and Mary Lawrence. "The Use of Films in Teaching
     English as a Second Language." Language Learning, 21, 1 (1971),
     117-129.
         Films can be an important source of material for in-class
     language practice if they are carefully selected and "utilized
     to their full potential." The authors maintain that the two
     main purposes of the film program are 1) informational and
     2) linguistic. Skills in listening, speaking, writing, and
     reading can be developed in the latter area. Some very helpful
     suggestions are made that can serve the ESL teacher well in
     making films more meaningful. The six criteria in selecting
     films are relevance, sequence continuity, quality, intelligi-
     bility, organization, and vocabulary.

53   Plaister, Ted. "On the Necessity for Specialized Materials in ESOL."
     TESL Reporter, 8, 1 (1974), 4, 5, 15.
         The writer explains how charts and graphs often found in maga-
     zines and newspapers, can serve as focal points for dialogue
     between teacher and student and stimulate note-taking. By call-
     ing on students to discuss the charts, the teacher encourages
     the student to use a "communicative pronunciation." Plaister
     maintains that students will benefit from a second rendition of
     the same lecture on the charts or graphs, even one presented by
     a different lecturer. Vocabulary learning will be spontaneous
     and "in a meaningful context."

54   Rainsbury, Robert C. "An Evaluation of the Use of Video-Tape in a
     Teacher-Training Program." Journal of English as a Second Language,
     2, 2 (1967), 93-106.
         This report offers some helpful suggestions regarding the use
     of video-tape in a teacher training course for students who wanted
     to teach English as a second language. The video-tape is expen-
     sive and should be used efficiently. Rainsbury discusses some
     advantages and disadvantages, and describes how the video-tape
     was actually used in such a training course, illustrating that
     it can be an effective aid.

55   Ramirez, Alfonso R. "H-200 Plus Five." Speech given at Fifth Annual
     TESOL Convention, New Orleans, La., 1971. ED 054622.
         A description of a series of ESL lessons for the primary
     grades including two aids used to reinforce what children learn
     in the daily lesson. The filmstrip accompanied by a recording
     offers stories, songs and language drills. A six-second record-
     ing reinforces language utterances on individual cards through
     repetition.

56   Selden, Sherman W. "Some Cultural Limitations to Visual Aids." Audio-
     Visual Instruction, 16, 1 (1971), 15-16.
         Since ESL teachers often utilize audio-visual aids in their
     classrooms, Selden offers some advice for them that should be
     helpful, suggestions that are not usually considered in using
     these aids. He states that students from developing nations

may lack the experience of viewing two-dimensional pictures and
are not used to the results obtained from complicated camera work.
He recommends that photographs and drawings used with these students should include some familiar object to help the student
judge the size of unfamiliar objects and suggests that the aids
should be at eye-level perception.

57   Sell, David. "Some Uses of Tape Recordings in the Classroom."
      The Modern English Journal, 1, 2 (1970). ED 036806.
             Tape recordings can be especially helpful in the language orien
      tion program before actual communication takes place. The author
      deals mostly with dialogues, narratives, drills, quizzes, and test
      Being able to stop and repeat the tape prevents monotony. For
      advanced students the recorder can extend the student's exposure
      to different dialects and language patterns.

58   So, Wu Hi. "A New Language Laboratory Program for Advanced Students.
      TESOL Quarterly,8,3(1974), 293-304.
             A description of a new language laboratory program for advanced
      students at the English Language Center at Michigan State Univer-
      sity. The tapes are divided into lectures, speeches, and dialogue
      covering a wide range of subjects of interest to foreign students
      and including different kinds of speakers' voices. Varied exer-
      cises cover many aspects of basic language skills. The program is
      especially designed to make it easier for students to derive more
      from their lectures in college.

59   Tidhar, Hava. "Using Television for Teaching a Second Language Throug
      Dramatized Every Day Situations; An Assessment of Effects on Active
      Speech and On Understanding Dialogues Presented by Other Media."
      Tel Aviv, Israel: Instructional TV Center, 1971. ED 053578.
             This paper reveals the benefits gained in using television to
      teach English to Hebrew-speaking students. Ninth grade students
      in an experimental group had English language instruction supple-
      mented by television, which presented spoken English in common
      situations. The ninth grade students in the control group re-
      ceived the standard English instruction. Improvement was parti-
      cularly noticeable in the control group students whose IQ was
      less than 110.

60   The Turners: An Audio-Visual Course for Students of English as a
      Foreign Language;Teacher's Book. New York: Longmans, Green, 1969.
      ED 042157.
             An audio-visual course for students of English as a second or
      foreign language that intends to help students use oral English
      more fluently. The program is designed for students with an
      elementary knowledge of English and for those who need review
      work. An interesting feature is that the lessons focus on an
      English family and life in Britain. The 30 levels each consist
      of a filmstrip and a dialogue and drills tape.

61 Valencia, Atilano A. Oral English Development among Non-English
Speaking, Spanish-Speaking, American Adults Based on Thirty
Innovative Video Programs and Related Paper/Pencil Lessons.
Albuquerque, New Mexico: Southwestern Cooperative Educational
Lab., 1971. ED 052441.
   A report of the findings of the 1970-1971 field study of the
Adult Basic Education Empleen Ingles video programs and paper
and pencil lessons that showed that the programs produced
significant gains in English comprehension, usage, and vocabulary; that the subjects were favorable to the program; that
the degree of English proficiency was noticeable after 20 days
of exposure to the program; and that a combination of the programs was more effective than a single method.

62 Valencia, Atilano A. The Relative Effectiveness of Three Video Oral
English Instructional Conditions for Illiterate or Undereducated
Non-Speaking Adults, Spanish-Speaking Adults. A report of Statistical Findings and Recommendations Based on a Field Testing Study.
Albuquerque, New Mexico: Southwestern Cooperative Education Lab.,
1969.
   A field testing program involving subjects exposed to films
to discover the worth of the lessons in each film in terms of
predetermined behavioral objectives. The study examined three
testing conditions: 1) a classroom with video exposure only;
2) a classroom with video and followup drills; 3) a home condi-
tion with video exposure only. Among other things the report
includes a summary, conclusions, and recommendations.

63 Williams, Frederick, et al. Carrascolendas: Effects of a Spanish/
English Television Series for Primary School Children. Austin:
Texas Univ., 1972. ED 066048.
   An evaluation of "Carrascolendas," a children's television
series in Spanish and English. Two experimental groups parti-
cipated--one watched the thirty programs only, while the other
participated in activities in English and Spanish relating to
the programs. A third group served as the control. Results of
tests showed that both experimental groups made significant
gains with greater gains for those who utilized extra activities related to the programs.

Cross Reference

37	Teaching Aids
38	Teaching Aids
39	Reading
42	Teaching Aids
43	Teaching Aids
44	Spoken English
50	Teaching Aids
51	Teaching Aids
52	Audio-Lingual
54	Teacher Preparation
59	Spoken English

BILINGUAL

64 Andersson, Theodore. "Bilingual Education and Early Childhood,"
1973. (Speech). ED 074868.
Part two of this paper contains a discussion of bilingual-
bicultural education for children that recommends that we
should exploit the great potential that children between two
and five have for learning language, culture, human relations
and many other things. It is advocated that we should take advantage of this great learning potential in bilingual-bicultural
education. Part one comments on the need for objectives, home,
community, and school cooperation, etc. in bilingual programs.

65 Andersson, Theodore, et al. An Experimental Study of Bilingual-
Affective Education for Mexican American Children in Grades K and 1.
Austin, Tex.: Southwest Educational Development Lab., 1970.
ED 056536.
An educational study to determine the best way to educate
Mexican American children among the three language teaching
methods--English as a second language, the traditional approach,
and the bilingual-affective approach. The teachers decided as
a group on goals, methods, and evaluation. Presented in the
report are the teachers' tasks, criteria for testing the program
effectiveness, and a description of the activities in the instructional activities characterizing the three methods.

66 Baker, Jean M. Bicultural Socialization Project: A Group Process
Approach to Bilingual Instruction-Title VII. Final Report, 1970-71.
Tuscon, Arizona: Arizona Univ., 1971.
Teachers of English as a second-language will be interested
in some of the material in this report, especially the results
of the Peabody Vocabulary Test, the Artola-Stewart Spanish-
English Vocabulary Test, and selected language samples in the
appendices. The report also includes information regarding
procedures that proved to be successful, and reasons for some
of the unsuccessful aspects of the program.

67 Barkman L. Bruce. "Some Psychological perspectives on Bilingualism
and Second Language Teaching." McGill Journal of Education, 1969.
Psychologically oriented studies of bilingual communities
which offer significant information about second-language teaching. The main topics are bilingualism and intelligence; language
aptitude; motivation; bilingual skill levels; stages of bilingual
development; and compound and coordinate models of bilingualism.
Barkman believes that information similar to what he includes is
necessary for the development of effective second-language programs in Canada.

68 Bauer, Evelyn. "Bilingual Education in BIA (Bureau of Indian Affairs)
Schools." TESOL Quarterly, 4, 3 (1970), 223-229.
In order to upgrade the academic achievement of Indian students
the Bureau of Indian Affairs carefully examined bilingual programs

26

and related research. Included in the recommendations after various studies and evaluations are the training of native-speaking teachers, and specific goals for the bilingual program to be selected. Final decisions would involve the results of a comparative study in Albuquerque examining 4 different combinations of Navajo and English with Navajo children in grades 1-3.

69   Benjamin, Richard O. "A Bilingual Oral Language Conceptual Development for Spanish-Speaking Pre-School Children," 1969. (Paper) ED 030087.
      This program describes the materials prepared for migrant pre-school children, most of whom speak a nonstandard dialect of Spanish. Oral language lessons provided for the teacher help her teach and learn. Spanish and English lessons are provided, each one of which takes about 15 minutes, to be used about three times a day for eight weeks. The non-English speaking children learn to comprehend and discuss practical subjects and familiar objects.

70   "Bilingual Education Project." The Linguistic Reporter, 13,3(1971), 5.
      A three-year bilingual education program developed by the School of Education at a state university is described. The program will train Spanish-speaking teachers to help students retain competency and pride in their first language and culture, and will present methods in teaching English as a second language. Workshops and a fellowship program will be utilized, and eventually the project will prepare educators to instruct other language groups in the Northeast.

71   A Brief Guide to Bilingual Education. Arlington, Virginia: Center for Applied Linguistics, 1974.
      This pamphlet answers many questions related to bilingual education and discusses Program Design, The Selection and Training of Teachers, Community Participation, and Needed Research. It offers a definition of bilingual education, its purpose, the people it serves, and how a program is started. The section on Needed Research offers challenges to all interested people, including the ESL teacher. Sources of information and addresses of materials centers appear at the end.

72   Capco, Clemencia S., and G. Richard Tucker. "Word Association Data and the Assessment of Bilingual Education Programs." TESOL Quarterly, 5, 4 (1971), 335-342.
      In order to investigate the relative language skills of a group of first grade children schooled bilingually compared with those schooled monolingually, the authors used a variation of the standard word association technique. The results indicated that the language of instruction and the language of testing affected the percentage of different responses. The profile of responses for the bilingual-with-kindergarten class was similar to that of the English control class when responding in English, and to the Filipino control class when responding in Tagalog. Other results indicate that the techniques could be relevant in North American settings although this research was in the Phillippines.

73   Carrow, Elizabeth. "Comprehension of English and Spanish by Preschool
      Mexican-American Children." The Modern Language Journal, 55, 5
      (1971), 299-304.
          A discussion of a study that attempted to describe the English
      and Spanish language performance of a group of Mexican-American
      children of a low economic level. At several day-care centers
      in Texas, 99 children from 3 years 10 months to 6 years 9 months
      were tested. It was found 1) that there was wide variation in
      the combination in which the two languages were known; 2) that
      among pre-school children from a low socio-economic level in
      Houston, most understood English better than Spanish; and 3) that
      both languages improved as the children got older. Findings
      offered some principles for educators to follow in developing
      programs.

74   Clemons, Elinor D. English As-A-Second-Language Methods in the Educa-
      tion of the Bilingual Child. Flagstaff, Arizona: Northern Arizona
      Supplementary Education Center, 1967. ED 039990.
          The application of the methods of teaching English as a second
      language at all levels and in all subjects is advocated since the
      bilingual student's academic success is very dependent on his
      ability to use the dominant language. Teachers from all disci-
      plines could contribute to the bilingual student's success by
      stressing language skills while teaching the subject matter.
      Parents and the bilingual committee should become involved in
      school activities.

75   Cohen, Bernard, et al. Final Evaluation Report of the 1970-1971
      New Haven Bilingual Education Program. New Haven, Conn.: New Haven
      Board of Education, 1971. ED 064459.
          This final evaluation report presents analyses of data com-
      piled on student performance in English oral language proficiency
      and English reading comprehension of interest to ESL teachers.
      The data revealed that the program classes showed positive and
      sometimes significant growth in word knowledge and reading.

76   DiPietro, Robert J. "Bilingualism and Bidialectalism." 1970.
      (Speech). ED 061824.
          Although bilingualism and bidialectalism should not be con-
      strued as linguistic equals, there are enough commonalities
      between the two that warrant comparison. Stable bilingualism
      results when each language is used frequently for different
      purposes in the community. Also, the fact that one language
      group can force the other to abandon its language (and its
      culture) in order to "share the wealth" may be common to both
      linguistic forms, although bidialectal people use both a
      "socially stigmatized and a prestige variety of the same lang-
      uage."

77   Ehrlich, Alan. "Bilingual Teaching and Beginning School Success,"
      1971. (Unpublished paper) ED 077279.
          The results of this study showed that a bilingual approach to
      reading was more effective than a monolingual approach in the
      education of Spanish-speaking second-grade children in New York
      City. In addition to a summary, there is a review of the pro-
      cedures along with tables that help to interpret statistical
      data.

78   Epstein, Erwin H. "English and Politics in Puerto Rican Schools."
      The Educational Forum, 33, 2 (1969), 225-230.
          The author comments on the language problems in Puerto Rico
      and remarks that the question of how much English should be
      taught in schools there "has been a vital concern since American
      occupation in 1898." He states that the purpose of English in-
      struction in Puerto Rico are socioeconomic and acculturative and
      that school children are expected to be bilingual. A comparison
      is made between the language problems of Puerto Ricans learning
      English and Mexican-Americans studying English. In referring
      to English vs. Spanish, Epstein states that "The fear of lang-
      uage loss" is not founded on their imagination.

79   Fischer, John C. "Bilingualism in Puerto Rico: A History of Frustra-
      tion." English Record, 11, 4 (1971), 19-24.
          Problems abound in teaching English to Puerto Ricans both in
      Puerto Rico and in New York City, mainly because of the lack of
      well trained teachers. In order to strengthen the ESL program,
      the Puerto Rican Department of Public Instruction granted aids
      to over 400 men and women to improve their teaching of English.

80   Fishman, Joshua A. Bilingualism in Barrio, Bloomington, Indiana:
      Indiana Univ. Press, 1971.
          Includes twenty-two articles that cover a scientific study of
      bilingualism conducted mainly in a Puerto Rican community in New
      Jersey. The book emphasizes the evaluation of linguistic method-
      ology and is primarily concerned with refining the ways in which
      bilingualism is examined. ESL teachers in a bilingual education
      program involving Spanish-speaking students can find some helpful
      articles to read here.

81   Fishman, Joshua A., and John Lovas. "Bilingual Education in Socio-
      linguistic Perspective." TESOL Quarterly, 4, 3 (1970), 215-222.
          A discussion of various kinds of bilingual programs and sugges-
      tions to help the reader decide what kind to establish. The
      broad categories that the authors discuss are 1) transitional
      bilingualism--native tongue is used in early grades until skill
      in English is developed; 2) monoliterate bilingualism--aural-oral
      skills in both languages but is not concerned with literacy in
      the mother tongue; 3) partial bilingualism--seeks fluency and
      literacy in both languages, but literacy in mother tongue is
      restricted to certain subject matter; and 4) full bilingualism--
      students develop all skills in both languages.

82   Franquez, Eleanor. Bilingual/Bicultural Preschool Education
      Program: Montessori Design, 1972-73. Compton, Calif.: Compton
      Unified School District, 1972.
           A report that contains information on project arrangements,
      organization, and preschool cu:riculum of the Montessori-
      designed bilingual/bicultural preschool education program of
      the Compton School District. Plans are presented for in-service
      development and parent involvement and education. The appen-
      dixes include salary schedules, job descriptions, and personnel
      policies.

83   Gonzalez, Josue, and Zenobia Verner. "English Language Teaching in
      a Texas Bilingual Programme." English Language Teaching, 25, 2
      (1971), 296-302.
           A description of a bilingual program in San Antonio, Texas,
      in which language was taught through subject matter so that
      language would not be taught in an "academic vacuum." Such an
      approach involved the development of new curriculum materials,
      but these were in the process of being developed. Emphases in
      a subject matter class taught in English were on subject matter
      and on reading and speaking English. Teachers participated in
      professional development classes for this kind of teaching which
      was tested and also found to be successful in the Bronx and in
      Harlem.

84   Goodman, Frank M. Compton Bilingual Plan: Review Report 1971-72.
      Compton, Calif.: Compton Unified School District, 1972. ED 072676.
           A review of the Compton Unified School Bilingual Plan during
      its third year of operation at Thomas Jefferson High School in
      South Central Los Angeles. The report provides the reader with
      information about personnel, community involvement, the new
      vocabulary developed for lexical references, services rendered
      under ESEA Title VII, in-service training for teachers, and
      bilingual curriculum and materials.

85   Goodman, Frank M., and Carolyn Stern. Bilingual Program Evaluation
      Report, ESEA Title VII., 1970-1971. Compton, Calif.: Compton City
      Schools, 1971. ED 054672.
           An evaluation of a bilingual education plan in its second
      year. The purpose of the program is to prepare Spanish-speak-
      ing students to be fluent in both English and Spanish by
      utilizing their native language abilities in Spanish as the
      primary agent of instruction at the outset. The report con-
      sists of a description and the extent of the program: curriculum,
      materials used, community involvement, personnel, budget, and
      the results.

86   Gudschinsky, Sarah C. "Literacy in the Mother Tongue and Second
      Language Learning." Paper given at Conference on Child Language,
      Chicago, Illinois, 1971. ED 060753.
           The paper answers some questions about the necessity for
      literacy in the mother tongue as a prerequisite for success in

a second language, and supports this principle. It is maintained that besides increasing the child's chances for academic success and minimizing cultural conflicts, the child who controls his own language will learn a second language easier since literacy in the mother tongue will give the child a basic understanding of the manner in which language works.

87   Guerra, Emilio L. "The Challenge of Bilingualism in Education in the City of New York." Paper presented at National Convention of American Assn. of Teachers of Spanish and Portugese, 1968. ED 030339.
A brief discussion of the New York City special programs for non-English-speaking students, especially Puerto Rican arrivals. Also discussed is the Puerto Rican Study of the New York City Board of Education that sought to improve educational opportunities for non-English speaking children. The paper offers eight recommendations for teachers and administrators involved in the programs.

88   Gumperz, John J. "Verbal Strategies in Multilingual Communications," in Language and Cultural Diversity in American Education, eds. Roger D. Abrahams and Rudolph C. Troike. Englewood Cliffs, New Jersey: Prentice-Hall, 1972, 184-195.
The author refutes the theory that people of minority groups living in "two social, cultural, and linguistic worlds" mix up their two languages and recognize no real grammar. He maintains that code-switching is a skill that these speakers use "as a verbal strategy to convey meanings." The problems of minority group students may be based more on different values and associations rather than on actual linguistic differences.

89   Gutierrez, Medardo. Bilingualism and Bilingual Education Programs. Albany: State Univ. of New York, 1972. ED 066979.
Relevant issues concerning the planning of bilingual education programs are discussed in this article which points out that a primary factor in developing such programs is a knowledge of the degree of language ability and cultural dominance which varies among individuals. Programs seeking to achieve bilingual-bicultural balance must first analyze community linguistic and cultural balance.

90   Helping Advance Bilingual Learning in Abernathy (HABLA). Evaluation Report, 1970-1971. Abernathy, Texas: Abernathy Independent School District, 1971.
This bilingual program was initiated to reduce the high dropout rate of Mexican-American students. Students in grades K-1 received instruction in English and Spanish with the program to be expanded one grade level each year. First-grade students were expected to write simple words in English and Spanish and respond to instruction in English and Spanish. A battery of tests indicated that the program was a promising one.

91   Holm, Wayne. "Bilagaana Bizaad (The English Language): ESL/EFL
      in a Navajo Bilingual Setting." Paper given at Fifth Annual TESOL
      Convention, New Orleans, La., 1971.
           This program involves team teaching in two languages with the
      English-language teacher and the Navajo-language teacher conduct-
      ing activities simultaneously, each one working with a small
      group at a time. The Navajo language teachers are in charge and
      teach content in the lower grades, especially. The English-
      language teachers stress language rather than content. The
      program was developed at Rock Point on the Navajo Reservation
      in New Mexico.

92   John, Vera. Cognitive Development in the Bilingual Child. Paper given
      at 21st Annual Round Table, Georgetown Univ., 1970.
           The paper protests against the traditional way "with standar-
      dized tools" that the bilingual minority child is tested and
      offers recommendations for educating non-English-speaking child-
      ren, especially those in pre-school and primary classes. These
      suggestions are concerned with comprehension, cognitive develop-
      ment, language fluency, and language use. The author maintains
      that "As yet, the new insights of linguists and psychologists
      have had little impact upon the education of non-English-speak-
      ing children."

93   John, Vera P., and Vivian M. Horner. Early Childhood Bilingual
      Education. New York: Modern Language Association, 1971.
           A monograph which describes bilingual education programs in
      the United States including program descriptions, teacher recruit-
      ment and training, curriculum materials, testing and evaluation,
      research in bilingual education, and other pertinent matters.
      For communities considering a bilingual program, this publica-
      tion could be very helpful since the authors summarize many
      projects in operation.

94   King, Paul E. Bilingual Readiness in Primary Grades; An Early Child-
      hood Demonstration Project. New York: City Univ. of New York,
      Hunter College, 1966.
           The project attempted to show that with two or more language
      and ethnic groups in an integrated classroom there would be
      bilingual readiness in both English and Spanish-speaking child-
      ren and there would be a native respect and a mutual respect for
      one another's language and cultural background. Fifteen kinder-
      garten and four first-grade classes participated. Results
      indicated that the kindergarten children demonstrated readiness
      for such a program.

95   Knowlton, Clark S. "Bilingualism--A Problem or an Asset," (Speech),
      1965. ED 010744.
           The author finds weaknesses in bilingual programs in New Mexi-
      co and Texas schools and offers suggestions for improvement. He
      maintains that in poor communities the staff and equipment are
      inadequate, the students fail to learn a variety of subject
      matter., and Spanish-speaking children learn to believe their

language and culture inferior. Students should be taught subject matter earlier and in their native tongue to help them gain an appreciation of their own language and culture.

96   Kolers, Paul A. "Bilingualism and Information Processing," in
      Language, Virginia P. Clark, et al., eds. New York: St. Martin's
      Press, 1972, 84-96.
             The ESL teacher can gather some interesting and helpful information about the mental operations utilized by bilingual subjects.
      Kalers designed a set of experiments to gather data about the
      "acquisition, storage, and retrieval of information." He discusses the "switch mechanism" that is necessary in using different languages and considers the differences between learning
      concrete and abstract words. Teaching people a skill in one
      language and finding out if the skill can be expressed in
      another language is a "phenomenon of bilingualism."

97   LaFontaine, Herman, and Muriel Pagan. A Model for the Implementation
      of the Elementary School Curriculum through Bilingual Education.
      Bronx, New York: P. S. 25 (Bilingual School), 1969. ED 066934.
             A description of a model for a program that provides seven
      years of bilingual instruction for a child from kindergarten
      through the sixth grade, enabling him to get half of his instruction in English and half in Spanish. After ascertaining
      the child's language dominance, teachers gradually increase
      second language instruction as the pupil advances through the
      grades.

98   Lambert, Wallace E. Language, Psychology, and Culture: Essays.
      Stanford, California: Stanford Univ. Press, 1972.
             A collection of 21 essays written by the author from 1955-
      1971 appearing in various journals and dealing with pertinent
      ESL topics like language learning and acquisition, attitudes
      toward language, and bilingualism. The essays discuss the
      performance of bilinguals and monolinguals on intelligence
      tests, motivation in language learning, the influence of
      psychology in studying language, and factors that influence
      teachers' attitudes toward pupils.

99   Lambert, Wallace E. "A Social Psychology of Bilingualism,"
      Journal of Social Issues, 23, 2 (1967), 106-108.
             The results of Lambert's investigation point out that although ethnocentrism is highly developed in Europe and American
      culture, bilinguals with bicultural experiences can take advantage of their bicultural backgrounds and capitalize on them.
      Being able to gain competence in both languages and participate freely in both cultures can be a distinct advantage. The
      author used a series of attitude scales with French-American
      students to obtain most of his results.

100   Lambert, Wallace E., and G. R. Tucker. <u>Bilingual Education of Children</u>. Rowley, Mass.: Newbury House, 1972.
      A study of the St. Lambert Experiment--a five-year program designed to teach non-native-speaking pupils in the target language. The book provides information about pupil achievement in non-language subjects when taught through a foreign language, the effect of bilingual experience on intelligence, the development of foreign-language skills, and an evaluation of teaching techniques used in the program.

101   Lance, Donald M. <u>A Brief Study of Spanish-English Bilingualism: Final Report, Research Project ORR-Liberal Arts-15504</u>. College Station, Texas: Texas A. & M. Univ., 1969. ED 032529.
      A report consisting of five papers, and a conclusion, which is perhaps the most significant part of the report because of some general implications which indicate that the use of non-standard English by bilinguals is caused by language development and use of common dialect forms as well as Spanish language interference.

102   Levinsky, Frieda L. "Research on Bilingualism," 1972. (Unpublished paper.). ED 062839.
      Many linguistic observations concerning the problems of language teaching in bilingualism and second language programs are considered here. The ideas of some outstanding linguists, the results of current research, and reports of observations in bilingual classes are also presented. Discussion of the purposes of bilingual education, types of bilingualism, bilingual problems, and second language learning are also included.

103   Logan, J. Lee. "One Will Do But We Like Two: The Coral Way Bilingual Project." <u>The National Elementary Principal</u>, 50, 2 (1970), 85-87.
      The principal of the Coral Way Elementary School in Miami, Florida, describes the development of his school's bilingual program that is considered to be the best of its kind, with each child learning his native language one half of the day and learning his second language in the other half. Logan lists some of the criteria in selecting teachers, the "prime contributors" to the success of the program, and the general activities of teachers and administrators in making the project work. Teachers involved in any bilingual program will find the article informative and encouraging.

104   Mackey, William F. <u>Bilingual Education in a Binational School</u>. Rowley, Mass.: Newbury House, 1972.
      The author describes a working bilingual educational system for a community of families using two languages--German and English. He includes a description of the school, the method of teacher selection and training, and the selection and preparation of materials. The book can be helpful to administrators and teachers planning a bilingual education program.

34

105   Materials Used in Bilingual Programs. New York: New York City
        Board of Education, 1973.
                New York City has had some measure of success in conducting
        its bilingual programs under difficult conditions and offers
        here a list of instructional materials used in bilingual pro-
        grams prepared by the Bilingual Resource Center in New York
        City. Included are audio-visual aids, textbooks, and various
        educational materials.

106   Model Programs: Compensatory Education. The Juan Morel Campos Bilin-
        gual Center, Chicago, Illinois. Washington, D. C.: U. S. Government
        Printing Office, 1972. ED 067959.
                A description of a bilingual program in an economically dis-
        advantaged neighborhood in Chicago. Intermediate level English
        and Spanish instruction were offered to Spanish-speaking pupils.
        Information in the report covers usual items: personnel, methods,
        texts, evaluation, community involvement, etc.

107   Morgan, Judith Claire. "The Effects of Bilingual Instruction on the
        English Language Arts Achievement of First Grade Children."
        Diss. Northwestern State Univ. of Louisiana, 1971.
                An investigation to determine whether first-grade pupils com-
        ing from bilingual families would obtain significantly higher
        scores through a bilingual education program than would first-
        grade pupils coming from bilingual families and who were enrolled
        in a monolingual educational program. Results of tests indicated
        that first-grade pupils from bilingual families who received
        instruction through a bilingual educational program developed
        greater competency in analyzing words without the aid of context,
        greater competency in reading comprehension and general reading
        achievement, and spelling.

108   Nedler, Shari, and Peggy Sebera. "International Strategies for
        Spanish-Speaking Pre-school Children." Child Development, 42
        (1971), 259-267.
                A study comparing three strategies of early intervention de-
        signed to increase the language skills of disadvantaged 3-year-
        old Mexican-American children. The first treatments, concentrat-
        ing on a Bilingual Childhood Education Program, made significantly
        greater gains than other treatment subjects on the basis of a
        performance scale and a picture vocabulary test in English and
        Spanish. The positive results were attributed to various skills
        taught in the Bilingual Program.

109   Ney, James W. "Predator or Pedagogue?: The Teacher of the Bilingual
        Child." The English Record, 21, 4 (1971), 12-18.
                A convincing argument for bilingual education programs that
        includes supportive evidence: ethnic group dropout rates and
        research in the area of bilingualism, especially those that
        describe successful programs. The author states that the
        teacher's role can be changed from "predator" to pedagogue
        by adopting a truly bidimensional bilingual program, increasing

the understanding of non-Anglo American culture, and recognizing that a grasp of "playground English" is inadequate for the
student to cope with problems created by using academic English
in the classroom.

110   Ng, Jolson Pak-leung. "The Effects of Bilingual Science Instruction
      on the Vocabulary Comprehension Achievement, and Conceptualization
      of Elementary School Chinese Whose Second Language is
      Chinese." Diss. Univ. of Calif., Los Angeles, 1970.
            The study attempted to measure the difference in vocabulary
      comprehension achievement and conceptualization between a group
      of Chinese children taught only English and a group taught bi-
      lingually (English and Cantonese) as revealed in several aspects
      of science learning. Statistical evidence revealed that the
      children taught bilingually surpassed children taught mono-
      lingually only in vocabulary at the 0.05 confidence level and
      in conceptualization at the 0.001 confidence level. As a
      result, "recommendations were made to teach vocabulary and
      concepts bilingually and comprehension monolingually."

111   Perez, Carlos V. "Auxiliary Personnel in Bilingual Education."
      Paper given at Fifth Annual TESOL Convention, New Orleans, La.,
      March, 1971. ED 052648.
            The introduction of auxiliary personnel into a bilingual edu-
      cation system may bring the schools and community together,
      provide more individualized instruction for children, and help
      the classroom teacher. The paper discusses the criteria, the
      activities of the auxiliaries, their training, and the certi-
      fication requirements.

112   Peso Bilingual Language Development Project. Project Evaluation,
      June 30, 1970. Amarillo, Texas: Peso Education Service Center,
      1970. ED 064010.
            A one-year pilot study involving 451 Anglo- and Mexican-
      American first- and second-grade students. One of the three
      components was the development of bilingual oral and written
      language skills and instruction in English, within the regu-
      lar school program. Testing revealed a need to develop
      Spanish oral language skills, and Spanish written skills, but
      the instruction in English achieved its objectives to a signi-
      ficant degree.

113   Ramirez, Arnulfo Gonzalez. "The Spoken English of Spanish-Speaking
      Pupils in a Bilingual and Monolingual School Setting: An Analysis
      of Syntactic Development." Diss. Stanford, Univ., 1974.
            The hypothesis tested was that if any significant difference
      between Spanish-speaking pupils schooled bilingually and those
      schooled monolingually in developing English grammatical con-
      structions occurred, pupils schooled bilingually would show
      greater syntactic development in their spoken English. Using
      115 Mexican-American pupils in grades K, 1, 2, and 3 as sub-
      jects, the researcher found that the bilingually-schooled

pupils produced more language and also performed with superiority in using numbers and types of sentence-combining transformations.

114   Ramirez, M. "Bilingual Program Bandwagon and the Psychodynamics of the Chicano Child." Claremont Reading Conference Yearbook, 1972, 68-72.

Ramirez found that the pupil's native language seemed to be best for teaching conceptual aspects and some curriculum skills. After the Mexican-American pupil becomes better adjusted to school, more English words will be taught. Using this method the teacher then increases the development of oral English as the pupils evidence their readiness for this process. The thesis behind this approach is that the pupil's native language is more completely developed than the target language.

115   Rebert, Robert J., et al., eds. Bilingual Education for American Indians. Washington, D. C.: Bureau of Indian Affairs, 1971. ED 061789.

Articles related to problems in bilingual education for American Indians appear in this curriculum bulletin. The essays cover past and present activities in bilingual education for American Indians and Eskimos, the history of language instruction in American Indian schools, bilingual education in Bureau of Indian Affairs schools, and the Bilingual Education Act. Among other items are case studies programs for Navajo children, and a bibliography.

116   Resource Material for Bilingual Education. Fort Worth, Texas: Fort Worth Public Schools; National Consortia for Bilingual Education, 1972.

A reference book to help the bilingual classroom teacher at the primary level by presenting material on language and other learning activities related to a bilingual program. There is an abundance of material on colors, letters, seasons, months, days, plants, family, the community, etc., and supplemental activities including stories and songs. The materials written in Spanish and English can be adapted to the language skills of the students by the teacher.

117   Rosco, Carole. "Developing Instructional Materials for a Bilingual Program." TESOL Quarterly, 6, 2 (1972), 163-166.

A helpful description of Project SELL (Spanish-English Language Learning), a bilingual program in Union City, New Jersey, where approximately sixty per cent of the school enrollment consists of Spanish-speaking children. Through a five-year curriculum, students were expected to achieve functional bilingual fluency in subject matter areas. The project, begun in one elementary school, was to be extended to all elementary schools in the town.

118   Sancho, Anthony R. "Spanish: A New Approach for Bilingual Programs."
       TESOL Quarterly, 6, 4 (1972), 333-338.
            A report of an innovative bilingual curriculum to make student
       coordinate bilinguals in Spanish and English. Spanish is taught
       to children whose first language is Spanish and as a foreign
       language to non-native speakers. In grades one and two English
       and Spanish are taught. The curriculum utilizes the activity
       of switching from one language to the other in these grades.
       Cultural corners with linguistic and cultural items enhance
       the bilingual switching lessons.

119   Saville, Muriel R., and Rudolph C. Troike. A Handbook of Bilingual
       Education. ED 035877.
            Designed for teachers and administrators in bilingual educatio
       programs, the book reviews the history of bilingualism and offers
       suggestions for developing bilingual programs. It also considers
       controversial topics related to bilingual education and offers
       useful teaching suggestions. One chapter is devoted to English
       phonology and grammar as contrasted with Spanish and Navajo. The
       introduction reminds the reader that "For thousands of the child-
       ren who enter school each year, English is a foreign language."

120   Spector, Sima. "Patterns of Difficulty in English in Bilingual
       Mexican-American Children," 1972. M. A. Thesis, Sacramento State
       College, Sacramento, Calif.
            This study makes an effort to discover the best methods to
       be used in providing language training for bilingual children.
       To ascertain patterns of difficulty, an experiment was con-
       ducted among 15 bilingual and 15 monolingual children. Results
       indicated that although areas of difficulty for bilingual
       speakers were confirmed, there were other influences affect-
       ing children in both groups. A comprehensive discussion of
       various aspects of bilingual education is also included.

121   Spell, Faralie S. "Practicalities in Teaching English as a Second
       Language to Navajo Children." Paper given at the Fifth Annual
       TESOL Convention, New Orleans, La., 1971. ED 053610.
            Better teacher education is advocated in this paper since
       English as a second language has often been taught without
       relationship to the learning needs of Navajo children.
       Teachers have to be properly trained so that they can gain an
       understanding of the English language and of the techniques
       of language instruction. The author also recommends that
       materials should be properly developed and used according to
       the needs of the pupils.

122   Spolsky, Bernard. "ESOL and Bilingual Education." Paper given at
       annual meeting of American Council for Teaching of Foreign Lang-
       uages, (ACTFL), New Orleans, La., 1969.
            The author discusses various organizations interested in
       bilingual education, realizing that schools have a responsi-

bility for preparing students to use the standard language if they are to share cultural and economic advantages. Furthermore, the student should be taught in his own language while he is learning English. Organizations discussed are ACTFL, ATESL, and TESOL.

123 Spolsky, Bernard. Evaluation of Research on Bilingual Education for American Indians. A Position Paper. Albuquerque, New Mexico: Southwestern Cooperative Education Lab., 1970.
In order to develop any successful bilingual education program a great deal of study is necessary, including teacher training methods, community participation, curriculum evaluation, methods, and other topics. In the case of American Indian education, even more studies are necessary because of limited evidence. These studies should include problems of curriculum development, and a language census, among others.

124 Spolsky, Bernard, ed. The Language Education of Minority Children. Rowley, Mass.: Newbury House, 1972.
The articles in this book are divided into three sections: 1) Multilingualism in the U. S.; 2) Bilingualism and Bilingual Education; and 3) Language Education in Practice; and include writings on the problems of minority groups in the United States. The essays can provide teachers with a background in language education of minority children, bilingual education, teaching English as a second-language, and foreign-language. As an introduction to the difficulties of starting bilingual education programs, the book is quite satisfactory.

125 Stern, Carolyn, and Diane Ruble. "Teaching New Concepts to Non-English Speaking Preschool Children." TESOL Quarterly, 7, 3 (1974), 309-317.
Since many Mexican-American children have language problems where English is the language taught, a study was made to ascertain the effects of new concepts taught to these children. Results indicated that Spanish-speaking children did no better when taught a new concept in Spanish and that there was no evidence that children taught a new concept in English would achieve a concept in English easier than those taught the concepts in Spanish. Other results are included.

126 Stern, H. H. "Bilingual Education: A Review of Recent North American Experience." Modern Languages, 50, 2 (1973), 57-62.
A very pertinent section of this report describes the development of a bilingual school for English children in Quebec Province called the St. Lambert Elementary School. Studies comparing bilingual and monolingual children showed that the bilingual children rated higher in verbal and non-verbal intelligence tests. Since there were opportunities for practicing the second language, bilingual education was more successful than conventional second-language-teaching methods.

127   Swickard, Sara R., et al. Language Arts and the Migrant Child,
       Diagnosis and Prescription. Lansing, Michigan: Michigan State
       Dept. of Education, 1969. ED 040789.
            The book is divided into three sections with suggestions for
       improving language arts instruction for the migrant child and
       covers behavioral goals for teachers working with pre-school
       to first-graders, goals for initial reading instruction, and
       language behavior desirable for those in grades four to six.

128   Taylor, Marie E. An Overview of Research on Bilingualism.
       California State Dept. of Education, 1970. ED 049876.
            The document provides some relevant information to the ESL
       teacher regarding the research about second language learning.
       Success in a second language depends on language aptitude,
       strong motivation and verbal intelligence. Some of the re-
       search indicated that Spanish-speaking students learn a second
       language better when they have regular instruction in English
       as a second language while using their native language.

129   Tipton, Robert L. "Problems of Cross-Cultural Communication in
       Developing Bilingual Bicultural Education Programs." Paper given
       at Annual Meeting of the Southern Speech Communication Assn.,
       1973. ED 081038.
            The author wants to stress the ideas that the purpose of bi-
       lingual, bicultural instruction is to develop behavior patterns
       acceptable in more than one culture and that such a program does
       not intend to change the student's language or culture. He
       reminds teachers that they must not try to force the language
       or culture of the dominant group upon minorities.

130   "Training Teachers for Bilingual Bicultural Education." Hispania,
       56 (1973) (Membership Issue), 762-766.
            This report which was commissioned by the Executive Council
       of the American Association of Teachers of Spanish and Portu-
       gese, will be of interest to ESL teachers working in bilingual
       education programs. It states the problems and objectives of
       bilingual education and discusses teacher training, develop-
       ment of curricula and the implementation of programs in both
       Spanish and Portugese.

131   Trevino, Robert E. Is Bilingual Education Shortchanging the Chicano?
       ED 077617.
            A report of a study indicating that bilingual education should
       support bilingual-bicultural opportunities and that the Chicano
       child's negative self-image can be corrected only through a
       worthwhile bilingual program that includes more than drill in
       English. The Bilingual/Bicultural Follow-Through Model for Grades
       K-12 at the University of California, Riverside, is described as
       a positive program involving participation of parents, the commun-
       ity, and home teaching.

132   Troike, Rudolph C. "Statement on Linguistic Concerns in Bilingual Education." Paper given to National Advisory Committee on the Education of Bilingual Children, 1974.
        The author states that linguists and anthropologists should provide more input in organizing bilingual education programs since cultural and socioeconomic factors may play a greater part than native language in the academic success of the student. The paper also discusses teacher training, certification, and staffing, reminding the reader that a person should not be hired to teach merely because he speaks a particular language.

133   Tucker, C. Allen. "The Chinese Immigrant's Language Handicap : Its Extent and Its Effects." Florida FL Reporter, 7, 1 (1969), 44, 45, 170.
        A very informative report of the plight of the Chinese immigrant's handicaps due to psychological, socio-economic, and linguistic factors. One can understand the special difficulties that confront the Chinese immigrants, and the reasons why it is so important for them to learn English. Tucker deals with the vast structural and intonational differences that make it so difficult for the Chinese to learn English. English word order, vowels, consonants, and verbs create additional problems. The reader agrees that they constitute a challenge to our society, especially a challenge to those concerned with teaching English as a second language.

134   Turner, Paul R. Bilingualism in the Southwest. Tucson, Arizona: Univ. of Arizona Press, 1973.
        A collection of 18 articles written by people with varied language interests. One segment is devoted to Mexican-Americans, another to American Indians, and the third to recommendations for needed research. Most of the essays add to the reader's information, although the anthology does not have a theme that holds the collection together or a definite pattern that is recognizable.

135   Walsh, Donald D. "Spanish-Speaking Children in American Schools: The Story of an Educational Crime." Paper given at Annual Meeting of National Council of Teachers of English, Philadelphia, 1973. ED 088103.
        Since the Spanish-speaking American child enters school without the knowledge of the English sound and structure system, a program aimed at making these children bilingual should be developed through an intensive course in English. The author advocates a truly bilingual system with the native-speaker of English studying subject matter using Spanish as the medium of instruction.

136   Zintz, Miles V. The Reading Process. Dubuque, Iowa: Wm. C. Brown, 1970. Chapter 14, 325-353.

A great deal of ground is covered in this chapter that
acquaints the teacher with the cultural expectations of the
school that teaches the bilingual student and presents information about the development of language arts skills, linguistic
reading programs, and teaching vocabulary. Zintz also spends
some time discussing bilingualism in the Southwest and includes a brief bibliography of materials along with some reading
references that could easily be expanded.

137   Zintz, Miles V., et al. The Implications of Bilingual Education
       for Developing Multicultural Sensitivity Through Teacher Education.
       Washington, D. C.: ERIC Clearinghouse on Teacher Education, 1971.
       ED 054071
          Since a multicultural program enables students to apprec-
       iate contributions of other cultures, teachers must recognize
       differences in languages, customs, and values of their students.
       The non-native speaker cannot succeed when a class is focused
       on the middle-classed Anglo student. Non-native speakers not
       only need training in various language skills but should feel
       that the teacher understands the cultural background. The
       students should acquire competency in two languages.

138   Zirkel, Perry Alan. "A Method for Determining and Depicting Lang-
       uage Dominance." Paper given at Annual Convention of TESOL,
       May, 1973. ED 086028.
          A practical model for detecting and illustrating language
       dominance is offered in order to identify language achieve-
       ment and needs of students in bilingual education programs.
       By testing the aural ability of students, teachers can also
       ascertain the extent of language dominance for placement and
       programmed instruction. The paper includes illustrations
       and tables.

Cross Reference

       70   Teacher Preparation
       72   Testing and Evaluation
       73   Methodology
       80   Teacher Preparation
       81   Language Learning
       98   Language Learning
       99   Socio-Cultural
      108   Testing and Evaluation
      124   Socio-Cultural
      126   Socio-Cultural
      128   Reading

CURRICULUM

139   Agun, James Ibitayo. "Determination of Media Materials and Methods
       for Teaching English as a Second Language in Nigeria." Diss.
       Univ. of Southern California, 1973.

The guidelines developed in this study provided procedures
and criteria used in selecting media materials and methods for
teaching English in Nigeria. The methods used in establishing
such procedures and criteria could be used in other geographical areas. In-depth interviews were conducted among co-ordinators of instructional materials centers; college experts in
English as a second language; co-ordinators of ESL programs.
A study was made of three ESL programs enrolling large popula-
tions; students with different cultural and linguistic backgrounds; and a study of models for media selection.

140 Bending, H. B. "Motivation for English in an Examination Geared
School System." Paper given at Annual Conference of International
Assn. of Teachers of English as a Foreign Language, 1974. ED 093165.
It was found that few students in the Egyptian school system
were able to master the English language well enough to use it
at the university level, where it is the medium of instruction
in all subject areas. English language study is begun in the
seventh grade. The author maintains that motivation would be
improved and better results would be obtained if English were
not required but would be elective, and if Arabic replaced
English as the language medium in the university.

141 Bowen, J. Donald. "Tesol Research for the Classroom." TESOL
Quarterly, 6, 4 (1972), 351-362.
The need for research in learning and teaching English as a
second and foreign language is important, but the author cautions
overzealousness in the search to provide programs and develop
theories in teaching language. He suggests that research be
carefully evaluated, that promising solutions should be fully
justified, that programs involving "political motivations"
should be closely examined, and that one listen to those who
question current popular trends.

142 Exemplary Programs in English as a Second Language, San Diego County.
San Diego, Calif.: San Diego City Schools, 1969. ED 032244.
A description of this 2-year project could serve as a guide
for school systems that are starting or expanding ESL programs.
The report, besides describing the usual objectives of such a
program--language skills, student participation, etc.--reviews
the in-service workshops for teachers, evaluations of ESL curriculum materials, conferences for educators and parents, and the
contributions of cooperating community agencies.

143 Garcia, Joseph J. "A Look at Minority Education Today with Implications for the Teaching of English," 1970. (Unpublished paper).
A forthright discussion which is critical of bilingual education programs which fail to distinguish the distinct separation
between the two languages and cultures but is complimentary
toward English-as-a-second-language programs that develop a

mutual respect for both American and foreign cultures. Standard English should be taught as a second language, and the ethnic heritage should always be primarily maintained.

144   Goldstein, Wallace L. General Principles for an ESL Program. Westfield, Mass.: Westfield State College, 1972.
       A guide for teachers and administrators in setting up an ESL program, first used in developing such a program at the West Street School Bilingual Project, Holyoke, Massachusetts. The guidelines cover the objectives, classroom activities, and general theories related to teaching English as a second language, the kinds of materials to be used, and the social and cultural patterns of the English-speaking community that should be stressed in the curriculum.

145   Hale, Thomas M., and Ena C. Budar. "Are TESOL Classes the Only Answer?" Modern Language Journal, 54, 7 (1970), 487-492.
       Although this article discusses the research conducted in the secondary schools of Honolulu, the recommendations could be applicable to many other areas in developing ESL programs for immigrant students. Some of the important recommendations are that pupils should attend special English classes as little as possible, that newly-arrived immigrants be given lightened academic loads, that pupils should have more exposure to English outside of school, and an American pupil should be assigned to each immigrant pupil.

146   Harasawa, Masayoshi. "A Critical Survey of English Language Teaching in Japan." English Language Teaching, 29, 1 (1974), 71-79.
       The writer feels that, based on his experiences as a learner and teacher, "the time and energy our students devote to English is mostly wasted." He offers specific reasons for this opinion: 1) The Japanese learners have never convinced themselves that living English is real, not abstract or artificial; 2) that there are grave teaching defects--poorly trained teachers, impractical teaching programs, and unsatisfactory language-teaching methodology; 3) that the Japanese are "intoxicated" by their own language, that the Japanese tend to "Japanese" anything foreign. An interesting and honest appraisal by a man who obviously cares about the subject and the people.

147   Hendrickson, R. H. "ESL--Who Needs It?" The English Record, 21, 4 (1971), 47-52.
       At the end of his article, Hendrickson states that ESL programs and who should be the students in them "is a lot more complicated than has generally been recognized," and the reader will agree with him. Many students are put into ESL classrooms when they should be in regular English language classrooms, and the ESL programs are often misused. In many instances they are used as "cure-alls" by assigning students

to them who need other kinds of remediation; teachers often fail to assess their students' language needs accurately, especially in differentiating between students who speak a nonstandard dialect and no English at all.

148 Honig, Lucille J., and F. William D. Love. Options and Perspectives: A Sourcebook of Innovative Foreign Language Programs in Action, K-12. New York: MLA/ACTFL, 1973.
Although the focus here is on foreign language programs, the discussion of factors related to the most successful foreign language programs in the country should be of interest to ESL teachers. The report is a survey of innovative foreign language programs from which 50 were selected because of the accomplishment of their stated goals. The book discusses language and culture, use of materials and community, and the parts played by students and teachers. Some of the innovations dealing with enrichment programs, programs for low- and high-ability students, and the student-centered techniques are especially interesting.

149 Johnson, Francis C. "The Failure of the Discipline of Linguistics in Language Teaching." Language Learning, 19/ 3, 4 (1969), 235-244.
Johnson points out some of the dangers in accepting linguistics as a panacea for second language learning. He believes that we have emphasized language interference rather than language facilitation. He does not reject linguistics as a useful discipline but asks educators to scrutinize this "raw material" and use it along with other associated disciplines. Linguistics should be only one of the "inputs of a total language strategy."

150 Kalantzis, Constantine P. "The Systems Approach to Instruction: English as a Second Language." Diss. Boston Univ., 1972.
Kalantzis believed that ESL teachers overlooked "the importance of viewing language as a form of human behavior" and usually did not include socio-psychological aspects of language learning in the curriculum. He therefore developed an instructional model that integrated various socio-psychological with pedagogical and linguistic aspects of language learning and, using experimental and control groups at a Boston public school, tested the model. A statistical analysis of objective post-tests showed that the experimental groups' scores were significantly superior.

151 Kaplan, Robert B. Guidelines: English Language Proficiency. Washington, D. C.: National Association for Foreign Student Affairs, 1971.
Since American colleges and universities enroll foreign students with varying degrees of English language skills, this book can be very helpful since it covers such things as admissions, testing, evaluation, funding, etc. In addition to a bibliography are a list of ESL tests, agencies in the international field, and recommendations for intensive English programs.

152   Kleitsch, Russell V. Teaching English as a Second Language, Grades
       7 through 12. San Diego, Calif.: San Diego Schools, 1968. ED 027128.
       The document presents guidelines for secondary schools offer-
       ing programs in English to Spanish-speaking students. Suggestions
       are made for placing students at various levels according to
       their English proficiency. It includes sample lessons that could
       cover a school year. Pronunciation, structure, spoken English,
       reading, and writing are all included.

153   Layne, Patsy Gaynell Pool. "Modern Linguistic Theory and Language
       Instruction in a Bilingual Milieu: Developing a Strategy for Primary
       English Instruction on Guam." Diss. Univ. of Pittsburgh, 1970.
       Although the setting of this study is Guam, the assessment
       of the program, the linguistic areas studied, and the strategies
       recommended are relevant to ESL teachers. The purpose of the
       study was to improve oral English instruction in the primary
       classrooms of Guam for children whose mother tongue was Chamorro.
       Sections of the study dealt with the use of a second language
       for formal instruction, the teaching of English, modern linguis-
       tic theory, the socio-political environment of Guam and its
       school system. The analysis of data gathered from various
       sources determined the syllabus and strategy recommendations.

154   Light, Richard L. "Our Language Arts and Minority Children."
       Speech given at Annual Convention of National Council of Teachers
       of English, Washington, D. C., November, 1969.
       Teachers working with children whose first language is not
       standard English should have an understanding of linguistic,
       cultural, and social elements in second language learning.
       The paper discusses the efforts of the USOE to support various
       kinds of programs to benefit minority group children, includ-
       ing the training of trainers of teachers in the Career Oppor-
       tunities Program.

155   Mason, Charles. "The Relevance of Intensive Training in English as
       a Foreign Language for University Students." Language Learning, 21,
       2 (1971), 197-204.
       The results of the experiment described in this article indi-
       cate that, for many intermediate to advanced foreign students,
       intensive EFL work may be irrelevant. The author questioned
       the theory that intensive EFL programs were the best means of
       increasing English proficiency. He therefore studied a control
       group of 15 students who took the compulsory Univ. of Hawaii
       English Language Institute program for foreign students, and an
       experimental group of 9 students who followed their regular
       programs. The author calls for further experimentation with a
       larger number of subjects who have varied backgrounds.

156   McKenzie, Keith S. "Language: The Great Barrier." The English
      Quarterly, 2, 2 (1969), 37-42.
            A problem that the author describes in this article is one
      that is faced by any minority group even though the focus of
      attention here is on the education of Indians and Eskimos in
      Canada. Noting that almost 60 per cent of the Indian children
      entering Canadian schools lacked fluency in English and that
      they had a higher medial age in every grade and a noticeable
      under-enrollment in higher grades, educators believed that
      lack of proficiency in English was the primary problem. It
      was recommended therefore that pre-school language instruction
      and an oral-aural program be offered from kindergarten to the
      sixth grade.

157   Mattran, Kenneth J. "Adult English as a Second Language Program in
      Chicago." Paper given at TESOL Convention, Chicago, Illinois,
      March 7, 1969. ED 030849.
            The largest program for adults learning English as a second
      language in Chicago is run by the Americanization Division of
      the Chicago Board of Education. The author applauds the pro-
      gram since it recognizes the necessity for providing language
      training for non-native speakers and does not accept the theory
      that people will learn English merely through "contact." ESL
      teachers will join in the applause. The program, a comprehen-
      sive one, is described and recommendations are made for its
      improvement, including teacher training.

158   Molina, Huberto. "Factors to be Considered in Designing an Instruc-
      tional Program in English for Spanish Speakers." Paper given at
      Fifth Annual TESOL Convention, New Orleans, La., 1971.
            Materials and information to be presented to new speakers of
      English must be properly selected, and should be based on what
      the learner must know in order to function in a different cul-
      ture. The teacher should know what to expect from materials,
      should know what the materials can do in the classroom, and
      should know the students well enough to utilize materials
      wisely.

159   Petrini, Alma Maria. ESOL-SESD Guide: Kindergarten. Ann Arbor:
      Univ. of Michigan, 1969.
            A carefully designed guide intended to help the kindergarten
      teacher teach English to speakers of other languages or teach
      standard English as a second dialect. There are 135 lessons
      each one of which covers a day's activities. The program
      stresses oral language development with the children repeat-
      ing language patterns after they have been uttered by the
      teacher. An imaginative teacher can make the program flexi-
      ble and fit it to the needs of the students.

160 Rahman, Binito Wajihur. "American Techniques of Teaching English as a Second Language and Their Application to the Schools of East Pakistan." Diss. Colorado State College, 1968.
  A survey of TESL programs and techniques of teaching English as a second language was made in order to examine the possibility and desirability of their application to the schools of East Pakistan. The results of a questionnaire sent throughout the United States and five territories revealed that fourteen states and Puerto Rico had one or more TESL programs, twelve states had none, and others had some informal programs or did not reply. The researcher believed the TESL programs in existence generally were not meeting the needs of non-English speaking students, but felt that certain techniques could be applied to English instruction in East Pakistan.

161 Roeming, Robert F. "Teaching English as a Second Language as a Model for Foreign Language Teaching." Paper given at Pacific Northwest Conference on Foreign Language, Portland, Oregon, 1970. ED 044975.
  In making suggestions for the improvement of foreign language teaching, the author advises that the principles he advocates could also be applied to teaching English as a second language. He suggests that language teaching should be linguistically oriented, should seek to develop proficiency, use new media, and offer a student-centered curriculum.

162 Rosen, Carl L. "Some Needed Research Regarding the Language and Reading Instructional Problems of Spanish speaking Children." Paper given at International Reading Assn. Conference, Kansas City, Mo., 1969. ED 031384.
  Presented here are three areas of research needed in language and reading development for children of Spanish-speaking backgrounds. The areas in need of research are in the descriptive studies of prelearning processes, compensatory educational programs, and curriculum and materials modifications. It is suggested that new curriculums should reflect current research results.

163 Rupley, William H. "Language Development and Beginning Reading Instruction." Elementary English, 52, 3 (1975), 403-408.
  This well researched article has important implications for ESL teachers and administrators involved in planning the curriculum for a language arts program, although the article was not written primarily for practitioners in second language teaching. The discussion focuses on the relationship between the pupil's language development and the reading process. The discussion presents opinions and the results of experiments by language authorities who offer a variety of ideas about the language curriculum and reading.

164   Sample Units for Use in Implementing an Effective ESOL Program.
      San Antonio, Texas: Our Lady of the Lake College, 1969. ED 031346.
           This is a collection of 20 sample units prepared by partici-
      pants of the NDEA Institute on ESOL at our Lady of the Lake
      College to be used in supplementing an ESOL program. The units
      cover science, spelling, arithmetic, language, and social
      studies with special stress being placed on using linguistics
      and oral-aural methods to teach English to non-native speakers,
      especially those who are Spanish-speaking. Units cover grades
      one through six.

165   Saville-Troike, Muriel. "Tesol Today: The Need for New Directions."
      TESOL Newsletter, 8/ 5, 6 (1974), 1-2, 6.
           Written by the President of TESOL, this article contains new
      ideas, points of weaknesses, and offers challenges to teachers
      of English as a second language. She is critical of the homo-
      geneous grouping of students for ESL instruction and advocates
      the use of integrated classrooms for non-native speakers. Such
      a system would require "major changes in our own preparation
      and in the materials we use." The article offers recommenda-
      tions for other changes that are worthy of consideration.
      Teachers and administrators should give careful consideration
      to the author's remarks.

166   Scarth, Peter, and Timothy F. Regan. "ESOL and the Mexican-American."
      Washington, D. C.: Center for Applied Linguistics, 1968. ED 016977.
           The article is critical of the ESOL programs that were de-
      signed for Mexican-American migrant workers because they dis-
      regarded the cultural background and psychological set of the
      learner and because the schools conducted all classes in English.
      The results of this kind of program have not been good as indi-
      cated by poor class performance, high dropout rates, and
      illiteracy in both Spanish and English. The authors call for
      more innovative programs and specially trained ESL teachers.

167   Smith Larry E. "What is Individualism in TESL?" TESL Reporter, 8,
      1 (1974), 1, 2, 12.
           The writer prefers the word "appropriate" to the word "individ-
      ualization" and questions whether teachers who claim to offer
      individualized programs in their ESL classrooms really do this.
      He offers some Theoretical Guidelines for Individualization in
      ESOL that are unorthodox, but refreshing: "I doubt that most
      people need to learn English at all. Those that do can decide
      for themselves what skills they are interested in." Smith
      offers some very worthwhile suggestions for the ESL teacher
      and lists questions at the end that can help teachers decide
      to what degree their classes are individualized.

168   Smith, Marquerite. "English as a Second Language for Mexican
       Americans." University Park, New Mexico: New Mexico State Univ.,
       1968. ED 016560.
              The author of this paper considers the students, teachers,
       school, and community as the four important factors for achiev-
       ing the objective of teaching Mexican-Americans to gain pro-
       ficiency in English. She stresses the listening-speaking-
       reading-writing sequence based on sound linguistic theory and
       recommends the use of games, songs, poems, and drills for use
       in the first grade.

169   Usmani, Mufti Ashfog Hasan. "A Study of the Teaching of English as
       a Foreign Language in the Secondary Schools of the Peshawar Region,
       West Pakistan." Diss. Texas Technological College, 1965.
              A study that attempted to provide data for improving English
       Instruction in the secondary schools of the Peshawar region of
       West Pakistan. Data were secured from 154 English teachers to
       determine current practices of teaching English, and a survey
       of related literature was made to determine the most effective
       techniques of teaching English. A contrastive analysis of
       English and Nrdu was also made to identify some of the teach-
       ing problems. Results of the survey revealed that the objectives
       of English teaching programs were unsound, that there was heavy
       reliance on the grammar-translation method, and that there was
       a lack of qualified teachers, materials, and visual aids.

                              Cross Reference

                    139   Methodology
                    143   Bilingual
                    144   Bilingual
                    146   Testing and Evaluation
                    150   Socio-Cultural
                    153   Bilingual
                    156   Adult
                    165   Methodology
                    167   Methodology

                                GRAMMAR

170   Aurbach, Joseph, et al. Transformational Grammar: A guide for
       Teachers. Portland, Oregon: English Language Services, 1974.
              An elementary course in transformational grammar to provide
       the teacher of English with an introduction to the theory and
       application of transformational grammar; it includes sections
       on syntax, morphology and phonology oriented to classroom texts
       using this grammar. The text moves progressively from elemental
       to more advanced language concepts and contains drawings and
       charts that reveal significant system relationships in new
       textbooks.

171   Brown, H. Douglas. "The Psychological Reality of 'Grammar' in the
      ESL Classroom." TESOL Quarterly, 6, 3 (1972), 263-269.
          Grammar has to be taught in the ESL classroom, but the mater-
      ial taught and the methods used can frequently be monotonous
      and, therefore, affect the achievement of the students. Lang-
      uage learning should be meaningful, without reliance on memor-
      ization or "over-learning." Teacher-student rapport is
      important so that students become responsive. Inductive drills
      should point toward a clear and specific grammatical goal;
      sentences should relate to real situations and all manipulative
      activities should "fulfill original conditions for meaningful
      learning."

172   Brown, T. Grant. "In Defense of Pattern Practice." Language Learn-
      ing, 19/ 3, 4 (1969), 191-203.
          Although recent theories of syntax and language learning
      have had an influence on second language teaching and should be
      respected, Brown believes that students studying foreign lang-
      uages still need "oral practice of grammatical contrasts" to
      overcome their native language structural habits; therefore,
      pattern practice is still essential despite the changes that
      have occurred in theories. He offers graphic definition of
      a pattern in relation to syntax and maintains that "the form
      of an abstract theory can have more effect on the form of the
      utterances of the language."

173   Byrd, Hazel Patricia. "Modals in Present-Day American English:
      Theories, Applications, and Resource Materials for the Teaching
      of English as a Second Language." Diss. Univ. of Florida, 1974.
          This study was conducted in order to provide ESL teachers
      who had a limited knowledge of English with a text that would
      explain how English works and provide resources for indepen-
      dent study. Taking the modal auxiliary as an import element
      to students of English as a second language, the researcher
      collected and analyzed 825 examples of modals and then de-
      vised exercises based on theoretical materials, ESL teaching
      methodology, and observation of modals obtained from techni-
      cal and scientific writing, since there is a need to teach
      English to technicians in various parts of the world.

174   Diller, Karl C. Generative Grammar, Structural Linguistics, and
      Language Teaching. Rowley, Mass.: Newbury House, 1972.
          A comparison of the audio-lingual and the generative grammar
      method of teaching English as a second language. The former
      method, based on repetition of patterns, is being re-examined
      and the author explains why he favors the latter approach, a
      rationalistic one, after evaluating the results of programs
      based on structural linguistics.

175　Dixson, Robert J., _Essential Idioms in English_. New York: Regents
　　　Publishing Co., 1974.
　　　　　　A book containing more than 600 frequently used idioms with
　　　　　definitions, illustrations, examples of use and exercises. The
　　　　　Appendix gives the French, Spanish, and German equivalents for
　　　　　each idiom. The illustrations and practice exercises should be
　　　　　helpful to students.

176　Elgin, Suzette Hoden, and John T. Grinder. _Guide to Transformational_
　　　Grammar: History, Theory, Practice. New York: Holt, Rinehart and
　　　Winston, 1973.
　　　　　　Intended to serve the college undergraduate who has little know-
　　　　　ledge of linguistics and for use by instructors who are not
　　　　　specialists in generative grammar, the text is considered by
　　　　　critics to be the best of its kind presently available. The
　　　　　authors' style and enthusiasm make the text attractive to students,
　　　　　and including answers to exercises provides immediate reinforce-
　　　　　ment. The major emphasis is on the syntax and semantics of
　　　　　language. A useful bibliography is included.

177　Eschliman, Herbert R., Robert C. Jones, and Tommy R. Burkett.
　　　Generative English Handbook. Belmont, California: Wadsworth, 1968.
　　　　　　An intoductory text to generative-transformational grammar with
　　　　　a discussion of rules of rhetoric and logic not often found in
　　　　　this kind of text. Most of the book is written simply and clearly,
　　　　　covering kernel rules, transformations, lexical rules, and diction.
　　　　　The exercises have been carefully prepared; the text includes a
　　　　　Glossary and Index. The book could be a helpful reference to
　　　　　people teaching intermediate and advanced ESL students.

178　Hill, L. A. _Programmed English Course: Stages 1-6, Pupil's Book_.
　　　New York: Oxford University Press, 1969.
　　　　　　The text for students of English as a second language uses
　　　　　149 steps that lead progressively through a variety of English
　　　　　language patterns including verb forms, questions, commands,
　　　　　and negatives. The programmed book makes use of various draw-
　　　　　ings of people and objects used in introducing words and
　　　　　grammatical structures.

179　Jacobs, Roderick A. "Linguistic Universals and Their Relevance to
　　　TESOL", in _Studies in Language_, Roderick A. Jacobs, ed. Lexington,
　　　Mass.: Xerox Publishing Co., 1973, 11-18.
　　　　　　Jacobs believes that more emphasis should be placed on the
　　　　　likenesses of languages and offers examples of universal pro-
　　　　　cesses in human languages. Based on his experiences as a
　　　　　teacher of English to non-English-speaking students, the
　　　　　writer recommends that teachers should know transformational
　　　　　grammar and "the relevant characteristics of the native lang-
　　　　　uage of their students." When a teacher can show how the pro-
　　　　　cesses in the student's language and in English are similar, it
　　　　　is then easier to teach correct usage.

180   Jacobs, Roderick A., ed. Studies in Language. Lexington, Mass.:
       Xerox College Publishing, 1973.
            A collection of articles about language and meaning, most
       of which are written by the editor with four articles written
       by "guest authors". The anthology covers various matters of
       language including syntax, phonology, dialect, and transfor-
       mational grammar. A careful reading of the articles reveals
       novel approaches to studying various aspects of language that
       should be of interest to ESL teachers who want more insights
       into language teaching.

181   Kapili, Lili Vasquez. "Grammatical Features Identified by Sector
       Analysis: Their Use as Criteria for Determining the Suitability
       of English and American Poetry for Filipino Second-Language
       Learners." Diss. New York Univ., 1970.
            A study that should interest college instructors who teach
       poetry to foreign students in their English classes. The
       researcher listed twelve syntactical combinations consistently
       used in fifty English and American poems of the seventeenth
       and twentieth centuries and then compared these with the
       grammatical patterns taught in Philippine high schools, thus
       identifying basic structural similarities and differences
       between the grammar taught and the combinations involved in
       the poems. It was found that the structural patterns taught
       to Filipino students did not prepare them "to meet the lin-
       guistic demands" of most of the poems.

182   Langendoen, D. Terence. The Study of Syntax: The Generative-
       Transformational Approach to American English. New York: Holt,
       Rinehart and Winston, 1969.
            One of the texts in the Trans-Atlantic Series in Linguistics,
       this book can be helpful to the ESL teacher who needs more in-
       formation about generative-transformational grammar. The text
       covers semantics, morphology, deep and surface structure, ling-
       uistic data, and transformations. Also included are a biblio-
       graphy and a glossary. At times, the explanations become
       unnecessarily complex, but the book, as a whole, achieves its
       purpose.

183   Lester, Mark. Introductory Transformational Grammar of English.
       New York: Holt, Rinehart and Winston, 1971.
            The book is intended for students who have little background
       in transformational grammar. It is an elementary book and one
       that could be helpful to ESL teachers who need guidance in this
       area of language study. It is divided into four sections:
       Simple Phrase Structure Rules, Simple Transformational Rules,
       Sentences Combined by Embedding Rules, and Sentences Combined by
       Joining Rules. The explanations are simply stated, and the
       examples are carefully selected. For the instructor with
       specialized training in transformational grammar, the book is
       too elementary, but for the uninitiated, it can be a valuable
       guide.

184   Marckwardt, Albert H. <u>Linguistics and the Teaching of English.</u>
       Bloomington, Indiana: Indiana Univ. Press, 1966.
           The material in this text provides the ESL teacher with some
       basic information about the use of linguistics on the elemen-
       tary and secondary school levels. Marckwardt discusses some
       historical perspectives and deals with traditional, structural,
       and transformational approaches to linguistic analysis. The
       book also covers the relationship between linguistics and
       composition, the difficulties of spelling, the teaching of
       reading, and the study of linguistics and literature. The
       author explains what linguistics can and cannot do, treating
       it more as an aid rather than a panacea.

185   Natalicio, Diane S., and Luiz F. S. Natalicio. "A Comparative Study
       of English Pluralization by Native and Non-Native English Speakers."
       <u>Child Development</u>, 42 (1971), 1165-1173.
           A comparative study in English pluralization by native and
       non-native English speakers. A total number of 144 males in
       first, second, third, and tenth grades were equally divided at
       each grade level according to native language and were pre-
       sented a randomized list of nonsense syllables for which the
       pupils would find plurals. Results showed that the pattern
       of acquisition of noun plurals in English was comparable for
       both native and non-native speakers of English.

186   Nilsen, Don L. F. "The Use of Case Grammar in Teaching English as
       a Foreign Language." Paper given at Fifth Annual TESOL Convention,
       New Orleans, La., 1971. ED 053584.
           In order to permit the non-native speaker of English to per-
       ceive certain vocabulary and semantic similarities between
       English and his native language, the author advocates the use
       of case frames. In addition the utilization of case frames
       would allow for situational and structural control and enable
       the student to use conceptual signs in learning new words.

187   Pincas, Anita. "'Transformational', 'Generative', and the EFL Teache
       <u>English Language Teaching</u>, 22, 3 (1968), 210-220.
           This article attempts to clarify the definitions and use of
       generative and transformational grammar. The author believes
       that those who believe that language teaching should be by
       transformational drills are misinterpreting the aim of trans-
       formational grammar which is to get students to produce
       acceptable English utterances. The rules of the grammar are
       discussed and graphically explained. Generative grammar is
       also defined, and Pincas stresses that it is useful when it
       "presents the data for work preliminary to the actual situa-
       tional use...."

188   Pinson, Rosie Barajas, et al. I Do and I Understand (Glen Helen
      Workshop: April 29 - May 1, 171). Columbus, Ohio: Ohio State Dept.
      of Education, 1971. ED 058976.
            The report contains four workshop presentations given during
      the teacher workshop seminar at the Glen Helen Outdoor Educa-
      tion Center at Yellow Springs, Ohio, where major emphasis was
      on training teachers to serve migrant children. One presenta-
      tion includes 12 pattern drills to be used by the teacher to
      help students master basic English language patterns. Another
      offers practice in word order and grammatical structure. Each
      section contains pictures and a narrative discussion of the
      presentation.

189   Praninskas, Jean. Rapid Review of English Grammar, 2nd ed. Engle-
      wood Cliffs, N.J.: Prentice Hall, 1975.
            A recently revised edition of a successful text that reviews
      basic grammatical patterns. The twenty lessons have four parts
      to them consisting of model paragraphs, explanations of grammat-
      ical patterns, and exercises and assignments. Students using
      the text should be at the high intermediate or advanced level
      of English. Although some of the grammatical elements are more
      traditional than current and not really reflective of contempor-
      ary usage, much of the material is very useful.

190   Ravem, Roar. The Development of Wh-Questions in First and Second
      Language Learners. Colchester, England: Essex Univ., 1970.
      ED 054654.
            A study of the development of English wh-questions in first
      and second language learners to find regular patterns of struc-
      ture and to compare these with transformational grammar struc-
      tures. The author points out that there is a need for language-
      learning theory that will include generalized learning factors
      as well as a consideration of linguistic principles.

191   Reeves, George. Idioms in Action: A Key to Fluency. Rowley, Mass.:
      Newbury House, 1975.
            A workbook for teaching the intermediate or advanced student
      to speak and write in idiomatic American English, containing 150
      essential idioms in a semi-programmed arrangement that is largely
      self-correctable. A series of dialogues between a Japanese and
      a French girl continue throughout the book in order to relate
      idioms to situations. Exercises are provided to enable the stu-
      dent to recite and write the idioms in appropriate contexts.

192   Ross, Janet. "The Transformationalists and ESL Teachers, 1972."
      TESOL Quarterly, 6, 4 (1972), 305-311.
            The gap between pattern practice used in audio-lingual approaches
      and the cognitive approach of transformational theory may not be
      as large as some people think it is. The teacher is advised to
      make use of the knowledge we now have of transformational grammar
      and apply it to some of the techniques (audio-lingual) that we

now use. "Deduction and induction may both play a role in language teaching." Such a view could reduce the confusion of the ESL teachers who believe that an eclectic approach is effective.

193   Rutherford, William E. "Pragmatic Syntax in the Classroom." Paper given at Annual Conference of Teachers of English to Speakers of Other Languages. San Juan, Puerto Rico, 1973. ED 086023.
       The author maintains that syntax and pragmatics can work harmoniously in a second language program and believes that the teacher should point out certain structures that the student should recognize even though he is interested in communicating. Various exercises closely related to the content of the communication are offered as examples of language control that the teacher can utilize.

194   Salus, Peter H. Linguistics. New York: Bobbs-Merrill, 1969.
       One of the Bobbs-Merrill Series in Speech Communication consisting of sixty-six pages and covering sounds, morphology, sociolinguistics, psycholinguistics, and other areas. The author takes special pains to be explicit so that the reader will be able to grasp each concept easily. The text could serve as an introduction to linguistics, followed by a text with more substantial coverage.

195   Saporta, Sol. "Applied Linguistics and Generative Grammar," in Trends in Language Teaching, Albert Valdman, ed. New York: McGraw-Hill, 1966.
       Saporta is critical of some of the suggestions that linguists have made in second language teaching including the primacy of speech over writing and the pattern-practice exercises and memorization that go with linguistic methods. He believes that generative grammar "enables textbook writers to base their material on the most adequate description," but also maintains that a grammar that advocates automatic performance and another which presupposes "the competency to be learned" must develop "pedagogical" theories.

196   Saville, Muriel R. "Language and the Disadvantaged," in Language and Cultural Diversity in American Education, Roger D. Abrahams and Rudolph C. Troike, eds. Englewood Cliffs, New Jersey: Prentice-Hall, 1972, 310-318.
       A compact and non-technical article that discusses some of the differences in grammar, sounds, and semantics between Spanish, English, Acadian, French, and Navajo. Teachers will find the essay helpful because it reveals problem areas that students will have in learning English, thus enabling teachers to anticipate such problems.

197 Smackey, Thelma R., and Richard Beym. "Tag Questions - Dangerous Psycholinguistic Territory for TESOL." <u>IRAL</u> 7, 2 (1969), 107-115.
The authors conducted experiments with native speakers (male and female) from various sections of the United States to test their understanding of tag questions. In responding to ten selected tag questions, both undergraduates and professionals in the experiment revealed a "broad range of emotional qualities and attitudinal meanings." Another experiment and passages from works of contemporary American authors support the hypotheses that tag questions are complex; that "two standard variations in their final intonation contours" convey a yes-no question to native speakers; and variations in voice quality influence the meanings gained by native listeners.

198 Stageberg, Norman C. <u>An Introductory English Grammar</u>. New York: Holt, Rinehart, and Winston, 1971.
A textbook of structural grammar with a chapter on transformational grammar. The material covered in the book offers the ESL teacher a rich background in English that is essential to teaching the language to non-native speakers. The text includes material on phonology, morphology, syntax, and transformational grammar. A key is provided for the many exercises that appear.

199 Stieglitz, Francine B. "Sentence Length, Grammatical Structure, and Repetition of Sentences." Paper given at the Sixth Annual TESOL Convention, Washington, D. C., 1972.
A report of a study that probes the effects of sentence length and grammatical structure on the ability of foreign students to repeat English sentences. It was thought that sentences with varied syntactic structure would be more difficult to repeat than those with the same length without varied structure. Also, longer sentences involved a more pronounced structure. Teachers should recognize the importance of sentence length, patterns, and the type of sentence development in developing drill sentences.

200 Topping, D. C. "Some Implications of Transformational Grammar for Language Teaching." <u>Regional English Language Centre Journal</u>, 1, 1 (1970), 37-49.
Topping defines transformational grammar and discusses its use in language teaching. He considers that transformational grammar, since it refers to unchanging rules that influence the generating of an infinite number of sentences, should be used in teaching language. He suggests that language texts should give the student a chance to use his innate ability to develop language, and this will motivate him more than the drills often found in texts, including ESL textbooks.

201   Wohl, Milton. "The Pedagogical Applications of Two Theories of Grammar
to the Teaching of English as a Foreign Language." Diss. Univ. of
Michigan, 1967.
    A classroom experiment was conducted in Quito, Ecuador, using
instructional materials with two groups of students, one of
which (experimental) received instruction consisting of a simplified transformational analysis prepared by the experimenter.
Statistical computations yielded no significant results at the
five per cent level. The experimenter discusses reasons for the
failure of the instructional variable to have as much influence
as had been hypothesized and expresses the need for "diagnostic
instruments capable of differentiating students" according to
their modes of learning.

Cross Reference

172	Audio-Lingual
173	Methodology
179	Methodology
194	Texts

LANGUAGE LEARNING

202   Allen, Virginia F. "A Second Dialect is Not a Foreign Language."
Monograph Series on Languages and Linguistics, No. 22. Ed. James
E. Alatis. Georgetown University, 1969.
    There are certain similarities between the programs for teach-
ing Standard English to speakers of other dialects and those for
teaching English as a foreign language that include the use of
contrastive analysis, the stress on habit-formation and structure, and recognition of the student's own language. Teaching
a second dialect, however, is different from teaching a foreign
language not only in regard to classroom techniques but in the
teacher's relationship to the students when the students learning Standard English must be taught to understand that "there
are new speech habits to be acquired," whereas the student
learning English as a foreign language has usually already
recognized this.

203   Andrade, Vincente de Paula. "The Role of Cognate Vocabulary in the
Teaching of English to Speakers of Portuguese." Diss. Univ. of
Texas, 1973.
    The researcher believed that teachers of English to speakers
of Portuguese should rely more heavily on cognate vocabulary in
the early stages of instruction, that enough recognition had not
been given to lexical similarities between English and the
Romance languages. The study reveals weaknesses in teaching
methods and in compiling word lists for the teaching of foreign
languages that have affected the use of cognates and concludes
that teachers should revise current assumptions concerning the
role of vocabulary in FL teaching and that materials for teaching English to speakers of Portuguese should use cognate ex-
tensively.

204 Anisfield, Moshe. "Psycholinguistic Perspectives on Language Learning," in Trends in Language Teaching, Albert Valdman, ed. New York: McGraw-Hill, 1966.
       The author does not attempt to offer any solution to language teaching problems through the application of psychology guidelines, but offers some ideas emerging from psychology and linguistics that are pertinent to language learning and teaching. Anisfield discusses the nature of linguistic competence, the psychological processes in language acquisition, and perception as a field of psychological inquiry. The section in Learning and Retention presents some information about language learning that is relevant to the task of ESL teachers.

205 Bates, Roberta Reed. "A Study in the Acquisition of Language." Diss. Univ. of Texas, 1969.
       This study should have some implications for second language learning although it deals with the acquisition of a first language. The results indicated that language acquisition is "not an accretion of adult rules," but that the order of acquisition of language is determined by the child's inductive strategies." The researcher's conclusions were based on the fact that truncated passives were easier to comprehend than full passives and get passives were learned earlier than be passives by 50 three-year-old children under study.

206 Bordie, John G. "When Should Instruction in a Second Language or Dialect Begin?" Elementary English, 48, 5 (May 1971), 551-557.
       The author, through research, seeks to offer some evidence that will provide some answers to the question of the best time or grade level for beginning second language instruction. He offers three possible answers: 1) If communication in the second language is all that is desired, the instruction may be begun at or near the time of need; 2) If pronunciation skill is of social importance, language study should begin as early as possible; 3) If the school program is not a strong one, due to various reasons, the grade at which a person begins the language is less important than having a "continuous sequence of offerings" --a period usually of four to six years.

207 Brown, H. Douglas. "Affective Variables in Second Language Acquisition." Language Learning, 23, 2 (1973), 231-244.
       The author believes that affective variables have not been adequately investigated in studying the acquisition of a second language. He mentions empathy, introversion/extroversion, and aggression as important social variables in understanding the social aspect of such learning. He advocates inter-disciplinary research in the affective area of the study of second language acquisition which could create improved approaches to language teaching.

208 Brown, H. Douglas. "Cognitive Pruning and Second Language Acquisitions." Speech given at the Fifth Annual TESOL Convention, New
Orleans, 1971. ED 056588.
In discussing rote learning and meaningful learning, the
author maintains that rote learning takes place through a con-
ditioning process and is effective only on a short-term basis;
meaningful learning involves abstraction, generalization, and
an established conceptual system. His theory is important to
ESL teachers and should be carefully considered in second
language teaching.

209 Burt, Marina K., and Heidi C. Dulay. "Natural Sequences in Child
Second Language Acquisition." Language Learning, 24, 1 (1974),
37-53.
In comparing the acquisition sequences of 11 English grammatical forms by native Chinese- and Spanish-speaking children
learning English, the authors found strong support for universal
child language learning tactics and believe that further research could describe such devices. They also contend that it
is the second language system rather than the first that "guides
the acquisition process" as shown in the authors' research.
Case, articles, plurals, possessives, auxiliaries, and copula
were some of the grammatical forms of study.

210 Cornejo, Richard J. A Synthesis of Theories and Research on the
Effects of Teaching in First and Second Languages: Implications for
Bilingual Education. University Park, New Mexico: New Mexico State
Univ., 1974. ED 092265.
A thorough paper that discusses first and second language
acquisition and bilingualism, reviewing theories, research,
present practices, and legislation in language acquisition
and language learning. The author's recommendations include
a bilingual curriculum for all bilingual students, a flexible
program for low and bright students, a bilingual education
major for all universities in the Southwest.

211 Dale, Philip S. Language Development: Structure and Function.
Hinsdale, Illinois: Dryden, 1972.
ESL teachers who want information about language development
in children will find this book both helpful and interesting.
The material is presented in non-scientific language covering
the basic terms and principles of linguistics, the child's innate
ability to learn language, syntactic development, and phonetic
development. The book covers language development comprehensively and offers the reader major viewpoints about the topics
discussed.

212 DeVito, Joseph A. Language Concepts and Processes. Englewood Cliffs
New Jersey: Prentice-Hall, 1973.
For the teacher of English as a second language who wants to
acquire knowledge about the acquisition of language, several

essays in this anthology will be very helpful. These include Chomsky's "Language and the Mind," Bellugi's "Learning the Language," and Whorf's "Language and Logic." Other articles consider language forms and functions, language and thought, and language and communication.

213 Dulay, Heidi, C., and Marina K. Burt. "Errors and Strategies in Child Second Language Acquisition." TESOL Quarterly, 8, 2 (1974), 129-136.
A study was made of 179 children from 5-8 years old learning English as a second language whose 513 utterances containing errors were classified as due to "interference" or "developmental." Results showed that children learning English as a second language do not use first language habits in learning the syntax of their new language. The author believes that "less explicit teaching of ESL syntax to children may produce better learning."

214 Emig, Janet A., James T. Fleming, and Helen M. Popp. Language and Learning. New York: Harcourt, Brace, 1966.
A revision and expansion of the 1964 Special Issue of the Harvard Educational Review. The collection of essays covers the child's acquisition of syntax, oral language development, psychological aspects in the teaching of concepts, the potential educational value of transformational grammar, the teaching of intonation and other topics. Although the book is primarily for the teachers of English to native speakers, the anthology offers cogent material for the ESL teacher.

215 Ervin-Tripp, Susan. "An Issei Learns English." The Journal of Social Issues, 23 (1967), 78-90.
A general discussion of the psychological factors in bilingualism in which the author states that many of the factors which interfere with the linguistic performance of a speaker learning English as a second language are the same as those affecting a monolingual speaker, although some are due to linguistic and sociolinguistic principles that the bilingual student must learn.

216 Ervin-Tripp, Susan M. "Is Second Language Learning Like the First?" TESOL Quarterly, 8, 2 (1974), 111-127.
This study was made to help determine the relation between first and second language learning and compares the process of native language acquisition with second language acquisition-- the learning of French by English speakers. It was found that the development of syntax comprehension and of morphology followed the order in native language studies. It might be surprising to some people that in the samples of children, ages four through nine, the older children learned faster than the younger ones.

217 Hepworth, Janice C. "The Importance and Implications of the 'Critical Period' for Second-Language Learning." English Language Teaching Journal, 28, 2 (1974), 272-282.

An assessment of "the importance and implications of the critical period (second-language learning that overlaps primary language learning) for second-language learning." The paper discusses the importance of the critical period for second-language learning and deals with the theory of Lenneberg's matrix idea. References are made to Penfield and Roberts, Kolers and Lambert, and Fillenbaum. Results indicate that primary-language learning sequence is applicable to second-language learning if the second language is learned during this critical period.

218 Higginbotham, Dorothy O. "Psycholinguistic Research and Language Learning." Elementary English, 49, 6 (1972), 811-817.

A well researched article that provides the teacher with some valuable information about language acquisitions and discusses the social and environmental variables "which may provide the key to understanding individual and group differences in language behavior." The article concludes that the period from ages 2 to 12 are the productive years for language learning, that all languages share the same potential for expression, and that children may be impeded in some aspects of school learning if their communication sphere is restricted.

219 Hunt, Kellogg W. "Do Sentences in the Second Language Grow Like Those in the First?" TESOL Quarterly, 4, 3 (1970), 195-202.

Since it has been found that children who are native speakers of English embed an increasingly larger number of sentence parts as they get older, it seems significant to see if this activity could measure a person's command of a second language and whether drill in sentence embedding should be part of second language instruction. The author maintains that one must differentiate between language acquisition, and language development and indicates that sentence embedding is important enough to warrant further investigation.

220 Hymes, Dell. "Models of the Interaction of Language and Social Setting." The Journal of Social Issues, 23(1967), 8-28.

The author states that speakers are not limited to a single linguistic code and that they switch to a code which is appropriate for signaling social intimacy or distance. If this switching is to be understood, emphasis must be placed on the interaction of language and its social contexts.

221 Kaneda, Michikazu. "Some Transformation Effects on Recording English Sentences." Bulletin for the Teachers of English (Hiroshima Univ.), 1972.

This report describes an experiment concerned with determining various levels of language acquisition based on the premise that a developmental procedure could be established in foreign language acquisition based on individual learning maturation. The experiment involved Japanese students who were asked to recall English kernel sentences and paraphrase and transform them. Results showed that the students were able to follow the transformational system only to some degree.

222   Kessler, Carolyn. "Syntactic Contrasts in Child Bilingualism." Language Learning, 22, 2 (1972), 221-233.
        The author's hypothesis in developing her experiment was that languages share deep structures and that "differences derive from language--specific rules." She conducted an investigation of a selected group of twelve children, ages 6 to 8, bilingual in Italian and English, to test the theory that structures shared by Italian and English develop in like order and rate in the bilingual child. Her findings indicated that children acquire structures shared by two languages in like sequence and rate. These results may have implications for the adult learner of English.

223   Lado, Robert. "Patterns of Difficulty in Vocabulary," in Teaching English as a Second Language, Harold B. Allen and Russell N. Campbell, eds. New York: McGraw-Hill, 1972, 275-288.
        Much of the thinking about vocabulary work in language learning has been over-simplified, according to Lado. The teacher is advised to consider three important aspects of words: form, meaning, and distribution. The author points out that the form of words varies "according to the formality of the situation, speed of talk," and other factors and states that "Some meanings found in one culture may not exist in another." In addition, words can be restricted geographically, and socially, and according to styles of speaking and writing.

224   Lambert, W. E. and G. R. Tucker. "The Home-School Language Switch Program: Grade K through Five." Paper given at Conference on Child Language, Chicago, Illinois, 1971. ED 060750.
        An experiment that utilized the criterion that priority should be given to the language least likely to be developed by a child who intends to become bilingual. English-speaking Canadian children studied in French in kindergarten and the first grade, and in grades 2 through 5 studied mainly in French except for brief lessons in English language arts. Evaluation of the children's language development are of special interest.

225   Langacker, Ronald W. Language and Its Structure. New York: Harcourt, Brace & World, 1968.
        The second chapter of the book provides some important language background for teachers of non-native speakers since it deals with language acquisition, sound and meaning, linguistic "subsystems," and language and thought. The entire section explains how languages differ in sound and grammar

and refers to many languages other than English. The material
on language learning is especially informative. Other chapters
offer helpful background material.

226   Lee, W. R.   "Language, Experience, and the Language Learner."
       English Language Teaching, 27, 3 (1973), 234-245.
              A discussion of the success in learning the mother tongue
       and the problems in learning a foreign language. The mater-
       ial presented here is relevant to learning English as a second
       language. Some of the discussion is repetitive and may seem
       almost contradictory, but Lee offers some worthwhile sugges-
       tions. Second-language learning lessons "must consist of
       experience as well as of language," and must be based on the
       student's interests at the time he learns the language. Signi-
       ficant conditions are situation, liveliness, and involvement.

227   Lindfors, Judith.   "The Michigan Oral Language Series: A Critical
       Review." Paper given to Language Research Seminar, Univ. of
       Texas: Austin, 1970.
              The author states that the primary Michigan program cover-
       ing mathematics, science, social studies, linguistics, and
       conceptualization attempts to accomplish too much and criti-
       cizes the lessons which focus on one subject matter area, and
       suggests that lessons should cross content areas so that the
       concepts from different content areas could be used. She also
       points out that the linguistic and conceptual emphasis was not
       used to identify basic concepts in the subject matter area.

228   Lugton, Robert, ed.   Toward a Cognitive Approach to Second Language
       Acquisition. Philadelphia: Center for Curriculum Development, 1971.
              A collection of thirteen papers dealing with the theories of
       second-language teaching. The papers have enough variety to
       offer the teacher a fairly good cross section of current theor-
       ies of language learning. Included among the authors are
       Jakabovits, Chastain,Wardhaugh, Bosco, and DiPietro.

229   Mackey, William F.   "Free Language Alternation in Early Childhood
       Education." Paper given at Conference on Child Language, Chicago,
       Illinois, 1971.
              Results accumulated over a ten-year period reveal that two
       languages need not be taught to children in different contexts
       to avoid linguistic confusion. If the pre-school child uses
       one of the languages with some efficiency, he can alternate
       languages in a mixed population to enhance his bilingualism in
       kindergarten and the primary grades. The two alternating lang-
       uages discussed here are English and German.

230   McNeill, David.   The Acquisition of Language: The Study of Develop-
       mental Psycholinguistics. New York: Harper and Row, 1972.
              For the teacher who needs background information about lang-
       uage acquisition and is not prepared for the technical aspects
       involved, this text can be helpful. The arrangement of material,

based mostly on the language theories of Chomsky, is orderly, enabling the reader to understand the psycholinguistic theory more easily. An appendix introduces the reader to transformational grammar.

231   Martinez-Bernal, Janet Ayers. Children's Acquisition of Spanish and English Morphological Systems and Noun Phrases. Diss. Georgetown Univ., Washington, D. C., 1972.
        Information about monolingual language acquisition in English and Spanish was used in developing a bilingual diagnostic language test that would help to ascertain the bilingual language acquisition of children aged five to eight years in Tucson, Arizona. Test results indicated that children seemed to be acquiring English and Spanish in much the same way as children who were monolingual acquired their language.

232   Milon, John P. "The Development of Negation in English by a Second Language Learner." TESOL Quarterly, 8, 2 (1974), 135-143.
        The paper compares the development of the system of negation in English in a seven-year-old Japanese immigrant's speech with the system of negation as it developed in the speech of three native English speakers. It was found that "native-like language learning ability could in principle remain a human characteristic up to the age of puberty." One can possibly conclude that a child learning a second language living within that culture uses the same learning tactics used by native speakers.

233   Nedler, Shari, and Judith Lindfors. "Bilingual Learning for the Spanish-Speaking Preschool Child." Paper given at Conference on Child Language, Chicago, Illinois, 1971. ED 060746.
        The principle of the program described in this report is that children of preschool age who are not English-speaking will learn new concepts better if they are introduced on their own language. The program was initiated for Mexican-American preschool children. The English program features practicality of language use, questioning, and initial emphasis on syntactic structure.

234   Oskarsson, Mats. "The Acquisition of Foreign Language Grammar by Adults: A Summary Report on Three Field Experiments." Paper given at International Congress of Applied Linguistics, Copenhagen, Denmark, 1972. ED 070353.
        A comparison of two approaches to teaching foreign language grammar to adults: one based on the audiolingual habit theory (Implicit Method), and the other based on the cognitive code-learning theory of language acquisition (Explicit Method). It was ascertained from the experiments that adult students acquire foreign language grammar better using a cognitive method. Results and procedures are included.

235   Prator, Clifford H. "Adding a Second Language." Paper presented at
       TESOL Convention, Chicago, Illinois, 1969.
            An important principle is stated in this paper: A student
       learning English as a second language does not learn English
       naturally as a child learns his mother tongue; therefore the
       second language usually must be taught to the student. The
       paper also discusses the various stages of first language
       learning and also includes such topics as motivation, linguis-
       tic interference, teacher responsibility, sequence of skills
       learned, and organization of the content of lessons.

236   Richard, Jack C. "A Non-Contrastive Approach to Error Analysis."
       Paper given at the TESOL Convention, San Francisco, March 1970.
       ED 037721.
            A discussion of structural difficulties in the native langu-
       age which interfere with the student's acquisition of his second
       language. There are errors in learning English not derived
       from transfers from another language not predictive from con-
       trastive analysis. These intralingual and development errors
       reveal some of the general traits of language acquisition. To
       distinguish among various kinds of errors, the author studied
       speakers of varied languages in order to define errors pro-
       perly.

237   Riegel, Klaus, Robert M. Ramsay, and Ruth M. Riegel. "A Comparison
       of the First and Second Language of American and Spanish Students."
       Journal of Verbal Learning and Verbal Behavior, 6, 4 (1967),
       536-544.
            The results of this experiment reveal how the method of
       training affects second-language learning. Twenty-four American
       and twenty-four Spanish students gave restrictive associations
       to a variety of stimuli and the researchers concluded that pro-
       gress in a second language cannot be measured only by knowledge
       of vocabulary. The Spanish students learned their English by
       living in an American environment with little formal English
       instruction. They showed rapid vocabulary growth but little
       knowledge of "conceptual semantic structure."

238   Rivers, Wilga M. "Rules, Patterns, and Creativity in Language Learn-
       ing," in Readings in English as a Second Language, Kenneth Croft,
       ed. Cambridge: Mass.: Winthrop Publishers, 1972, 49-56.
            After discussing Chomsky's theories and his contributions to
       language learning, the writer defines two levels of language
       behavior 1)the level of manipulation of language elements (habit
       formation) and 2) "a level of expression of personal meaning at
       which possible variations are infinite" (the understanding of a
       complex system). The writer believes that practice at the
       second level should not be delayed until the student learns
       "all the common features of the manipulative type," and that
       the student must learn to apply what he learns at the appro-
       priate time. The article should convince ESL teachers that
       they must "induce language behavior at the second level."

239 Rogers, R. S., and E. N. Wright. The School Achievement of Kinder-
     garten Pupils for Whom English is a Second Language: A Longitudinal
     Study Using Data from the Study of Achievement. Toronto, Ontario:
     Toronto Board of Education, 1969. ED 066220.
          A presentation of data concerning children for whom English
     was a second language. Sources included pupil profile folders,
     teacher rating questionnaires, various standardized tests and
     psychological service referrals. Results showed that pupils
     learning English as a second language overcame their language
     difficulty by grade 3; they were more likely to enter separate
     school systems; and they were less likely to be referred to
     Child Adjustment Services. These results have led researchers
     to other pertinent questions involving students in bilingual
     programs.

240 Rubin, Joan. "What the 'Good Language Learner' Can Teach Us."
     TESOL Quarterly, 9, 1 (1975), 41-51.
          The writer believes that there are certain strategies used
     by successful learners of a second language that can be used
     in teaching poorer learners. Three variables are involved:
     aptitude, motivation, and opportunity. The good language
     learner is a willing and accurate guesser, needs to communi-
     cate, is not inhibited, attends to form, practices, monitors
     his own speech and the speech of others, and attends to mean-
     ing. The article discusses how learner strategies vary and
     states that further research will help lessen the difference
     between good and poor learners.

241 Scott, Charles F. "Transformational Theory and English as a Second
     Language/Dialect," in Report of the 20th Annual Round Table Meeting
     on Linguistics and Language Studies, Linguistics and the Teaching
     of Standard English to Speakers of Other Languages or Dialects,
     1970. ED 035892.
          The significance of transformational theory in the teaching
     of English is discussed, and the information should be helpful
     to teachers and language students. Chomsky's theories on
     language acquisition are reviewed as they relate to their impor-
     tance in second language/dialect learning, especially the
     usually accepted audio-lingual approach. An informative and
     stimulating article.

242 Seliger, Herbert William. "A Comparison of an Inductive Method with
     a Modified Deductive Method in the Teaching of English Syntax
     Patterns to Adult Learners of English as a Foreign Language." Diss.
     Columbia, Univ., 1969.
          Using foreign students attending the English Language Insti-
     tute of Queens College, New York, as subjects, the researcher
     compared the inductive and modified deductive method in teaching
     English as a foreign language. The results achieved by groups
     using either the inductive or modified deductive method were
     significantly higher than those achieved by the control group

receiving no special experimental treatment. Results indicated that learning a foreign language can be made easier and a more lasting effect achieved for adults if "the learner first focuses on the concept which he is expected to learn...."

243   Sepulveda, Betty R. "The Language Barrier and Its Effect on Learning." Elementary English, 50 (February, 1973), 209-217.
      Since language can be a barrier to the disadvantaged (non-native) speaker, educators must pinpoint the linguistic problem and develop means to meet the needs of the pupil. The author maintains that the K-3 level is the one at which the highest percentage of children become "retarded," and offers suggestions for helping these children, emphasizing the view that the child understands that both standard English and the child's dialect or first language are useful.

244   Spolsky, Bernard. "Some Psycholinguistic and Sociolinguistic Aspects of Bilingual Education." Paper given at Conference on Teaching the Bilingual Child, Univ. of New Mexico, 1968.
      Questions about the possible differences in conceptualization in speakers of different languages and the possible effects of bilingualism on language development are discussed. The author offers probative conclusions that indicate a possible loss in linguistic ability when two languages are learned, maintaining that it is possible that only a certain amount of language ability may be available to an individual and, if divided between languages, each one will be weaker.

245   Steiner, Violette G., and Irla Lee Zimmerman. "Assessing Bilingual Language Ability in the Mexican-American Preschool Child." Paper given at the Annual Convention of the Western Psychological Assn., Portland, Oregon, 1972. ED 073831.
      This paper describes a diagnostic study of ninety pre-school children in Mexican-American communities who were assumed to be Spanish speaking and were sent to a summer program to study English. Results of the Pre-school Language Scale showed that investigation of the pre-school child's language status should be made in establishing a bilingual program since competency and language dominancy may be falsely assumed.

246   Tarone, Elaine. "Speech Perception in Second Language Acquisition: A Suggested Model." Language Learning, 24, 2 (1974), 223-233.
      This article discusses the growing importance of strategies and procedures influencing the learner of a second language that are universal for "decoding the meaning of the second language." Until recently, language learning studies have focused on linguistic grammars and rules, but it would be advantageous to study the influence of the newer strategies regarding the second language learner. The author refers to various studies which support more recent theories and maintains that data can be described in terms other than linguistic rules.

247 Thonis, Eleanor. <u>The Dual Language Process in Young Children</u>.
     Quebec: Laval University, 1971. ED 061812.
          A report that offers some pertinent and novel information
     about learning two languages in childhood. Problems caused by
     dual language learning have been exaggerated. Recommendations
     are made for more studies about language learning and thinking.
     To ensure the best dual language acquisition conditions, the
     two languages should be kept in separate contexts; the best
     language models must be available and children should have
     respect for their native languages. Intensive oral language
     development and readiness for literacy in the second language
     are necessary for success.

248 Thornhill, Donald Edward. "A Quantitative Analyses of the Develop-
     ment of Syntactical Fluency of Four Young Adult Spanish Speakers
     Learning English." Diss. The Florida State Univ., 1969.
          An experiment with four young adult Columbians learning Eng-
     lish at Tallahassee Junior College to test the hypothesis that
     development toward second language maturity recapitulates first
     language learning. Data were gathered from eight weekly tape-
     recorded conversations, the first part consisting of answers to
     a set series of questions and the second part a discussion of
     pictures chosen for their conversation-stimulating possibilities.
     Analysis of data showed that trends in language behavior of the
     second language learners "suggest remarkable parallels with that
     reported by other investigators of first language behavior of
     school children."

249 Titone, Renzo. "Some Factors Underlying Second-Language Learning."
     <u>English Language Teaching</u>, 27, 2 (1973), 110-120.
          There are psycholinguistic factors that must be considered
     in helping the student to gain mastery of a language, and the
     author discusses some aptitude and personality variables
     closely related to language study. He defines what linguistic
     aptitude is and how important it is in learning a second lang-
     uage. In addition, the article considers personality factors
     in the language-learning process, and then discusses recent
     work on the subject presenting a section on "Cautions and pros-
     pects." A lengthy bibliography is included at the end.

250 Wilkinson, Andrew. <u>The Foundations of Language: Talking and Reading
     in Young Children</u>. London: Oxford University Press, 1971.
          A short book of fifty pages offering helpful information about
     how children acquire language, how oral communications skills
     are learned, and the relation between language and society. In
     addition, there is a section devoted to the teaching of reading.
     Each chapter is summarized, and the book includes a general and
     an annotated bibliography.

251　Williams, George M., Jr.　Puerto Rican English: A Discussion of Eight
Major Works Relevant to Its Linguistic Description. Cambridge, Mass.:
Language Research Foundation, 1971.　ED 051709.
A valuable document for teachers and curriculum coordinators
working with Puerto Rican students.　The author discusses eight
works pertinent to a linguistic description of Puerto Rican
English in an effort to develop a more unified theory of bilingualism and second language acquisition.　Included among
the topics in the works are the sounds and grammatical structures of Spanish and English, the education of Puerto Ricans
in Public Schools of New York, and Spanish phonology.

Cross Reference

210	Bilingual
214	Methodology
215	Bilingual
218	Socio-Cultural
220	Socio-Cultural
222	Bilingual
229	Bilingual
239	Bilingual
241	Grammar
242	Methodology
244	Bilingual
245	Bilingual
250	Reading
251	Bilingual

METHODOLOGY A

252　Abberton, Evelyn and A. J. Fourcin.　"A Visual Display for Teaching
Intonation and Rhythm."　ELT Documents, 5 (1973), 2-6.
A method for teaching intonation based on immediate speech-
pattern feedback used with an audio-visual system developed at
University College, London.　The pattern is presented on an
oscilloscope screen with a curved line that rises and falls in
relation to the speaker's intonation.　It was found that students
needing a visual stimuli easily learned to produce contours and
remember them when this method was used along with auditory
stimuli.

253　Afolayan, A.　"Contrastive Linguistics and the Teaching of English as
a Second or Foreign Language."　English Language Teaching, 25, 3
(1971), 220-229.
Certain weaknesses are identified in the use of contrastive
studies in EFL/ESL teaching, and a new approach is offered by the
writer who maintains that a new approach should be a more practical one.　He discusses the major weaknesses and then presents his
new method based on his experiences in teaching Yoruba, a major
Nigerian language.　Classical contrastive analysis is used in new

EFL/ESL learning situations and is later replaced by "a more effective comparative study" that is described.

254 Aid, Frances M. "Semantic Universals in Instructional Material." TESOL Quarterly, 8, 1 (1974), 52-71.
The author believes that a semantic grammar can provide materials that will help students in learning English or Spanish as a second language since the two languages have common semantic structures. In addition, if we utilize an approach to language analysis based on the fact that meaning determines structure, better communication will result. A generative case grammar is suggested as a basis for "comparing the semantic structures of English and Spanish."

255 Allen, Robert L. "The Use of Rapid Drills in the Teaching of English to Speakers of Other Languages." TESOL Quarterly, 6, 1 (1972), 13-32.
Mechanical drills are important for gaining proficiency in a second language, but the author maintains that students should understand how each new structure is put together and be given an opportunity to create their own sentences. He states that drills should be short and to the point with some variety to eliminate boredom. Learning the models should come first, but drills should be carefully structured and done at a rapid pace. An appendix contains examples of eight drills involving some problems faced by non-native speakers.

256 Asher, James J. "The Total Physical Response Approach to Second Language Learning." Modern Language Journal, 53 (January 1969), 3-17.
By involving psychomotor activities and skills, the author was able to create improvement in second language learning. Cognitive skills were developed as pupils became aware of situations in which they should apply certain language responses. In learning to type, for example, students could express their thoughts through typewriting after they learned the skills of typing and the use of appropriate responses to language situations.

257 Banathy, Bela, Edith Trager, and Carl Waddle. "The Use of Contrastive Data in Foreign Language Course Development," in Trends in Language Teaching, Albert Valdman, ed. New York: McGraw-Hill, 1966.
The authors offer a "blueprint" for a foreign language program containing elements of phonology, morphology, and syntax; lexical items; and cultural and situational patterns. They believe that, in developing foreign language teaching materials, the initial step is to make contrastive statements about "the two languages and cultures involved." Then the teacher can help students understand differences between the two languages and identify target elements for each lesson.

258   Barclay, Lisa Frances Kurcz. "The Comparative Efficacies of Spanish, English,and Bilingual Cognitive Verbal Instruction with Mexican-American Head Start Children." Diss. Stanford Univ., 1969.
       The researcher hypothesized that 1) the use of a structured language training program for two periods daily during a seven-week Head Start program would produce greater language development than the use of music and art for commensurate time periods with bilingual and Spanish-speaking Mexican-American Head Start children and 2) a bilingual presentation of this language program would produce better results in English than either a Spanish or English presentation alone. The first hypothesis could not be sustained and the second hypothesis had to be rejected in 18 out of 20 instances.

259   Barkman, L. Bruce. On the Uses of Dialogs in Learning English. Montreal: Etudes Anglaises, Univ. of Montreal, 1970. ED 043030.
       The paper deals with the importance of dialogues in language learning and emphasizes that dialogues, in order to be useful, must be used in a realistic setting in the classroom so that the student will realize that what he is learning will be useful to him in the community. In addition, the author maintains that when dialogues are used on the levels for which they are designed the students can find them useful.

260   Beattie, Nicholas. "Teaching Dictionary Use." Modern Languages, 54, 4 (1973), 161-166.
       The material in this article is relevant to teaching English as a second language as well as to foreign-language teaching in general. Teachers want their students to use dictionaries but not become too dependent on them. The author suggests that students have a firm knowledge of the lexicon and syntax of the language before using the dictionary and that the students should then learn about the special dictionaries and their use. The article also discusses practical uses of the dictionary by students.

261   Bedford, Richard C. English Experienced. Detroit, Michigan: Wayne State Univ. Press, 1972.
       This text offers a novel approach to teaching English as a second or foreign language that emphasizes physical activity in communications including learning behavior patterns, mimicry, posture, gestures, etc.--performing the language. Bedford maintains that the aural-oral method does not ensure carry-over after the student's formal language classes have ended. The book introduces the writer's theories and then the major part is devoted to "Stagings" or short plays preceded by an explanation of the purpose of the play. Useful in drama classes.

262   Boucher, Charles R., and Morris L. Krear. "A Comparison of Special Programs or Classes in English for Elementary School Pupils." Modern Language Journal, 51, 6 (1967), 335-337.
       This study could have implications about the manner in which pupils in the elementary school are taught English as a second

language. The purpose was to determine whether the ESL program is more effective when a specialist works with small groups apart from the self-contained classroom or when instruction is given by the classroom teacher trained in teaching ESL. Group I stayed in self-contained classrooms and received no formal ESL instruction; Group II received thirty minutes of daily language instruction outside the regular classroom; Group III received similar language instruction from the regular classroom teacher. Although the researchers state that the results should "be approached with caution," a formal ESL program was found to be essential, and children receiving ESL instruction in the regular classroom appeared to have acquired a larger vocabulary and achieved greater ability in using sentences.

263   Bradkey, Dean. "A Student-Led-Tutorial Approach in Sri Lanka."
      TESOL Quarterly, 8, 2 (1974), 161-169.
          In an effort to provide students with English language skills
      at Vidyodaya campus of the University of Sri Lanka, an experimental ESL program was initiated. The procedures used could be helpful to other campuses seeking to provide conversational and reading guidance in English to its students. Groups of six students met daily and tutored one another with occasional guidance from professional ESL teachers. The article describes the student-directed system in detail and suggests that the success of such a program depends on the enthusiasm and morale of teachers and students.

264   Burt, Marina K. "Error Analysis in the Adult ESL Classroom." TESOL
      Quarterly, 9, 1 (1975), 53-63.
          The article offers suggestions for correcting student errors
      and deals with errors from the listener's or reader's point of view. The criteria for determining communicative importance of errors by adults are based on several thousand English sentences containing errors made by adult EFL learners from many different countries and the United States. "Global" errors are those affecting overall sentence organization, and "local" errors are those that "do not usually hinder communication significantly." Selective error correction is considered to be more effective than comprehensive correction.

265   Burt, Marina K. "Goof Analysis in English as a Second Language,"
      1971. (Speech). ED 061838.
          A novel approach toward exposing common errors made by students
      in the ESL classroom. The teacher records common errors (goofs) made by the students and then states the rules to correct the goofs. This process enables the teacher to recognize where students need help and then concentrate on these areas. The most important goofs are sorted out to see how they affect the understanding of the sentences in which they appear.

266 Burt, Marina K., and Carol Kiparsky. The Gooficon: A Repair Manual for English. Rowley, Mass.: Newbury House Publishers, 1972.
A teacher who is selective can make good use of material in this book even though the text has some weaknesses. It includes a collection of about three hundred common errors and each type of deviation from English grammar is explained. The book, designed mostly for secondary schools teaching English as a second language, avoids technical language. Correctional devices in the book could be more constructive by explaining positive rather than negative examples of English language use.

267 Campbell, Russell N. "The Contributions of Linguistics to the Teaching of English as a Second Language." Speech given at the English as a Second Language Conference, San Diego, December, 1967.
One of the valuable aspects of this paper in Campbell's presentation of the similarities and differences between English and Spanish in order to demonstrate to the ESL teacher teaching Spanish-speaking students the elements that will be easy and difficult to teach. Campbell points out that "sames and differences in two or more languages" can be revealed by linguistic analysis, and the teacher can take advantage of the similarities and prepare to counteract the differences. The specific details presented here are invaluable for teachers dealing with Spanish and English.

268 Carroll, John B. "Current Issues in Psycholinguistics and Second Language Teaching." Paper given at Fifth Annual TESOL Convention, New Orleans, La.: 1971. ED 052643.
The field of language instruction is one that is beset by uncertainties and needs more study and research. Significant topics related to language instruction and these uncertainties include linguistic rules and their relevance to language habits, the nature of language learning, the relationship between grammar and language teaching, and differences in language teaching techniques.

269 Carroll, John B. "Some Suggestions from a Psycholinguist." TESOL Quarterly, 7, 4 (1973), 355-367.
Several suggestions are offered to teachers of English as a foreign language that are worthy of consideration. Recent studies indicate that emphasis should be placed first on listening comprehension, postponing speech production until later. The author also suggests that students should "be trained to practice retrieving items from immediate memory" in order to improve permanent memorization. In addition, rules which build sentences up from "left to right" may offer teachers ways of adapting them to second language teaching.

270 Cooney, David T. "English as a Second Language: Meeting the Needs of the Foreign Student," in Changing Patterns in Foreign Language Programs: Report of the Illinois Conference on Foreign Languages in Junior and Community Colleges, Wilga M. Rivers et al. eds. Rowley, Mass.: Newbury House, 1972.

Cooney describes an alternative program for foreign students studying at American colleges where an ESL program is not available. At Polk Community College in Winter Haven, Florida, an ESL instructor works with the academic instructors to provide special training for foreign students who need help. Working together, the instructors plan a program for the student in areas in which he is deficient.

271   Corder, S. Pit. Introducting Applied Linguistics. Middlesex, England: Penquin Books, Inc., 1973.
The most important section of this book for ESL teachers is Part Three which covers, among other things, contrastive linguistics and error analysis. The latter material is important because the teacher can "describe the nature of the learner's interlanguage and ... compare this with the target language." The book also contains a lengthy Bibliography and a Subject-Author-Index. For the beginning teacher or the college student with little or no linguistic experience, the book could be helpful.

272   Cortez, Emilio G. "The ABC Principle and the Second-Language Learner." TESL Reporter, 8, 1 (1974), 3, 14.
A series of activities intended to give the non-English speaker help in learning the alphabetic principle. Cortez recommends using names from class lists, the telephone directory, and recently learned words to teach the alphabet. He also mentions game-like activities and suggests the use of flash cards to emphasize the placement of words. The activities are simple and original.

273   Cortez, Emilio G. "Lip-reading--A Viable Approach to Language Teaching in the EFL Classroom." English Language Teaching Journal, 28, 2 (1974), 135-138.
Cortez states that the sense of sight has been neglected in language teaching and maintains that the EFL teacher should "instill in the pupil a more focused awareness of the vocal apparatus." He believes that lip-reading can help to overcome consonant-sound problems and help to correct pronunciation difficulties. He offers suggestions regarding the proper use of lip-reading in the classroom. His system, if properly followed, will focus the pupil's attention on the vocal apparatus, stimulate the child's curiosity, and provide aural reinforcement.

274   Darian, Steven G. "A History of the Teaching of English as a Foreign Language in American Colleges and Universities." Diss. New York University, 1968.
A study of EFL teaching in the United States that covers trends, language teaching, political and economic influences, and the role of federal, state, and private agencies in establishing courses and developing materials. One of the constant aims has been the "development of aural-oral mastery" for the

student. The report also studies current problems and practices to identify future trends and needs and discovers, after surveying EFL methodology, that the aural-oral method is used less frequently than writing in the teaching of grammar at intermediate and advanced levels.

275 D'Arrigo, Peter. "Variables and Instructional Arrangements for the Non-English Speaking Child in the School Program." Elementary English, 49, 3 (1972), 405-409.
Certain variables were found to be significant in working with non-English speaking pupils: 1) the level of ability of the child to speak English; 2) the child's makeup--age, grade, and personality; 3) the pupil population of the school; and 4) the teacher's willingness to work with non-English speaking pupils. Different school personnel can become involved: classroom teachers, remedial reading teachers, librarians, speech therapists, and others. In addition, various instructional arrangements can be developed to meet the needs of the non-English speaking pupil.

276 Diller, Karl C. "Some New Trends for Applied Linguistics and Foreign Language Teaching in the United States." TESOL Quarterly, 9, 1 (1975), 65-73.
Diller points out that language teaching is undergoing many changes in the United States and discusses five trends that he considers as important for improving the teaching of foreign languages. Teachers of English as a second language should be familiar with these trends: 1) Chomsky's theories have undermined mimicry and pattern drills as teaching methods; 2) Language is characterized by "rule-governed creativity; 3) Error analysis is replacing contrastive analysis; 4) Oral and written language is being emphasized in new methods; 5) Eclecticism is being replaced by more definitive methods.

277 Dobbyn, Michael. "First Things First: A Page for Beginners Planning Good Lessons." TEFL, 5, 3 (1971), 4, 5, 7.
This is a guide to using a plan book for the entire year and dividing such a book into small sections. The author offers suggestions that should enable EFL/ESL teachers to have some unity and order in their teaching. Patterns should appear at the beginning of the plan book along with a number of daily lesson plans accompanied by the time necessary for teaching the lesson and when tests are given. The article also discusses unit plans and the proper division of time for each aspect of the subject taught.

278 Dodson, C. J. Language Teaching and the Bilingual Method. London: Pitman, 1967.
This book describes experiments to investigate the best way to insure the retention of meaning and the ability to imitate and remember sentences taught in class to ESL/EFL students. Tests were administered to students on the primary, secondary,

and college levels and consisted of 1) foreign-language sentences with pictures showing the meanings; 2) FL sentences with mother tongue equivalents and pictures; and 3) FL sentences with mother tongue equivalents without pictures. The important results indicated that translation is harmful to second-language learning. Dodson presents a convincing argument here.

279 Donen, Erika. "Poetry as an Aspect of Foreign-Language Teaching to Children." English Language Teaching Journal, 28, 2 (1974), 331-336.
The article contends that poetry should be taught to pupils who study English as their second language since it is a part of a nation's cultural heritage and can enrich the pupil in several ways. The writer uses Katherine Mansfield's "The Pillar-Box" and Christina Rassetti's "Colours" to illustrate how a teacher can help pupils to expand their vocabulary, arouse pupil interest, stimulate their imaginations, and provide them with a "point of departure for oral or written work."

280 English as a Second Language for the Culturally Depressed Children at Rogers School, Leflore County, Mississippi. Little Rock, Ark.: So. Central Regional Education Lab. Corp., 1969. ED 033368.
A study was made to ascertain the effects of introducing programmed English as a second language in the elementary program by measuring the influence it had on the achievement of first-year elementary students. Follow-up studies were made of second, third and fourth grade students from culturally disadvantaged Negro homes. No definitive results were attained, indicating that more than one year of ESL training is needed to measure definite effects.

281 Finocchiaro, Mary. "Myth and Reality in TESOL: A Plea for a Broader View." TESOL Quarterly, 5, 1 (1971), 3-17.
Anyone who teaches English to non-native speakers has learned that restrictive techniques limit the teacher and student and that an integrated approach, making use of many options, usually gets the best results. The author suggests that teachers recognize the need for modification of methods depending on the students, teachers, and the community; and the need for students to retain pride in their native tongue and to experience success. As a result, the article offers many helpful suggestions that should be profitable to any ESL teacher.

282 Garwood, C. H. "The Teaching of English to the Non-English-Speaking Technical Student. 1: The Context of the Situation." English Language Teaching, 24, 2 (1970), 107-112.
The first part of a discussion offering recommendations for developing an English program for the non-English-speaking-technical student. The English teacher should learn some of the sample vocabulary items in the pupils' technical studies, become acquainted with their technical studies in general, and develop those skills that will help these pupils. Teachers can use contexts which require simple scientific descriptions, experiment writeups, and accounts of procedures.

283   Gay, Charles W., et al. Learning English Through Typewriting.
Portland, Oregon: English Language Services, 1974.
       The objectives of this text are to improve the proficiency
of students in spelling, vocabulary, writing, and the use of
structure and idioms, in addition to developing skill in typing letters, reports, and manuscripts. While the student
learns how to type, he becomes familiar with basic sentence
patterns and progressively is expected to use transforms of
the patterns.

284   George, H. V. Common Errors in Language Learning: Insights from
English. Rowley, Mass.: Newbury House, 1972.
       The causes and prevention of errors in foreign language learn-
ing with particular reference to English as a second language,
are discussed. Especially helpful to the teacher are a survey
of error analysis and a model of error production in the first
part of a three-part discussion. Other relevant topics on the
subject include comments on mother-tongue interference in pronunciation, vocabulary, and syntax, and the difficulties in
dealing with homonyms and similar kinds of language sets. The
relationship between errors and learning motivation is also
discussed.

285   George, H. V. "English for Asian Learners: Are we on the right road?"
English Language Teaching, 25, 3 (1971), 270-277.
       George presents some criticisms about the "performance-oriented
prescription" of people who design EFL/ESL courses for Asian
learners and offers alternative methods and approaches. The
learner's brain is economy-oriented and George sees no sense in
stressing standard English which is "far from the real life
prospects" of Asian children. He believes that we have neglected
psychological and social considerations and that there should be
more simplified grammatical items to make the results worthy of
the efforts expended in learning English.

286   Goldberg, J. Philip, and Marcia B. Bordman. "English Language Instruction for the Hearing Impaired: An Adaptation of ESL Methodology."
TESOL Quarterly, 8, 3 (1974), 263-270.
       A unique use for ESL procedures is described. Since students
with hearing impairments showed severe language problems, instructors noticed that they had the same difficulties in English
as non-native speakers in ESL classes, so ESL techniques were
applied. Modifications had to be made for the hearing-impaired
people; therefore, language practice was written and an additional step was added which forced students to express concepts.
Results revealed significant improvement in the students' use
of English.

287   Hagen, John W., and Daniel P. Hallahan. "A Language Training Program
for Pre-school Migrant Children." Exceptional Children, 37 (1971),
606-607.

A report of an evaluation of the effectiveness of English oral language lessons for Mexican migrant pre-school children. Two experimental groups were taught English sentence structure, and a control group made up of children with experience in a free-play nursery school program was used for comparison. Results showed that a short-term language training program can improve English language performance although no noticeable gains were made in language understanding and production in the classroom.

288 Harding, Deborah A., et al. A Microwave Course in English as a Second Language (For Spanish Speakers). LaJolla, Calif.: Lingoco Corporation, 1969.
     Based on Stevick's approach to foreign language teaching, the "microwave" course emphasizes communicative use of each structural element as soon as it appears. Short "cycles" are utilized, each beginning with new material and ending when that material has actually been used. Included are 107 cycles in a bilingual format: English on the right and Spanish on the left. The Teacher's Manual contains teaching guides with instructions for teaching each cycle.

289 Harris, David P. "Current Issues in ESL." TESOL Newsletter, 6, 1 (1972), 3-5.
     A look at the current issues in ESL teaching in order to make the teacher aware of the issues and how to respond to them. Harris discusses the audio-lingual habit theory and its validity compared with the cognitive code learning theory; the individual needs of the learner and the use of methods and materials to meet those needs; and the practicality of current linguistic theory in ESL teaching.

290 Harrison, Grant Von, and John C. Wilkinson. "The Use of Bilingual Student Tutors in Teaching English as a Second Language." Paper given at Annual Concention of TESOL, San Juan, P. R., 1973. ED 086030.
     A lack of properly certified teachers and the imposition of too much material on children were reasons for creating a tutorial system in which bilingual Indian children at upper-grade-elementary levels served as tutors for kindergarten and first-grade Indian children. Six specific phases are recommended that cover testing, materials, and the preparation of the tutors.

291 Hatch, Evelyn. "More Problems for the Elementary School ESL Teacher." Workpapers in English as a Second Language, 4 (1970), 87-92.
     A paper that stresses the need for more information about teaching ESL regarding the level of mastery one should expect from young children, specific items that should be taught, and the sequence of material for people of various ages. The writer believes that the language of the young native English speaker should be studied to determine what he knows about his language at an early age in order to offer appropriate help for the young ESL student.

292   Henry, Richard A. "The Individualization of Instruction in ESL."
      TESOL Quarterly, 9, 1 (1975), 31-40.
            A description of an individualized program in English as a
      Second Language at Washington Irving Educational Center in
      Schenectady, New York, including the classroom floorplan, grad-
      ing practices, record-keeping methods, progress charts, and
      materials. The author points out that the teacher in an individ-
      ualized classroom "is not the single focal point of the room as
      in the traditional classroom; there is no single focal point."
      The philosophy of teaching ESL in an individualized program is
      in getting learners to learn how to learn.

293   Hill, L. A. "Programmed Instruction and the Classroom Teacher."
      English Language Teaching, 21, 1 (1966), 45-50.
            Hill believes that programmed instruction, if properly formu-
      lated and used, can be advantageous to the student and the
      teacher in the English language classroom. Each student can
      progress at his own speed; his mistakes are not exposed; and
      both slow- and fast-moving students can receive specialized
      instruction. He points out, though, that the material should
      teach students "a new set of behavior patterns" and that they
      should be tested constantly in order to help them learn. Multi-
      ple choice and constructed response tests are preferred.

294   Hines, Mary Elizabeth. "Transitional Expressions in Written English:
      Psychological Versus Logical Order." The English Record, 23, 2
      (1972), 64-67.
            Teachers working with students studying English as a second
      or foreign language often find it difficult to teach the use of
      transitional expressions to their students. Hines suggests using
      a free association exercise in class to demonstrate that ideas
      which come to our minds are not necessarily in the order that
      we should receive them. In this way, students will understand
      the need for addition transitional expressions to show the re-
      lationships of ideas.

295   Hok, Ruth. "The Concept of 'General Specific' to TESOL Problems with
      Particular Attention to the Teaching of 'the/a' and 'some/any'," 1969.
      Paper presented at TESOL Convention, Chicago, 1969. ED 031691.
            The paper discusses some word choices that pose few problems
      to native speakers but are difficult for non-native students of
      English. Regarding the occurrence of "the/a" it is found that
      count nouns and non-count nouns govern the choices and when the
      choice is between "the", "a" or nothing, choice depends on the
      speaker's position. The use of "some" and "any" depend on whe-
      ther the speaker refers to parts or wholes.

296   Imhoof, Maurice L., ed. Viewpoints. Bloomington, Indiana: Indiana
      University, 1971.
            Seven articles comprise this bulletin devoted to teaching stan-
      dard and nonstandard English and English as a second language.
      Each article is clearly written and is preceded by relevant pre-
      fatory comments by Maurice Imhoof. The articles by Fishman on

language attitudes of Puerto Ricans, and by Rosenbaum on instructional product designs should be of special interest to ESL teachers.

297   Jakobovits, Leon A. "Implications of Recent Psycholinguistic Developments for the Teaching of a Second Language." Language Learning, 18/ 1, 2 (1968), 89-109.
      Recent developments in linguistics have influenced our theories about language learning and will affect second language teaching. The psycholinguistic theory of language acquisition stresses the developmental nature of language and gives the child innate capacities for learning the system of a language. Jakobovits discusses the effects of the new developments and tells how pattern drills, discrimination of sounds, and phonological drills might be replaced by transformation exercises at various levels.

298   Jacobs, Roderick A. "Linguistic Universals and Their Relevance to TESOL," in Studies in Language, Roderick A. Jacobs, ed. Lexington, Mass." Xerox College Publishing, 1973.
      The author identifies areas of linguistics in which non-native speakers will have difficulties and advocates that more emphasis be placed on comparative elements rather than only contrastive elements. He maintains that "likenesses between languages and even the universal characteristics are inadequately exploited." Recent developments in transformational grammar show that likenesses can be emphasized.

299   Jacobson, Rodolfo. "The Teaching of English to Speakers of Other Languages and/or Dialects: An Oversimplification." TESOL Quarterly, 4, 3 (1970), 241-253.
      The author maintains that, despite many similarities, the teaching of a second dialect requires a methodology that is different from teaching English as a second language. Psychological, sociological, cultural, and linguistic aspects are different in each case. These aspects involve motivation, student reaction against adopting standard English, and the failure of educators to recognize the linguistic system in non-standard dialects. Second language teaching principles should be adopted to specific problems of the speaker.

300   Johnson, Francis O. "The Discipline of Teaching English as a Second Language: A Theoretical Framework." Paper read at Regional English Language Seminar, Singapore, June, 1969. ED 032530.
      The author questions the significance of linguistic theory in the teaching of language skills, maintaining that the goals of the linguist and those of the teacher are different. Students who have passed tests supposedly showing competency in English have frequently been unable to communicate effectively. The suggestion is made that the present methods of language teaching must be revised if communication skills are to be learned.

301 Johnson, Kenneth Roy. "A Comparison of Traditional Techniques and Second Language Techniques for Teaching Grammatical Structures of Standard Oral English to Tenth-Grade Negro Students Who Speak a Nonstandard Dialect." Diss. Univ. of Southern California, 1969.
        An important study for those people who want to consider using second language techniques in teaching English to students speaking a non-standard dialect. A total of 67 students matched on the basis of I. Q. and reading achievement scores took part in the study. One experimental group received ESL instruction and regular instruction for a semester; another received regular instruction for 12 weeks and only ESL instruction for six weeks. The control group received only regular instruction. Tests revealed that ESL teaching techniques were "significantly more effective than traditional techniques."

302 Johnson, Sabina Thorne. "Remedial English: The Anglocentric Albatross." College English, 33, 6 (1972), 670-685.
        The material in this article that pertains to minority students will be of interest to ESL teachers on the college level. The author discusses the program in "Subject A" at the University of California, Berkeley, including the length of classes, course content, the texts that were used, the purposes of the course, etc. Special attitudinal problems had to be faced by instructors working with minority groups. It was reported that the Chicano Section of students was strongly motivated and accounted for their "high pass rate." The author suggests that we should move minority students away from purely ethnic concerns, though, "and provide them with a second and equally useful cultural and linguistic frame of reference."

303 Kelly, C. G. "English as a Second Language: An Historical Sketch." English Language Teaching, 25, 1 (1970), 120-132.
        Kelly offers historical perspectives on English as a second language making comparisons between early and current theories and methodologies. For example, translation was a dominant means of teaching structure in the nineteenth century although some preferred the object-lesson method. Harold E. Palmer appears to be the twentieth century originator of pattern practice, and in this century cultural and contrastive teaching were introduced. The author predicts that "no one method...will ever come to supersede all others in a permanent sense."

304 Klyhn, Joan. "On the Integration into School of Young Immigrant Children." English Language Teaching, 23, 2 (1969), 261-268.
        Immigrant children present special problems to ESL teachers since for some of them, English is their native tongue, for others a foreign language, and some speak a nonstandard English dialect. The author suggests that English-speaking students should be used as aides and that school and community resources be made available to these children who should not be taught English in special classes.

305   Kreidler, Charles W. "Teaching English Spelling and Pronunciation."
        TESOL Quarterly, 6, 1 (1972), 3-12.
                In teaching English as a second language, teachers have placed
        emphasis on the student's mastery of the sound system, but the
        author contends that the new English speaker will have to deal
        with spelling, and this aspect of the language should not be
        neglected. Maintaining that there is a spelling system to teach
        in English, he mentions the inner structure of words, the stress
        patterns, and parts of speech. He discusses three patterns of
        vowels since vowel sounds create spelling difficulties.

306   Lado, Robert. "Maintaining Interest." Modern English Journal, 1, 2
        (1970), 99-101.
                Lado maintains that interest in learning a foreign language
        can be sustained in several ways. For example, students seem to
        be stimulated by oral work. In addition, the goals that the
        teacher expects the student to reach should not be beyond his
        capabilities. Students should also know, after their efforts
        to learn a particular phase of language, whether or not they
        have been successful. Emphasis should not be on obtaining high
        marks.

307   Lancaster, Louise. Introducing English. New York: Houghton, Mifflin,
        1971.
                A text for Spanish-speaking primary pupils designed as an
        oral-pre-reading program to prepare children to participate in
        regular language activities. It emphasizes language patterns
        and includes attractive activities related to the patterns. It
        can be especially helpful for an ESL teacher who has had little
        training in teaching non-native speakers.

308   Lugo, Mabel Erb de. New Directions and Changes for Teaching High School
        English as a Second Language in Puerto Rico. Univ. of Puerto Rico,
        1972. ED 084926.
                A monograph that reviews the teaching of English in Puerto Rico
        and evaluates the English language program. The writer suggests
        that the recent theories on language acquisition and transforma-
        tional generative grammar should be applied to the teaching of
        English as a second language and makes recommendations for the
        improvement of the Puerto Rican English language program.

309   Lund, Elizabeth. "Vital Role of Language Requires Best TESL Methods,
        Knowledge." TESL Reporter, 5, 3 (1972), 4, 13, 14.
                A plea for teaching English as a second language in the most
        effective way possible since America's influence in the world is
        so great. The author calls for more emphasis on the natural
        skills--speaking and listening--which she feels were ignored in
        the past. New methods, however, recognize the importance of oral
        work and create more of a balance between oral and written prac-
        tice. The article also discusses various methods of instruction
        and the requirements of teachers.

310   Medina, T. Rene. "Planning the Teaching Unit in the Instruction of
       English as a Foreign Language." Lenguaje y Ciencias, 11, 2 (1971),
       44-54. ED 057655.
              A discussion of the teaching unit in classes for students learn-
       ing English as a Foreign language including such things as objec-
       tives, materials, activities, evaluation, time allotment, culture,
       etc. A rather complete example of a teaching unit is included
       which contains materials, goals, and activities. Also included
       are bibliographies for teachers and students. A useful article
       for ESL teachers who want ideas on organizing their lessons.

311   Michael, Alice. English as a Second Language for Speakers of Spanish.
       Monterey, Calif.: Educator Press, 1967. ED 032175.
              Many students of English as a second language are native
       speakers of Spanish, and this report intends to help the teacher
       deal with the problems of these students. Various techniques,
       materials, and lessons are presented, and annotated bibliograph-
       ies offer listings of books for teachers, instructional materials,
       charts, and pictures. There is also a bibliography of materials
       helpful to ESL teachers.

                             Cross Reference

                   254   Grammar
                   258   Bilingual
                   262   Curriculum
                   267   Grammar
                   274   Testing and Evaluation
                   279   Teaching Aids
                   283   Teaching Aids
                   288   Bilingual
                   289   Testing and Evaluation
                   290   Curriculum
                   293   Testing and Evaluation
                   296   Teacher Preparation
                   299   Socio-Cultural
                   304   Bilingual
                   307   Teacher Preparation
                   308   Grammar
                   309   Spoken English
                   310   Curriculum

                            METHODOLOGY B

312   Monnot, Michel, and Jon Kite. "Pun and Games: Paranomasia in the ESL
       Classroom." TESOL Quarterly, 8, 1 (1974), 65-71.
              Puns used either in introducing a unit or in complementing a
       lesson can be useful teaching tools. They can help the students
       increase their vocabulary and help them to understand the incon-
       sistencies in speech,syntax,and spelling. In addition, they help
       the students get accustomed to variations of English and help
       prepare them for the shades of differences in reading poetry.

The authors maintain that although teachers should exercise caution in presenting puns, the student can "effortlessly and amusingly learn much that is useful to him."

313 Morrow, K. E., and Marilyn Shaw. "L1 Techniques in EFL Teaching." English Language Teaching Journal, 28, 3 (1974), 197-202.
Projects consisting of a connected series of assignments based on a single theme can encourage students "to become aware of different 'varieties' of English." The authors describe a project used with a class of five intermediate students learning English as a foreign language. A photograph of an injured man on a stretcher, a damaged car, an ambulance, and a group of onlookers were used. Students were asked to provide data (date, time, weather, etc.) about the scene, act as witnesses, and write a police account, a playlet, and a news account about the scene.

314 Newmark, Leonard. "How Not to Interfere with Language Learning." International Journal of American Linguistics, 32 (1966), 77-83.
The author is critical of the teaching of language by applied linguists who emphasize structural drills based on contrastive analysis of the learner's language and the target language. Strict structural drill without recognition of context can create a special kind of interference. The learner should be taught to extend his ability to new situations. Students should learn in "chunks" rather than by item.

315 Ney, James W. "Towards a Synthetization of Teaching Methodologies for TESOL." TESOL Quarterly, 7, 1 (1973), 3-11.
This article is an important one for teachers of non-native speakers of English since the author suggests that language teachers utilize features of both the audio-lingual approach and the cognitive-code learning theory. Using a combination of theories, a teacher recognizes recent linguistic theories and makes it easier for him to solve the problem of contextualizing language exercises.

316 Oller, John W., Jr., and Nevin Inal. "A Cloze Test of English Prepositions." TESOL Quarterly, 5, 4 (1971), 315-325.
The authors found that the cloze technique as a basis for measuring the skill of non-native speakers in handling English prepositions was "highly useful." Three groups of subjects were tested: 19 native speakers of English, 53 native speakers of Turkey, and 110 foreign students entering UCLA from a wide variety of language backgrounds. The test worked best with students of varied backgrounds but was also useful for the Turkish group.

317 Pack, Alice C. "Form Class Baseball: A TESL Game." TESL Reporter, 4, 1 (1970),10-11.
The objects of this game are to help students learn the four English form classes and provide more practice for students whose

native languages do not contain specific words and alternate form (persuade-persuasion). Regular baseball rules are followed. The batter is "thrown" a verb, noun, adjective, or adverb and then must supply a correct form of the word. Whether he hits safely or strikes out depends on the answer the student gives. The game can be entertaining while it teaches.

318   Pack, Alice C. "A TESL Game for Constructing Sentences." TESL Reporter 7, 4 (1974), 3.
        The objective of the game is to give students practice "in creating acceptable sentences" using prepositions, articles, and singular and plural forms. Different colored file cards are used for location, time, nouns, and verbs; white cards contain determiners. Students take a word from the colored pack and then write a sentence. The game is simple, yet especially useful in teaching students to use function words in developing sentences.

319   Paik, Kee Duk. "Common Difficulties in English for Non-Native Speakers." Diss. Univ. of Illinois, 1972.
        Although this study was made of Korean students learning English as a second language, the procedures and many of the recommendations are applicable to all non-native students of English. The author paid special attention to the use of determiners, prepositions, two-word verbs, vocabulary, and basic structures and recommended that listening, speaking, reading, and writing skills must be more thoroughly integrated. He also suggested that grammar should cover common difficulties more completely and that Korean-English dictionaries be replaced by English-English dictionaries to provide better definitions of words.

320   Parker, Candy. Doing Your Own Thing in and Out of School. Miami: Dade County Public Schools, 1971. ED 063843.
        A description of a course intended to acquaint students with people through the use of language practice dealing with contrasting verb forms. By using language orally with their teachers and teaching machines, working on written and oral exercises, and reading selected material, the students are able to reinforce language learning.

321   Parkinson, Frank C. "Levels of Usage: A Systematic Approach." English Language Teaching, 21, 1 (1966), 15-18.
        The foreign student in intermediate and advanced English class is confronted by many language difficulties because he is not familiar enough with usage. Parkinson contends that the process of learning usage can be speeded up by using a "language usage diagram" which shows the written language on one side, the spoken on the other, and the various distinctions—formal, standard, colloquial, and slang in the center. Such a diagram, the author points out, provides "a visual stimulus and reinforcement to the teacher's oral instructions" and provides an immediate visual

reference. Such a diagram, it seems, could make students much
more aware of usage.

322   Paulston, Christina Bratt. "The Sequencing of Structural Pattern
      Drills." TESOL Quarterly, 5, 3 (1971), 197-208.
            A re-examination of the role and function of structural pattern
      drills in language learning, a technique that has been advocated
      by descriptive structural linguists but which has also been under
      close scrutiny in recent years. In summary, the paper states
      that mechanical drills are really necessary in beginning courses
      in learning a second language. However, teachers must also
      "employ meaningful and communicative drills" to enable students
      to express themselves with "fluency in appropriate situations."

323   Prieto, Muriel H. "An Experimental Study of the Value of Teaching
      Certain Word Roots and Prefixes Through Spanish-English Equivalents
      to Native Spanish-Speaking Students of English as a Second Language
      at the College Level." Diss. Boston Univ., 1973.
            The investigator attempted to determine whether the teaching
      of prefixes and roots through Spanish-English cognates or word
      equivalents improved the identification of the meanings of words
      containing the studied elements in English and Spanish and
      whether this teaching increased the students' general English
      vocabulary and reading comprehension in English. Semi-programmed
      lessons were prepared for 197 students divided into four experi-
      mental and four control groups. In spite of certain limitations
      of the study, it was ascertained that improvement was signifi-
      cantly greater in groups using the semi-programmed materials in
      contrast to those using traditional materials.

324   Rainsbury, Robert C. "Getting Meaning into the Drill--a Few Observa-
      tions and Checkpoints." Journal of English as a Second Language,
      4, 2 (1969), 49-56.
            If drills are going to be meaningful, the sentences should
      make sense and should be those that are likely to be used by a
      native speaker in his daily experiences. The author suggests,
      therefore, that the teacher consider the semantic aspect of the
      drills. Rainsbury believes that there is nothing wrong with
      using pattern drills but their content should be expanded and
      have more meaning.

325   Ramirez, Inez Ruiz. "The Effect of English as a Second Language
      Instruction on Oral English Proficiency, Self-Concept, and Scholastic
      Achievement of Kindergarten-Age Mexican-American Students." Diss.
      East Texas State Univ., 1973.
            A study to discover if there were significant differences in
      mean scores on oral English proficiency, self-concept, and scholas-
      tic achievement between kindergarten-age Mexican-American students
      taught English as a second language in an experimental group using
      the Teaching English Early Program and those in a control group
      receiving traditional English instruction. Results of tests
      showed that in the areas tested there were significant differences
      in favor of the experimental group.

326 Rees, Albin, L. W. "The Trainee Teacher and His Practice Class:
Fifty Pointers for the Student Teacher." Lenguaje y Ciencias, 33
(1969). ED 035889.
A handbook for student teachers who intend to work with non-
native English students in the secondary school. Based on the
author's experience in supervising student teachers the book
offers many practical suggestions dealing with realistic matters
including homework assignments and lesson plans.

327 A Resource Manual for Implementing Bilingual Education Programs. Austi
Texas: Good Neighbor Commission, 1972. ED 070552.
ESL teachers will be interested in the discussion of the role
of linguistics and a student's first language in a bilingual program, methods for teaching a second language, techniques for
teaching reading and writing, and sample lessons in subject
matter areas. The report is intended to help people develop
bilingual programs, especially for Mexican-Americans.

328 Rosenbaum, Peter S. "Aspects of Instructional Product Design," in
Viewpoints, Maurice L. Imhoof, ed. Bloomington, Indiana: Indiana
Univ., 1971, 103-124.
/ The final sections of this article will be of special interest to teachers of English as a second language since the author
discusses "a peer-mediated learning system" in which instruction
is carried out by students rather than teachers. Rosenbaum discusses this system in regard to the ESL classroom maintaining
that students enjoy playing the role of teacher and that "student
can provide extremely high quality remediational supervision for
one another...." The author maintains that in order to improve
instruction, the classroom behavior of teachers must be changed.

329 Saitz, Robert L. "Remember the Pupils." English Language Teaching
Journal, 28, 3 (1974), 220-222.
Teachers of students learning English as a second language are
advised that they must follow methods that focus more upon the
learner than on the language and Saitz describes some successful
activities that were derived "primarily from the teachers' sensi-
tive consideration of the learners." One of the activities
centered around the production of class poems by Puerto Rican
students and another involved the teaching of the structures of
English through subject matter areas in order to solve problems
related to the students' need to use English outside of class.

330 Sarantos, Robin L. How Much English Do You Know? Miami, Fla.: Dade
County Public Schools, 1971. ED 064966.
A course that intends to meet the language needs of students
in the ESL classroom including a study of government and citizenship. Many aspects of language study are covered, with emphasis
on correct usage of singular and plural nouns, clauses beginning
with adverbs,and irregular verbs and verb tense. Also included
is a list of objectives and recommended activities.

331 Sawyer, Jesse O., and Shirley Kling Silver. "Dictation in Language
Learning," in Teaching English as a Second Language, Harold B. Allen
and Russell N. Campbell, eds. New York: McGraw-Hill, 1972, 222-229.
The authors believe that dictation can be an effective teaching device that probably hasn't been used because the emphasis
has been on spoken language in language learning and teaching.
Dictation, however, can be used with classes of various sizes,
can quiet the class down at the beginning of a session, enables
the teacher to spot many errors in a short period of time and is
easy to correct. There are also many advantages to the learner.

332 Schuman, John H., and Nancy Stenson, eds. New Frontiers in Second
Language Learning. Rowley, Mass.: Newbury House, 1972.
The readings are divided into two parts: the first is addressed
to the teacher and offers suggestions on dealing with language-
learning errors; the second part is for those readers who are
interested in social, psychological, and linguistic influences
in second-language learning.

333 Scovel, Thomas. "Getting Tense in English: A Linguistics for Our Time."
TESOL Quarterly, 5, 4 (1971), 301-307.
The article discusses an approach to the teaching of English
tense to speakers of tenseless languages. The presentation,
although short on specific recommendations, does offer some ideas
that could be utilized in the classroom. In addition, the author
reviews the various ways in which tense is indicated in English,
many of which are unorthodox and therefore create confusion in
the minds of non-native speakers.

334 Slager, William R. "Creating Contexts for Language Practice." TESOL
Quarterly, 7, (1973), 35-50.
The textbook writer should prepare his material so that sentence
structure in drill work should combine grammar and context, and
structure and situation. Disconnected sentences tend to destroy
contextualization, but it is sometimes difficult to have consist-
ency in subject development and desired sentence variety. The
teacher should adapt the text to his needs, but the textbook
writer must make his drills adaptable.

335 Smith, Larry E. "Don't Teach-Let Them Learn." TESOL Quarterly, 5, 2
(1971), 149-151.
By using a flexible approach to teaching his students at the
East-West Center on the University of Hawaii campus and in
Bangkok, Thailand, the author was able to give his students more
responsibility for learning. He found that "an environment prepared for individual difference...was a place where learning
thrived." He used a cassette tape recorder, typewriters, SRA Rate
builders, and other materials for student use. Better students
assisted others and students made progress using individualized
materials helpful in learning English as a second language.

336   Smith, Philip D., Jr. <u>A Project to Develop Pre-Vocational Literacy</u>
       <u>Materials for Spanish-Speaking Students</u>. West Chester, Pa.: West
       Chester State College, 1972. ED 074824.
                Descriptions of the development of prevocational English lang
       uage and literary materials for non-English-speaking students.
       Special materials and techniques were tested in order to provide
       skills and practice in linguistic areas that posed problems for
       the non-English-speaking student and therefore impeded progress
       toward vocational preparation.

337   Stieglitz, Francine B. <u>Teaching a Second Language</u>. Urbana, Illinois:
       N.C.T.E., 1973.
                The sub-title of the book is <u>Sentence Length and Syntax</u> and
       it contains the results of a study to deal with difficulties in
       language drill construction. Mainly the text studies the abili
       of foreign students to use English sentences according to their
       structure and length. The author demonstrates that there are
       certain syntactic structures and lengths that offer students the
       most favorable conditions for learning through drill sentences.

338   Sutherland, Beatrice. <u>Teaching American English: A Syllabus and Hand</u>
       <u>book</u>. Rowley, Mass.: Newbury House, 1975.
                Primarily a reference book for teachers of English, the text
       describes sentence patterns and offers suggestions for vocabular
       development within such patterns. It aims at providing the
       teacher with information about teaching, learning, and testing.
       The Handbook offers suggestions for teaching the material found
       in the Syllabus.

339   Tachibana, K. "The Supervisor's Point of View." <u>Modern English</u>
       <u>Journal</u>, 1, 2 (1970), 71-81.
                The author believes that the ESL/EFL teacher should modify t
       materials in textbooks in order to meet the needs of the class
       and should plan his own beginning oral course based on informa-
       tion found in the textbooks. These materials should then be use
       in place of the textbook at the beginning of the course. In
       fact, the author suggests that the textbook not be taken into
       the classroom. He also emphasizes the need for closer communi-
       cations in devising curriculum, from the secondary school throug
       college.

340   Tezer, Phyllis. "A Contrastive Approach in Teaching English."
       <u>Research in the Teaching of English</u>, 4, 2 (1970), 157-167.
                The writer believes that a contrastive linguistic approach to
       teaching English as a second language can be helpful to adult
       learners. She makes a comparative-contrast analysis of some
       Turkish and English grammatical elements to illustrate how these
       English constructions can be explained to Turkish students. If
       the teacher understands the students' language and uses material
       that shows the differences between the languages then, Tezer
       states, the students will benefit.

341 Twaddell, Freeman. "Vocabulary Expansion in the TESOL Classroom." TESOL Quarterly, 7,1 (1973), 61-78.
     In discussing the development of vocabulary skills by the foreign language learner, the author maintains that the traditionally used methods of word-matching or "laborious pseudo-translation" should be replaced by the sharpening of skimming skills and an intelligent use of clues in context. He advocates helping students to learn to guess at meanings of unfamiliar words and phrases and to learn to tolerate some vagueness in understanding words. The student must cooperate with the teacher to make such a program successful.

342 Upshur, John A. "Four Experiments on the Relation Between Foreign Language Teaching and Learning." Language Learning, 18/ 1, 2 (1968), 111-124.
     The article reports the results of four experiments, three with students at the English Language Institute, the University of Michigan, and one with participants in the 1966 Orientation Program in American Language. Test results indicated that the most efficient foreign language learning is informal, and when the learner must make communicative use of the language. Also, language learning is not related to the amount of formal language instruction, and sequential mastery is not essential in an intensive foreign language program.

343 Valdman, Albert, ed. Trends in Language Teaching. New York: McGraw-Hill, 1966.
     The fourteen articles on foreign language teaching offer a variety of approaches to teaching by authors who disagree somewhat about the theories of psychology, language learning, and methods of instruction. The selections most relevant to teachers of English as a second language are those by Fishman, Banathy et al., Saporta, and Carroll who deal with bilingualism, contrastive analysis, grammar, and educational research, respectively. Brief sections on technical terms and symbols, and articulatory diagrams appear at the end of the book.

344 Vito, Lawrence. The Teaching of English to Non-English-Speaking Migrants. Naples, Florida: Collier County Board of Public Inst., 1966.
     In addition to the usual linguistic areas covered by textbooks for non-native speakers, this guide contains English-Spanish comparisons for names of children, commonly used classroom expressions, and more formal expressions to be used with adults. The author recommends various teaching materials and teacher guides.

345 Wardhaugh, Ronald, "The Contrastive Analysis Hypothesis." TESOL Quarterly, 4, 2 (1970), 123-129.
     The author contends that the influence of contrastive analysis in second language teaching no longer seems to be as important as it once was. It has not proved workable in the strong version but will continue to be helpful only in its weak version. Wardhaugh

adds that contrastive analysis, though, is one of "many uncertain variables which one must re-evaluate in second language teaching."

346 Wardhaugh, Ronald. "Some Current Problems in Second-Language Teaching." Language Learning, 17/ 1, 2 (1967), 21-26.
     Wardhaugh reminds the reader that two important facts about language cannot be overlooked: 1) voluntary characteristics of language (non-mechanical) create problems that remain unsolved; 2) language is mainly a human possession regardless of habit formation theories. He discusses variables like student motivation and personality, and the problems associated with language description and contrast. He believes that more must be done with deep structure and deep analyses of language which will show language similarities and that "fresh directions have to be found in the gradation of materials and in productivity."

347 Wardhaugh, Ronald. "TESOL: Current Problems and Classroom Practices." Paper given at TESOL Convention, Chicago, Illinois, March 5-8, 1969. ED 030847.
     The author points out that ESL teachers must recognize individual learning patterns of students along with their motives and desires and that teachers cannot depend on any one restricted approach in teaching language. Maintaining that a knowledge of language, psychology, and an educational philosophy is required of each teacher, the author stresses the significance of these three areas. Mastery of various language patterns is secondary to overall language competency by the student.

348 Wasserman, Paul, and Susan Wasserman. "No Hablo Ingles." Elementary English, 40, 6 (1972), 832-835.
     Although the authors concentrate on the Mexican-American child who needs to learn English as a second language, the information in the article is applicable to children of other backgrounds. The authors present material that can be helpful to ESL teachers since they are concerned about the non-English speaking Mexican-American school children; they also dicuss the kind of background the ESL teacher must have in order to work effectively with each child. Sensitive and imaginative teachers "who help Mexican-American children retain their own language while acquiring English as a Second Language" will offer a distinct language advantage to these people.

349 Whitman, Randal L. "Teaching the Article in English." TESOL Quarterly, 8, 3 (1974), 253-262.
     Since the proper use of articles in English is difficult for foreign students, the author offers suggestions for the presentation of the article in teaching non-native speakers in five steps. These steps involve the principle of quantity, the generic plural, non-count nouns, the introduction of determiners, and noun phrases that contain a quantifier and a determiner.

350   Widdowson, H. G. Language Teaching Tests. London: Oxford University
      Press, English Studies Series, 8, 1971.
            A book containing forty-two passages in English for use by ad-
      vanced students of English as a second language. ESL teachers
      who need a text that offers reading practice and practical ling-
      uistics should find this text useful. Passages are accompanied
      by notes and exercises to test comprehension, vocabulary, and
      syntax.

351   Williams, George M., Jr. "Some Errors in English by Spanish-Speaking
      Puerto Rican Children." Language Research Report No. 6, 85-102.
      Cambridge, Mass.: Language Research Foundation, 1972. ED 061850.
            The results of this investigation could be useful in develop-
      ing curriculums in ESL programs because it presents information
      on phonetic and morphological deviations from standard English
      in the spontaneous speech of Puerto Rican children. The range
      of errors include those of pronunciation: vowels, diphthongs,
      consonants, and stops. Examples of these errors and those of
      syntax are provided for the teacher.

352   Willink, Elizabeth W. "A Comparison of Two Methods of Teaching Eng-
      lish to Navajo Children." Diss. Univ. of Arizona, 1968.
            A different method than the traditional one in teaching English
      to Navajo children was experimentally used at Shiprock, New Mexico,
      from 1960 through 1965, and at Rock Point, Arizona, from 1964 on.
      This TESL method assumed that language played an important part
      in developing concepts and that structure is essential to language
      and language learning. To measure the effect of TESL on achieve-
      ment in English, the Basic English Test for Navajos was given to
      students in the third grade of Rock Point and comparison schools.
      The Rock Point mean of third grade scores was significantly higher
      than the mean of the comparison group at one per cent level of
      confidence. It is assumed from this result that TESL had had a
      favorable effect on achievement in English.

353   Willink, Elizabeth W. Needed Research as a Contribution to the Prob-
      lem of Teaching English to American Indians. A Position Paper.
      Albuquerque, New Mexico: Southwest Cooperative Education Lab., 1970.
      ED 057955.
            Although English as a second language is being taught to large
      numbers of American Indian children, the language is being learned
      very slowly. As a result, the author advocates increased research
      to study current second language learning theories and methodology
      and recommends certain short-term and long-term research projects
      to test current approaches and recommend new ones.

354   Wissot, Jay. "HESL and MESL: The Teaching of History and Math as
      Components of an English as a Second Language Program." English
      Record, 11, 4 (1971), 68-73.
            Worthwhile suggestions are offered to those involved in a pro-
      gram which teaches English as a second language. In classes in
      which history and math are taught, both subjects can be presented

to ESL students in terms of the linguistic capabilities of the students by ESL teachers who are familiar with their capabilities. As soon as the foreign-born student can compete linguistically with native speakers, he can move into regular classes in these subjects.

355 Woodsworth, John A. "On the Role of Meaning in Second Language Teaching." Language Learning, 23, 1 (1973), 75-87.
       The article offers food for thought about tendencies in second-language teaching methods by attacking 1) the emphasis that is placed on surface structure and often ignoring deep structure; 2) and the treatment of strong "print-speech correspondencies" as an important part of the ordering of ESL learning. The author intended the article to bring some new considerations on the subject of meaning to the attention of practitioners in the field of teaching English as a second language.

                              Cross Reference

               312   Teaching Aids
               313   Writing
               316   Testing and Evaluation
               317   Teaching Aids
               318   Teaching Aids
               321   Teaching Aids
               326   Teacher Preparation
               327   Bilingual
               331   Teaching Aids
               332   Teacher Preparation
               335   Teaching Aids
               338   Teacher Preparation
               339   Spoken English
               340   Adult
               341   Reading
               342   Language Learning
               347   Language Learning
               348   Bilingual
               350   Texts
               351   Spoken English
               352   Language Learning

                                READING

356 Adkins, Patricia G. "Teaching Idioms and Figures of Speech to Non-Native Speakers of English." Modern Language Journal, 52, 3 (1968), 148-152.
       The article discusses two difficult areas for non-native speakers learning English: idioms and figures of speech, and focuses on these difficulties encountered by Spanish-American and Mexican-Americans. Experiments involved the frequency of occurrence of idioms and figures of speech in reading materials, and a teaching program for 15 students who were taught idioms and figures of

speech in reading materials, and a teaching program for 15 students who were taught idioms and figures of speech for a six-week period.

357   Alesi, Gladys, and Dora Pantell. _Family Life in the U.S.A._ Regents Publishing Co., 1974.
        A book for adult students who are beginning to read English. The plot centers around the everyday activities of an immigrant family living in the United States. The subject matter is on the adult level, but sentences and vocabulary are simplified. Each lesson includes exercises in comprehension, conversation, grammar, and pronunciation.

358   Allen, Virginia French. "Trends in the Teaching of Reading." _TESL Reporter_, 6, 4 (1973), 1-2 and 15-19.
        Since students have to be trained to read material suitable for native speakers, unsimplified prose should be taught to them instead of using the old methods of limiting vocabulary and controlling grammatical constructions. Students should be trained to make rapid predictions about what will follow from the beginning of a sentence in order to identify the purpose of the sentence more quickly. It is also shown that when reading is learned at the same time as spelling, better results are obtained.

359   Alvarez, Juan, and Marie Jo Kwapil. _Five Stories Written in Spanish and English_. Dallas, Texas: The Leslie Press, 1972.
        Five stories comprise this textbook which introduces new words in both English and Spanish with a color coding intending to help the bilingual child identify his native and the second language. The material is supplementary for children who need a K-4 interest-level and K-2 skill-level reader in either English or Spanish. The stories use short simple sentences, the present tense, and dialogue. Translations are not literal.

360   Arnold, Richard D. "Retention in Reading of Disadvantaged Mexican-American Children During the Summer Months." Paper given at International Reading Association Conference, Boston, 1968. ED 020089.
        This paper describes a study of three groups of disadvantaged Mexican-American children to determine changes in reading achievement between the second and third grade. One oral-aural English group received intensive English instruction; one oral-aural Spanish group received intensive Spanish instruction; whereas the control group received no intensive language instruction. The Spanish group showed significant gains on the vocabulary test, while the English group showed no significant changes. The control group, however, showed significant losses over the summer vacation.

361   Barnard, Helen. _Advanced English Vocabulary, Workbook Two_. Rowley, Mass.: Newbury House, 1972.
        Designed for students who need a non-technical vocabulary to enable them to read English textbooks and other professional material. The course contains four workbooks which are mainly

self-instructional and cover word study, dictation exercises, reading passages, vocabulary for each section, and a short word-completion test. The course is based on a 2,000-word vocabulary.

362   Bedotto, Sr. M. Jean Rosaire. "The Effect of Non-Native Speech upon the Reading Achievement of Spanish-Speaking Students at Different Levels of Intelligence and Upon their Ability to Use Syntactic Clues to Meaning in Reading English." Diss. New York Univ., 1973.
Non-native speakers of English who learned to speak Spanish as their first language and native speakers of English from eighth grades of parochial schools in low-socio-economic areas in New York City were the subjects of this study to investigate the effect of non-native speech upon the reading achievement and the ability to use syntactic clues of Spanish-speaking children at different levels of intelligence. Important conclusions were: 1) non-native speakers of English of high and average intelligence scored lower in English reading achievement than the English-speaking students of similar intelligence; 2) students of low intelligence of both groups achieved low in reading achievement.

363   Berg, Paul Conrad. "Language Barriers of the Culturally Different." Paper given at College Reading Assn., Boston, 1969.
There are some important barriers that the culturally different pupil faces in learning to read English. Linguistic differences create one of the major problems, but the effects of language on the complete adjustment of the pupil also affects his reading performance. The author suggests that the best way to help the culturally different student is to use the language experience approach. Role playing and other language experience activities should prove helpful.

364   Blossom, Grace A. The Talleson Story: The Talleson Six School Reading Project: A Pilot Project to Help All Students Read Grade Level Textbooks with Adequate Comprehension, 1973. ED 086967.
A report of a pilot program for building reading comprehension that was conducted in six school districts near Phoenix, Arizona, in 1972-1973. More than half of the high school students were bilingual or bi-cultural. Teachers gave copies of difficult vocabulary and idiomatic phrases to students and found that the program resulted in an average gain of 3.2 in reading comprehension in the freshman class.

365   Burling, Robbins. "Some Outlandish Proposals for the Teaching of Foreign Languages." Language Learning, 18/ 1, 2 (1968), 61-75.
The author believes that we must give people access to the vast amount of English written matter and points out the need for courses that will teach reading skills. For many, the reading skill is more essential than oral and writing skills. His "outlandish proposals" include the following steps: 1) Teaching the student to read a word-for-word translation; 2) Introducing a few foreign terms; 3) Introducing the smaller classes of morphemes; 4) Introducing basic vocabulary. Burling admits that the course presents problems but is worth trying.

366   Carton, Aaron S. Orientation to Reading. Rowley, Mass.: Newbury
       House, 1972.
              This book can provide the ESL teacher with valuable informa-
       tion for understanding the reading process. The author shows the
       relationship between structural linguistics, generative-transforma-
       tional grammar, psycholinguistics, and the function of language
       as an educational process; and he supports his view of the reading
       process by referring to linguistic and psycholinguistic experi-
       mentation.

367   Clark, John. "Making Literature Real." TEFL, 5, 4 (1971), 3, 8.
              Recommendations for teaching literature in English to ESL/EFL
       students in the secondary school. The author favors the dis-
       cussion of novels, poems, stories, and plays,with the teacher as
       a moderator or questioner rather than a controller. He suggests
       that poetry should be read first to the students; a short story
       read by the students preceding discussion; and maintains that
       short scenes from plays could be acted out by the teacher and
       students. One of the objectives of reading the literature is
       to relate it as closely as possible to reality.

368   Cowan, J. R. "Lexical and Syntactic Research for the Design of EFL
       Materials." TESOL Quarterly, 8, 4 (1974), 389-399.
              The style of technical prose can be identified by vocabulary
       and syntax and this style can be difficult even for students who
       have had intermediate or advanced EFL training. In an effort to
       devise better EFL reading materials by analyzing the lexicon and
       syntax of technical prose, the author conducted a research pro-
       gram investigating these two factors. He discusses the relevancy
       of actual words appearing on vocabulary lists and the meaning of
       complex structures found in technical prose. The article con-
       cretely points out the problems that the reading of scientific
       prose presents to EFL readers.

369   Debyasuvarn, M. L. B. "Acculturization and Reading." Regional
       English Language Centre Journal, 1, 1 (1970), 82-88.
              A student learning to read in a foreign language must develop
       the ability to "acculturize" to a new cultural environment so
       he can enjoy and understand the material. In order to do this,
       the author suggests that language teachers must be trained in
       the teaching of reading and that cultural background should be
       a dominant topic of concern when people discuss language teaching
       problems.

370   Digneo, Ellen Hartnett, and Tila Shayn, eds. The Miami Linguistic
       Reading Program, 1965-1968. Report. Santa Fe, New Mexico: New
       Mexico Western States Small Schools Project, 1968.
              Since this reading program has been used with success in Miami,
       it has become very well known. Teachers will be interested in
       learning about its use with Spanish-speaking and American Indian
       children in six New Mexico school systems. The report contains
       a program evaluation, the program objectives, new developments,
       and pupil and visitor reactions regarding the program in each
       school system.

371   Dixon, Rebecca Giles. "A Project in the Development of English-as-a-Second-Language Materials for Puerto Rican Elementary School Pupils. Diss. Univ. of Illinois, 1973.
A reading text and teacher's manual were developed for use in the fifth grade in schools in Puerto Rico upon request by Puerto Rican English teachers. The text aims to provide reinforcement of linguistic elements and to motivate students to read. Students through a story-line, use games and other activities to reinforce what they acquire in English study. After using the text in a pilot study, teachers and students were enthusiastic about it.

372   Eskey, David E. "A Model Program for Teaching Advanced Reading to Students of English as a Foreign Language." Language Learning, 23, 2 (1973), 169-184.
For advanced foreign students, the development of reading skill is very important and should not be treated as a mere supplement to the development of oral skills. Instruction should be provided in those skills that are essential at each level of the reading process. The author describes a model reading program which includes classroom instruction and outside reading. Students are expected to master the syntax and lexicon of written English. The cloze procedure is recommended for both teaching and testing advanced reading. A good reading program, though, depends on "human variables" that include teacher talents and dedication and student motivation.

373   Felsten, Evelin. "The Non-English Speaking Child and Learning to Read." The English Record, 23, 3 (1973), 93-97.
The author refutes the assumption that reading should be taught to the non-English child only after he has some control over other English language areas. She maintains that words can be decoded by children who do not know the word meanings and refers to the GLASS-ANALYSIS method used in New York City schools utilizing decoding to teach the non-native speaking children to read English. The process is one that should interest ESL teachers.

374   Fries, Charles C. "Learning to Read English as Part of the Oral Approach," in Readings in English as a Second Language, Kenneth Croft, ed. Cambridge, Mass.: Winthrop Publishers, 1972, 168-173.
Fries maintains that a pupil learning to read a foreign language must develop "discrimination and recognition responses" to the signs he sees and in order to do this, he must master the writing system of Modern English. Fries then offers examples of word, syllable, and alphabet writing as writing systems representing a language. In Part II he advises us to give pupils practice in reading materials that they learn orally to grasp the language symbols and progressively move to silent reading of new materials. Part II of the paper will be of greater interest to the teacher.

375   Griese, Arnold A. "Focusing on Students of Different Cultural
       Backgrounds The Eskimo and Indian Pupil--Special Problems in
       Reading Comprehension," Elementary English, 48, 4 (1971),
       229-234.
            The article presents the special reading comprehension prob-
       lem of the Alaskan Eskimo and Indian, believing that many of
       their problems are the same facing other minority groups learn-
       ing English. The author maintains that children's literature
       can be used effectively "to improve reading comprehension of
       culturally-different pupils," and suggests that pupils' volun-
       tary reading and the teacher's reading stories to the class
       should be basic approaches to improving reading comprehension.
       Pupils should be able to relate emotionally to stories and en-
       couraged to use their imagination.

376   Hall, Richard. Learning to Read in Two Languages: Statements from
       the Research Literature on Reading in Bilingual Programs.
       Philadelphia, Pa.: School District of Philadelphia, 1970. ED 057653.
            Since the problem of the teaching of reading is even a more
       complicated one in bilingual education than it is in monolingual
       schools, this collection of statements should be helpful to those
       who teach reading in bilingual schools. In the Philadelphia pub-
       lic school bilingual reading program native Spanish speakers
       learn to read first in Spanish and are taught to read in English
       only after mastering the aural-oral skills of listening and
       speaking. Relevant material on interference, transfer of skills,
       and learning readiness is presented.

377   Harris, David P. Reading Improvement Exercises for Students in Eng-
       lish as a Second Language. Englewood Cliffs, New Jersey: Prentice-
       Hall, 1966.
            The text is designed for high-intermediate and advanced learn-
       ers of English as a second language who want to increase their
       reading speed and comprehension skills. A set of diagnostic
       tests are included at the beginning, followed by exercises using
       individual words, then sentences, paragraphs and finally complete
       compositions. Included are techniques for use in scanning and
       dictionary work. Keys to exercises are provided. This is com-
       prehensive, and can be helpful to the foreign student studying
       in American universities.

378   Herbert, Charles H., Jr. "The Bilingual Child's Right to Read."
       Paper given at the Claremont, California Reading Conference, 1972.
       ED 062841.
            A discussion of initial reading instruction in bilingual educa-
       tion that attempts to teach two languages at the same time. The
       "Initial Reading in Spanish" project presented a comprehensive
       analysis of methods used to teach Spanish-speaking children in
       Mexico to read in their native language. The results of the
       evaluations of the Mexican reading techniques used in the
       United States reveal that the project was successful in help-
       ing students read in both Spanish and English.

379 Herbert, Charles H., Jr. Initial Reading in Spanish for Bilinguals.
     Quebec: Laval University, 1971. ED 061813.
           ESL teachers should be interested in reading programs in bi-
     lingual education since there are varying theories concerning
     when and how to teach reading in the student's native and second
     languages. This report describes the methods used in formulating
     and evaluating a reading program used to teach Spanish-speaking
     children in the United States to read in their native language.
     Teaching methodologies, evaluations, and general results are
     included.

380 Hielerich, Robert L. "ERMAS: A Beginning Reading Program for Mexi-
     can American Children." The National Elementary Principal, 50, 2
     (1970), 80-84.
           ERMAS (Experiment in Reading for Mexican American Students)
     sought to determine whether Mexican-American children who began
     reading in Spanish also learned to read better by the end of
     the second grade than children who began reading only English
     in the first grade. The experimental group began to read in
     English after completing prereading skills in Spanish. The
     control group was given all instruction in English. It was
     noted that those who learned to read Spanish applied their
     skills to English and read "with a pleasure and enthusiasm long
     overdue."

381 Hirschorn, Howard H. Technical & Scientific Reader in English.
     New York: Simon and Schuster, 1970.
           Spanish-speaking students who want to develop their under-
     standing of scientific and technical English will find this text
     helpful since it includes 50 reading selections covering a var-
     iety of subjects. Included are comprehension, vocabulary, and
     conversation exercises, complete with answers. Items requiring
     special explanation appear in Spanish in the margin of pages
     where they appear.

382 Horn, T. D. "Three Methods of Developing Reading Readiness in
     Spanish-Speaking Children in First Grade." The Reading Teacher,
     20, 1 (1966), 38-42.
           The study compared the effectiveness of three methods of develop
     ing reading readiness in Spanish-speaking children in grade one.
     Group I received oral-aural English language instruction for one
     hour a day. Group II was given oral-aural Spanish language in-
     struction for the same amount of time, while Group III received
     no oral-aural language instruction. The only clear-cut conclu-
     sions that can be drawn from the study reveal a distinct need
     for measuring a variety of language related variables of these
     children.

383 Inouye, Margaret G., and Mary Jayne Larson. "A Total Involvement
     Reading Program." Elementary English, 51, 2 (1974), 249, 250, 294.
           A writeup of a program, initiated mainly because of the poor
     reading skills of the pupils, that incorporated ethnic back-

ground as a positive ingredient, and used parents, teachers, and pupils in developing an individualized multimedia reading program focusing on the immediate environment. The location is the island of Maui in Hawaii with a community composed mostly of people of Filipino ancestry. Kits were developed from materials used and will be designed for other subject matter areas. This is the kind of program that puts TESOL theories into practice.

384   Jenkins, Esther C. "Multi-Ethnic Literature: Promise and Problems." Elementary English, 50, 5 (1973), 693-699.
       The author found that even though there are people with various kinds of ethnic backgrounds living together in Hawaii--Japanese, Chinese, Blacks, Koreans, Portuguese, etc.--"there are still many misconceptions which we hold about each other." A worthwhile multi-ethnic literature program would be one way of providing people with information about their own culture and the culture of others. A strong recommendation is made to have well trained teachers work together with librarians and people in the community.

385   Jensen, Sidney L. "Children's Literature and ESL." TESL Reporter, 7, 4 (1974), 1-2.
       The author maintains that "any reading material will work as long as it is the proper grade level for the student," and then describes a reading program he conducted with nineteen second-language students whose abilities ranged from the fourth to the seventh grade. The objective of the class was to read English rapidly and silently but not to translate,and students were encouraged to read books completely even though the material was far below their reading ability. The contention is that the way to develop the habit of reading is by reading.

386   Kelly, Ernece B. Searching for America. Urbana, Illinois: N.C.T.E., 1972.
       One of the few reports of its kind and one that ESL teachers should become familiar with since it deals with the broadening of the scope of literature teaching to include wider cultural backgrounds. Essays deal with Afro-American, Asian-American, Chicano, and native American literature. Twelve frequently used American literature texts are evaluated according to the NCTE "Criteria for Teaching Materials in Reading and Literature."

387   Kline, Carl L., and N. Lee. "A Transcultural Study of Dyslexia: Analysis of Language Disabilities in 277 Chinese Children Simultaneously Learning to Read and Write in English and in Chinese." Journal of Special Education, 6 (1972), 9-26.
       An analysis of language disabilities of 277 bilingual Chinese children in grades 1-3 who were learning to read, spell, and write in English and Chinese. The incidence of reading disability in each language and in both languages is presented along with other data. Analyses are also made of various tests concerning reading disabilities.

388 McCanne, Roy. "Approaches to First Grade English Reading Instruc-
     tion for Children from Spanish-Speaking Homes." The Reading
     Teacher, 19, 8 (1966), 670-675.
          The main object of this study was to determine if there were
     any differences in achievement in reading English in first grade
     between pupils who speak Spanish at home and are taught by a) a
     basal reader approach; b) a modified TESL approach; and c) a
     language-experience approach. Results indicated that the experi-
     mental approach developing the highest achievement in reading
     skills was the basal reader approach, although the researcher
     points out that the TESL and LEA approaches can be recommended
     for language development skills other than reading.

389 Medina, Edward, and Francis H. Pope. English Alphabet Book 1:
     Spanish Phonetic Reading Program. Champaign, Illinois: Research
     Press Co., 1972.
          A concise reading program based on pictures providing indica-
     tors to speech sounds in the language. By matching an English
     speech sound with its alphabetical symbol, pupils can indicate
     an understanding of their auditory and visual discrimination.
     This is one of a series of documents for teaching reading
     phonetically to Spanish-speaking pupils, both in English and
     Spanish.

390 Miami Linguistic Readers. Boston: D. C. Heath, 1965.
          A series that is designed to help the student gain aural-oral
     control of the material he is going to try to read by giving him
     a great deal of practice in pronouncing the English language cor-
     rectly. The approach is a linguistic one for English-Spanish
     bilingual children, planned as a two-year program. The teacher
     can progress at a rate that is dependent upon the abilities of
     the children. The manual is very helpful to teachers. The only
     criticism of the series is that formal reading is introduced
     too early in the program.

391 Modiano, Nancy. "Reading in Bilingual Education." Paper given at
     Sixth Annual TESOL Convention, Washington, D. C., 1972. ED 065000.
          The author maintains that reading in the second language should
     not be indicated until the pupil is fully literate in the first
     language; therefore, reading in a bilingual program should be
     introduced in the pupil's first language. In addition, the role
     of reading in each of the two languages needs to be carefully
     examined to determine emphasis.

392 Moss, Kenyon. "Oral-Aural Proficiency Required." TESL Reporter,
     5, 3 (1972), 5, 12.
          A discussion of the prerequisites that should be met before
     a student reads English. Moss believes that a student should be
     proficient in oral work before he reads. He should know the
     sounds and structure of his native tongue; be familiar with the
     mechanics of reading; be able to recognize printed symbols; know
     some basic patterns of English sounds and structure; and have
     some knowledge of the culture of speakers of English.

393   Oller, John W., and James R. Tulluis. "Reading Skills of Non-
      Native Speakers of English." IRAL, 11, 1 (1973), 68-80.
           The authors maintain that the skill of reading has been largely
      overlooked in teaching English as a foreign language to college-
      level foreign students studying in the United States. In order
      to gather information about these students, the authors tested
      50 of them participating in the ESL summer program at the Univer-
      sity of California at Santa Barbara representing 21 language
      groups, and compared the results with native speaker norms on
      eye movement photography (EMP) tests. Results showed that read-
      ing difficulties of non-native speakers are different in type and
      numbers from the reading problems of natives.

394   Paterno, A. "Using Grammar to Help Reading Comprehension." MST
      English Quarterly, 20, 3 (1970), 305-322.
           The main principle of this article is that students learning
      English as a second language will be better able to understand
      English sentences if they can see how each sentence can be re-
      duced to one of the basic sentence patterns. By recognizing the
      basic pattern, the student sees the basic thought of the sent-
      ence. A knowledge of grammar that includes English syntactic
      structure and transitive and intransitive verbs will also help
      the student to understand complicated sentences.

395   Pierce, Mary Eleanor. "Sentence-Level Expectancy as an Aid to
      Advanced Reading." TESOL Quarterly, 6, 3 (1973), 269-277.
           Advanced EFL/ESL students usually have difficulty making a
      transition from reading material for ESL students to material in
      texts for native speakers. The application of expectancy as an
      aid in interpreting complex sentence patterns found in textbooks
      is considered. Emphasis is placed on identification of the sub-
      ject as a unit from which the rest of the sentence develops. Also,
      an awareness of the reasons for the complexity of sentences may
      help students increase their understanding of the sentences.

396   Povey, John F. "Literature in TESL Programs: The Language and the
      Culture," in Teaching English as a Second Language, Harold B. Allen
      and Russell N. Campbell, eds. New York: McGraw-Hill, 1972,
      185-191.
           The author justifies the teaching of literature in TESL pro-
      grams as something more than just a subject to teach when grammar
      is not being taught. He sets up some general reasons for teach-
      ing literature based on his own experience: it will increase all
      language skills; serve as a cultural bridge; give the student
      "awareness and human insight"; and guide gifted students towards
      creating their own writing.

397   Reed, Estella E. "An Investigation of the Relative Effect of the
      Study of Syntax and Paragraph Structure on Reading Comprehension
      of Monolingual and Bilingual Pupils in Grade Seven." Diss.
      Indiana Univ., 1966.
           A study that has implications regarding the methodology for
      teaching bilingual students in junior high school. An experi-

mental group of students followed a definite program of reading instruction based on 1) recognition of sentence elements and 2) recognition of paragraph structure. Although there was no significant difference between monolingual students in the experimental and control groups, a significant difference at the .01 level favoring the experimental group existed between bilingual students. Gains were noticeable for the experimental groups, monolingual and bilingual, on the Paragraph Comprehension Test.

398   Rich, Gene. "Teaching Reading to the American Indian." Paper given at Annual Meeting of the International Reading Assn., Denver, Colorado, 1973. ED. 075799.
      Since Indian children have special problems associated with learning to read, this paper offers guidelines for those involved with teaching reading to American Indian children who must first be taught to speak and read in their own language. The emphasis is on applying teaching techniques which are applicable to the special problems confronting Indian children.

399   Rosen, Carl L. Assessment and Relative Effects of Reading Programs for Mexican Americans. A Position Paper. Albuquerque, New Mexico: Southwestern Cooperative Educational Lab, 1970. ED 061000.
      Reviews of research in dealing with the problem of teaching reading in English to Mexican-American children whose first language is Spanish are presented. Of special interest is the research covering linguistic and language-experience approaches and directions for research in language and reading processes, and research in the teaching of English as a second language. A substantial bibliography is provided.

400   Saitz, Robert L., and Dennis Baumwolt. Advanced Reading and Writing: Exercises in English as a Second Language. New York: Holt, Rinehart, and Winston, 1965.
      A challenging text for ESL students who will find the book difficult unless they read well and write satisfactorily. The reading selections, serving as examples of standard formal English, have not been simplified. Some of the words on the vocabulary lists are not widely used. Word selection and sentence structure exercises can be useful. Explanations on theme development would be helpful additions to the text.

401   Saitz, Robert L., and Donna Carr. Selected Readings in English: For Students of English as a Second Language. Cambridge, Mass.: Winthrop Publishers, 1972.
      A collection of essays, mostly contemporary, that are useful for intermediate and advanced students studying English as a second language in providing them with reading and writing experience. Vocabulary, comprehension, and morphology exercises accompany each essay, and explanations are provided for difficult words and cultural references that might be troublesome to non-native speakers.

402 Saitz, Robert L., and Francine Stieglitz, eds. Ideas in English: Readings in English as a Second Language. Englewood Cliffs, New Jersey: Prentice-Hall, 1974.

A book for use with secondary, college or adult education students who have a limited command of English. The selections are of high interest and low reading difficulty concentrating on important ideas and attitudes that students can understand and communicate. Among the authors represented are Hemingway, Vonnegut, Saroyan, Agee, Maugham, and Sherwood Anderson.

403 Sandberg, Karl C. "Uses of Programmed Materials in Teaching Reading and Aural Comprehension." Paper given at the Third Annual Meeting of ACTFL, New Orleans, La., 1969. ED 035873.

The author suggests an intensive concentration on the teaching of grammar structures and function words since the latter account for about 50 per cent of the words on any given page of prose. He points out that programmed learning can be useful in solving reading and aural comprehension problems in English as a second language, and contends that the methods of teaching reading and aural comprehension haven't changed recently. Programmed materials can help the foreign student develop skill in reading.

404 Saville-Troike, Muriel. "Reading and the Audio-Lingual Method." TESOL Quarterly, 7, 2 (1973), 395-405.

The author contends that except for person-to-person communication, "training in oral production to the exclusion of other modes is of limited value." The ability to read fluently is often more important than understanding oral language. A reassessment of the audio-lingual method will show that developing reading skills will gain more significance in the ESL classroom. Some specific examples offered by the author help to make her theory a convincing one.

405 Seliger, Herbert W. "Improving Reading Speed and Comprehension in English as a Second Language." English Language Teaching, 27, 1 (1972), 48-55.

According to the author, it is necessary to increase the reading speed of ESL students in order to increase their comprehension, and he states that teachers must devote more attention to this area after teaching the basics of reading. The article discusses some of the difficulties of teaching reading to students learning English as a second language and offers some suggestions for increasing reading speed and comprehension. The author believes that previewing, scanning, directed reading, and the use of the finger can help the student to increase his reading speed. He recommends that teachers must help students to develop a reading approach "which will focus on units beyond individual words."

406 Sopher, E. "An Introductory Approach to the Teaching of Scientific English to Foreign Students." English Language Teaching Journal, 28, 2 (1974), 353-359.

Since some foreign students will want to read scientific texts with which they are unfamiliar, Sopher considers that a scientific English language course should enable foreign students to read such materials. Among the difficulties encountered by the student will be the vocabulary and sentence structure, especially the scientific terminology, jargon and idioms; and the complex sentences that one often finds in scientific writing. Sopher would stress the skill of extracting the main ideas in a passage and would also require the student to prepare a scientific report.

407 Tang, Benita T. "A Psycholinguistic Study of the Relationships Between Children's Ethnic-Linguistic Attitudes and the Effectiveness of Methods Used in Second-Language Reading Instruction." TESOL Quarterly, 8, 3 (1974), 233-251.
The article discusses the psycholinguistic investigation that studied the relationships between Chinese children's attitudes toward their native dialect and English, the second language, and the effectiveness of certain methods used in teaching second-language reading. The results showed that the Translation Method is the best one for children who have a positive attitude toward their native language and culture, but the Non-Translation Method is superior for those who do not have high esteem for their native tongue.

408 Thonis, Eleanor Wall. Teaching Reading to Non-English Speakers. New York: The MacMillan Co., 1970.
A compact and comprehensive book that takes the teacher from the pre-reading level of the learner through the evaluation of his growth. The author analyzes the problems of the learner and offers suggestions to enable the teacher to help solve these problems. She discusses many different approaches: reading in the content areas, developing various reading skills, and selecting materials. A rather complete list of references is included after each chapter. Very highly recommended for the ESL teacher at all levels.

409 Tuers, Elizabeth Ruth. "Culture Through Literature: A Guide to the Preparation of English Language Reading Materials for Speakers of Arabic in Egypt and the Levant." Diss. Univ. of Michigan, 1969.
The thesis states that motivation to acquaint students in the Middle East with American culture--culture being a significant factor in language learning--can be accomplished through the medium of the students' native literature in English translation. By starting with familiar material (one's own culture) and learning about one's culture patterns, students will then be motivated to learn about a different culture. Model reading materials therefore included a mixture of Arabic and American short stories in five different categories.

410 Ulibarri, Mari-Luci. "Reading in the ESL Program." Paper given at Fifth Annual TESOL Convention, New Orleans, La., 1971.

The author maintains that the teacher of reading in an ESL classroom must be familiar with the cultural background of the students and that a successful reading program must be measured by the students' feeling toward the program as well as a progressive development of reading skills.

411   Wilson, Lois Irene. "Reading in the ESOL Classroom: A Technique for Teaching Syntactic Meaning." TESOL Quarterly, 7, 3 (1973), 259-267.
The paper presents a technique for teaching grammar patterns in ESL or EFL reading classes in the belief that "sentence structure presents clues that the reader needs to understand the written language." The teacher presents the sentence pattern to the class and helps students understand the reasons for word order and the important function words. Exercises are given the students to help reinforce recognition of the sentence pattern, but students are never asked to produce the pattern.

412   Wilson, Robert D. "A Reading Program for ESL Primary Students." Speech given at Fifth Annual TESOL Conference, New Orleans, La., 1971. ED 056574.
A description of a reading program developed by Consultants in Total Education for primary students learning English as a second language. Four general stages comprise the program, and each stage includes certain educational concepts, from linguistic preparation to read, to reading for learning.

413   Withers, Sara. The United Nations in Action: A Structured Reader. New York: Thomas Y. Crowell, 1969.
Intended primarily for adults and young adults working in English as a second language on the intermediate grammar and vocabulary level. The reader can provide help to the student in his writing and speaking with topics provided for class discussion exercises in oral idioms. Dictionary practice, conversation questions, dictation, and pronunciation drills are also incorporated in the text.

414   Wolk, Elsie. "Reading Disabilities of Children Learning English as a Second Language." Elementary English, 49, 3 (1972), 410-414.
The Puerto Rican Study, a four-year research effort sponsored by the Ford Foundation and the Board of Education of the City of New York, recommended that "a direct attack be made on the problems of teaching reading" to non-English-speaking pupils. After surveying the situation, the author makes many recommendations to the teacher including teaching needed sight words and giving children the chance to read words used in a variety of contexts.

415   Yoes, Deck, Jr. "Reading Programs for Mexican-American Children of Texas." The Reading Teacher, 20, 4 (1967), 313-318, 323.
An examination of some of the Title I projects in Texas that are"designed to strengthen instruction in reading for children of Mexican-American backgrounds." Many of the children have

Spanish as their first language and have the added disadvantage of family migrancy. An assessment of the results of the projects showed better individualized instruction, teacher enthusiasm, and improved pupil work habits, skills, and attitudes.

416   Yorio, Carlas Alfredo. "Some Sources of Reading Problems for Foreign-Language Learners." Language Learning, 21, 1 (1971), 107-115.
Since foreign students consider vocabulary to be their most difficult problem in reading English, the author focuses on words in discussing approaches to dealing with this problem. He suggests that overall comprehension should be emphasized and tested; passages with a story-line should be chosen first; initial passages should not be lengthy; reading in the early stages should be done outside of class; speed should be emphasized as students progress; individual differences must be recognized; and, generally, reading should be "taught progressively."

Cross Reference

357	Adult
359	Bilingual
362	Socio-Cultural
364	Bilingual
365	Methodology
369	Socio-Cultural
370	Texts
376	Bilingual
377	Texts
378	Bilingual
379	Bilingual
382	Testing and Evaluation
383	Audio-Visual
386	Testing and Evaluation
391	Bilingual
392	Spoken English
394	Grammar
397	Bilingual
400	Writing
407	Methodology
410	Socio-Cultural
411	Writing
415	Bilingual

REFERENCE

417   Allen, Harold B. Linguistics and English Linguistics. (Goldentree Bibliographies in Language and Literature). New York: Appleton-Century- Crofts, 1966.
A bibliography for graduate and advanced undergraduate students that includes sources in English language, linguistics, and re-

lated areas. The book contains one section on English to Speakers of Other Languages and one on Bilingualism. Helpful to researchers, and teachers of advanced students.

418 Allen, Virginia F., and Sidney Forman. English as a Second Language-a Comprehensive Bibliography. New York: Teachers College Press, Teachers College, Columbia Univ., 1966.
A catalog of books dealing with English as a foreign or second language that appear in the Teachers College Library. Each book is listed according to subject and, in addition to the usual bibliographic information, includes price and language of the book. An author, title, and publisher index are included.

419 Altus, David M., Comp. Mexican American Education, A Selected Bibliography. Supplement No. 1. Los Cruces, New Mexico: New Mexico, 1971. ED 048961.
This reference book contains research findings and developments in the education of Mexican American children and adults. It includes many citations and abstracts appearing in "Research in Education" from June 1969 through December 1970 and some citations in "Current Index to Journals in Education" from January 1969 through June 1970. Bilingual education and teaching English as a second language are subjects covered that ESL teachers will be interested in.

420 Bibliography of Materials Available for Use in English as a Second Language Classes. San Diego, Calif.: San Diego City Schools, 1967. ED 026153.
This 23-page bibliography lists approximately 230 resource materials, books, and articles for English-as-a-second-language classes. For the teacher who needs more materials, this can be helpful since it includes lists for various subjects, songs and music, Spanish and English texts, and materials for adults. Descriptions of the materials are brief.

421 A Bibliography of (Mostly) Generative Synchronic Phonological Studies of TESOL Languages, 1971. ED 057649.
An unannotated bibliography which lists over 400 works published between 1924 and 1971 that deal with the sound systems of languages used by people who frequently are taught English. An attempt is made to include mostly those studies within the generative classification. Works on contrastive analysis are also included along with a language index.

422 Book of Educational Prescriptions for English as a Second Language. Santa Ana, Calif.: Orange County Board of Education, 1973. ED 083876.
A manual that offers teachers of English as a second language some pertinent information about their students on the kindergarten and primary levels and also presents lessons for instruction. A profile sheet helps to identify pupil academic needs along with prescribed materials which include vocabulary improvement, language usage, sentence structure, and aids for developing motor skills.

423 CARTEL: Annotated Bibliography of Bilingual-Bicultural Materials
No. 12. Austin, Texas: Education Service Center, 1973. ED 086429.
Books, curriculum guides, journals, and resource materials
published between 1967 and 1973 appear in this reference book
of bilingual-bicultural materials for American Indians, French,
Portuguese, Chinese, and speakers of Spanish. Materials are
related to the Title VII Elementary and Secondary Education Act
or other bilingual programs.

424 Carter, Thomas P. "Cultural Content for Linguistically Different
Learners." Elementary English, 48, 2 (1971), 162-175.
A bibliography of 43 sources accompanies this article which
is especially well researched and discusses the problems facing
the teacher of English to linguistically and culturally different pupils. The author maintains that a careful analysis of
these pupils' backgrounds and the perceptions they have of
their relationship with the school and society must be made.
He calls for a modification of curriculums and "massive school
reorientation and reorganization." He states that we should
teach "coping," the process of taking advantage of the culture
and language of the dominant society.

425 Ching, Doris O. "Reading Language Development, and the Bilingual
Child." Elementary English, 46, 5 (1969), 622-628.
An annotated bibliography of 36 articles compiled by Ching
to help educators understand the language needs of bilingual
children and to make teachers aware of various ideas used in
teaching these children. The annotations are long enough to
give the reader a clear idea of the purpose of the article.
The compiler includes some older articles (1939, 1945) that
she believes are still relevant.

426 Colflesh, Madeline. Curriculum Guide for Non-English Speakers,
Grades 9-10. West Chester, Pa.: West Chester School District,
1972. ED 071521.
Communities that are trying to begin an ESL program should
find some helpful suggestions in this curriculum guide for
English which describes a program for Spanish-speaking students
aged 14-17 that can also be adapted for speakers of other languages. The program contains thirty-six lessons for English,
mathematics, history, and science.

427 Cordasco, Francesco, and Eugene Bucchioni.. Puerto Rican Children
in Mainland Schools. A Source Book for Teachers. Metuchen, New
Jersey: The Scarecrow Press, 1968.
This book of collected readings can provide the ESL teacher
who works with Puerto Rican children with a better understanding of their needs, culture, and experiences. The text also
includes readings about the Puerto Rican family and Puerto
Rican children in North American schools. A lengthy bibliography is included.

428 Daniels F. J. Basic English Writers' Japanese-English Wordbook.
     Tokyo, Japan: The Hokuseido Press, 1969.
          This is designed mainly for use as an aid to the preparation
     of teaching material and as a reference for teachers although
     it has other uses. Entries appear in Japanese orthography
     followed by their representation in Chinese characters or
     phonemic transcription. It is also advocated for use by trans-
     lators from Japanese into English and by learners of Japanese.
     A list of basic words of English on which the book is based is
     included.

429 Decker, Donald M. "The Use and Teaching of English in Mexico,"
     1972. (Unpub. paper).
          Since English is the main foreign language taught in Mexico
     and extends from the pre-school level to college, this report,
     with its description of English language instruction at all
     levels, is a worthy reference. Included are course and pro-
     gram details and relevant material on texts, students, and
     teachers. Both public and private schools are discussed.

430 English as a Second Language in Elementary Schools--Background and
     Text Materials. Washington, D. C.: Center for Applied Linguistics.
     ED 012919.
          A bibliography, briefly annotated, of publications available
     in teaching English as a second language in kindergarten and
     elementary schools. The publications deal with materials, tech-
     niques, and theories, with age and learning levels. Materials
     prepared for ESL students in New York City: El Centro, Califor-
     nia; Miami, Florida; and Austin, Texas; are included.

431 English for Speakers of Other Languages. A Bibliography. London,
     England: English Teaching Information Centre, 1973. ED 093159.
          An annotated bibliography of 58 pages that is divided into
     14 sections including reference books and dictionaries, testing,
     reading, writing, linguistics, and general courses. The anno-
     tation for the last-named section indicates the student popu-
     lation for which the particular course was designed. One
     section is devoted mainly to entries concerning British History
     and English language history.

432 English Language and Orientation Programs in the United States.
     New York: Institute of International Education. 1973.
          A listing of programs and courses in English language orien-
     tation, and English as a foreign and second language, the
     result of a survey through a grant of the U. S. Department of
     State, Bureau of Educational and Cultural Affairs. The report
     includes course descriptions, tuition, housing available, en-
     trance requirements, and other pertinent information.

433 ESL Reference List of Materials for English as a Second Language.
     Los Angeles, Calif.: Los Angeles City Schools, 1972. ED 058557.
          An annotated bibliography of 19 pages with listings of books
     for students at beginning, intermediate, and advanced levels.

Books are divided into basic texts, supplementary language skills, and reading skills. A list of resource books for teachers is included. Although limited, the bibliography can be helpful to ESL teachers looking for more resources.

434   Finocchiaro, Mary. "Education of Puerto Ricans on the Mainlands: Overcoming the Communication Barrier, 1970." Paper delivered at Conference on Education of Puerto Rican Children on the Mainland, San Juan, 1970. ED 043871.

      ESL teachers in the United States can get some much needed information about the problems concerning the teaching of English to Puerto Ricans, and the author's discussion makes it apparent that the difficulties are manifold, difficulties not usually encountered in teaching native speakers. Problems include lack of previous English language training, illiteracy in Spanish, broken patterns of schooling, cultural conflicts, and others.

435   Flaherty, Jane F., comp. Resources for the ESL Teacher. Union, N. J.: Newark State College, 1970.

      A resource list for teachers of English as a second language, primarily in the field of adult education including textbooks and visual aids, filmstrips, and readings for instructions. Lists of organizations, resource centers, and information on testing are also included.

436   Fox, Robert P., ed. Essays on Teaching English as a Second Language and as a Second Dialect. Urbana, Illinois: N.C.T.E., 1973.

      This anthology includes eleven essays covering a variety of related topics about ESL teaching including a history of this kind of teaching, different teaching techniques, and difficulties encountered by non-native speakers and speakers of non-standard English. Suggestions for teaching are non-technical.

437   Gamez, Tana d., Ed.-in-Chief, Simon and Schuster's International Dictionary: English-Spanish, Spanish-English. New York: Simon and Schuster, 1973.

      A comprehensive and contemporary bilingual dictionary that covers the many meanings of colloquial, technical, scientific, and humanistic areas. It could be a useful tool to an ESL teacher teaching Spanish-speaking students since it is so inclusive and reflective of current usage. The size of the type and the style in which the definitions are written make this an especially good dictionary.

438   George, H. V. "An Inventory of Simple Sentence Patterns of English." Te Reo: Proceedings of the Linguistic Society of New Zealand, 10, 11 (1967-68), 62-66.

      The material in this brief report could be helpful to ESL teachers since it deals with the frequency of patterns used in spoken and written English. Thirteen sentence elements, such

as subject, and object, were inserted into a computer in order
to acquire transformations. Items for which no examples could
be found were eliminated, but a list of 518 patterns was retained ranging from very frequent to very infrequent.

439   Hartmann, R.R.K., and F. C. Stark. Dictionary of Language and
      Linguistics. London: Applied Science Publishers Ltd., 1972.
          A reference book consisting mostly of general language and
      linguistic terms with clear, concise definitions and some ex-
      amples of the use of such terms. The terms included are
      traditional (subjunctive mood) and modern (stratificational
      grammar). The book also includes I.P.A. graphically illus-
      trated, and a 24-page bibliography divided into ten sections
      that includes periodicals, reference books, glossaries, and
      other publications. An excellent dictionary for the ESL
      teacher.

440   Hornby, A. S. Oxford Advanced Learner's Dictionary of Current
      English. New York: Oxford University Press, 1974.
          A reference dictionary especially designed for non-native
      speakers containing idiomatic expressions, words used in
      phrases, and definitions that are uncluttered and commonly
      expressed. The vocabulary is current, and the explanations in
      the introduction facilitate the student's use and understand-
      ing of the dictionary. More illustrations would be helpful
      but would, naturally, expand the length of the book.

441   Jacobson, Rodolfo, ed. Studies in English to Speakers of Other
      Languages & Standard English to Speakers of a Non-Standard
      Dialect. Urbana, Illinois: N.C.T.E., 1971.
          The collection includes twenty-four articles on teaching
      English as a standard dialect and teaching English as a foreign
      language. The former includes historical approaches and atti-
      tudes, while the latter includes bilingualism, cultural inter-
      ference and curriculum. The studies, as a group, encourage
      linguistic and cultural pluralism.

442   James, Charles J., comp. A Selected Bibliography of Doctoral
      Disserations in Modern Language Education. New York: MLA/ERIC,
      1972.
          This bibliography of over 800 doctoral dissertations com-
      pleted from July 1961 through June 1971 in modern language
      education includes such categories as linguistics, culture,
      curriculum in foreign languages, teaching English to speakers
      of other languages, bilingualism, and others. Abstracts are
      not included but each entry has a reference to Dissertation
      Abstracts International.

443   Keck, Mary Ellen B., et al. A Selective Annotated Bibliography for
      the Language Laboratory, 1959-71. New York: ERIC Clearinghouse on
      Languages and Linguistics, 1972. ED 065006.
          The bibliography includes 163 articles, books, and reports
      about the language laboratory published from 1959 to 1972,

intended for people seeking information on various aspects of
planning and operating a language lab. Items include the history of the language lab, language and linguistics, audiolingual
and reading-translation methods, language lab techniques, and
future uses of the lab.

444 Kindergarten Bilingual Resource Handbook. Fort Worth, Texas: National
Consortia for Bilingual Education, 1971. ED 059636.
A helpful manual designed to aid kindergarten teachers working with bilingual five-year-olds. The guide contains information dealing with early childhood education, use of bulletin
boards, schedules and plans, resource material in Spanish,
teaching aids, curriculum, and other items. The ESL teacher
who has access to this information should find it easier to
acquaint the child with second language skills.

445 Lange, Dale L., comp. 1970 ACTFL Annual Bibliography of Books and
Articles on Pedagogy in Foreign Languages. New York: ACTFL/MLA ERIC,
1971. ED 050651.
The fourth annual bibliography published by the American
Council on the Teaching of Foreign Languages (ACTFL) lists
1,734 items about pedagogy in modern foreign languages, Latin,
Greek, English as a second language, and applied linguistics.
Sections are divided into areas of linguistics, culture, curri-
culum, psychology of language teaching, teacher education,
testing and others.

446 The Language Development Project: A Pilot Study in Language Learning.
A New York State Urban Aid Project. Mid-Year Report, February,
1969. ED 037724.
A project intended to give help to disadvantaged primary-
grade children learning English as a second language or using
non-standard speech patterns. Children used special language
development materials daily and received assistance in language
development during their other instructional time. The report
includes a list of schools and staff in the project, duties of
the demonstration teachers, and an evaluation of the Project's
first year (1967-68).

447 A Language Teaching Bibliography. Second Edition. London: Cambridge
University Press, 1972.
This annotated bibliography contains 837 entries covering
various aspects of language teaching. ESL teachers will be
particularly interested in the division entitled English for
Speakers of Other Languages and in the sub-divisions on language teaching and the psychology of language acquisition,
learning and teaching. Readers would probably like to have
more information about each entry regarding its philosophy of
language teaching and the direction it takes, but the reference work is comprehensive and can be serviceable.

448   Lesley, Tay. <u>Bilingual Education in California</u>. Master's
        Thesis, Univ. of California, Los Angeles, 1971.
           A report of the development of bilingual education in Cali-
        fornia with a special focus on programs for Mexican-Americans.
        The author offers a comprehensive study of most of the state's
        bilingual programs and includes information about community
        involvement, curriculum, methods, teachers and teacher train-
        ing, and goals. In addition to a list of state programs, the
        author includes the questionnaire used in the survey. Sections
        on methods and materials and curriculum will be of interest to
        ESL teachers.

449   Lugton, Robert C., ed. <u>English as a Second Language: Current</u>
        <u>Issues</u>. Philadelphia: The Center for Curriculum Development, 1970.
        ED 044671.
           A collection of articles on teaching English as a foreign
        language, covering a variety of topics: audio-visual aids,
        programmed instruction, psycholinguistics, transformational-
        generative grammar, phonology, and others.

450   Madsen, Betty M., and William R. Slager, eds. <u>Language in American</u>
        <u>Indian Education</u>. Salt Lake City, Utah: Utah University, 1972.
        ED 076067.
           Teachers engaged in teaching English to American Indians will
        find a variety of information in this book that contains arti-
        cles on language, book reviews, short stories, films, local
        resource materials, Title 7 projects for Indian languages, and
        summaries and excerpts from conference papers.

451   Malkoc, Anna Maria, comp. <u>A TESOL Bibliography: Abstracts of ERIC</u>
        <u>Publications and Research Reports, 1969-1970</u>. Washington, D. C.:
        Center for Applied Linguistics, 1971. ED 047295.
           The bibliography is divided into two parts, the first con-
        taining resumes of works in English for non-native speakers
        appearing in "Research in Education" mainly in 1969-70. The
        second presents articles in journals listed from January 1969
        through August 1970 in "Current Index to Journals in Education."
        Resumes cover the teaching of reading and composition, testing
        and evaluation, teaching guides, bilingual programs and related
        subjects.

452   Marckwardt, Albert H. "The Dictionary as an English Teaching
        Resource." <u>TESOL Quarterly</u>, 7, 4 (1973), 369-379.
           Since English is not always uniform and since no one grammat-
        ical approach can deal with the entire language, the dictionary
        should be used because it can offer language information not
        found anywhere else. It can provide information on usage,
        grammar, synonyms, and material about written and spoken English
        not often found in textbooks. It is important, however, that
        the teacher selects a dictionary of at least collegiate size
        that can furnish this necessary information.

453   Marckwardt, Albert H. <u>Teaching English as a Foreign Language</u> --
       <u>A Survey of the Past Decade.</u> Washington, D.C.: Center for
       Applied Linguistics, 1967.
           A look at the development of the teaching of English to non-
       native speakers in the United States and elsewhere, including
       programs in Africa, Europe,and the Far and Near East. Mention
       is made of the teaching methods and use of materials and the
       courses and degree programs available to teachers in American
       colleges. Marckwardt stresses the need for more research in
       language learning and methodology, and the development of
       materials and teacher training programs.

454   <u>Materials for Those with a Spanish-Speaking Background</u>. Madison,
       Wisconsin: Cooperative Children's Book Center, September, 1969.
           An annotated bibliography listing more than 150 books and
       audio-visual material of interest to students with a Spanish
       language background and to those who teach them. Items are
       classified according to subject,geographical area, and reading
       difficulty. Librarians and teachers who want to expand their
       acquisitions and materials will find this useful.

455   Ortego, Philip D., and Carl L. Rosen. <u>Issues in Language and</u>
       <u>Reading Instruction of Spanish-Speaking Children. An Annotated</u>
       <u>Bibliography.</u> Newark, Delaware: International Reading ASsn.,
       1969. ED 075804.
           The sections of this bibliography that will appeal most to
       ESL teachers are those that deal with the language arts
       teacher of Spanish-speaking children and the articles on read-
       ing achievement. The introductory section, however, offers
       information that is relevant for a teacher of English in a
       bilingual school.

456   Pedtke, Dorothy A., ed. <u>Teaching English to Speakers of Other</u>
       <u>Languages, United States Activities: 1968.</u> Washington, D. C.:
       <u>Center for Applied Linguistics,</u> 1969. ED 030115.
           The report summarizes various activities in the United States
       related to the teaching of English to non-native speakers in
       1968. Each category is listed separately and includes English
       language teaching and training overseas and in the United States;
       and the testing and development of materials. Sources of
       information are from universities, foundations, published arti-
       cles, and reports from city, state, and federal organizations.

457   Pedtke, Dorothy A., et al. <u>Reference List of Materials for English</u>
       <u>as a Second Language. Supplement: 1964-1968.</u> Washington, D. C.:
       Center for Applied Linguistics, 1969.
           This annotated bibliography is divided into eleven sections
       including references to texts, teaching aids, methodology, langu-
       age testing, American readers and other groupings with sub-
       groups. An author index appears at the end of the work which
       contains 207 pages.

458   Recorded Materials for Teaching English. London, England: National
      Committee for Audio-Visual Aids in Education, 1971. ED 065997.
         A 50-page catalog that includes records, films, slides, and
      books to be used in teaching English as a second language.
      Information is presented that describes the materials, the cost,
      and place of purchase; most of these materials are available
      from Britain. The various segments of the catalog contain
      materials on pronunciation, films for students, teacher mater-
      ials, and publishers' addresses.

459   Research: Annotated Bibliography of New Canadian Studies. Toronto,
      Ontario: Board of Education, 1969. ED 061136.
         Some of the material in this bibliography will be of interest
      to ESL teachers since some aspects of the twenty-one research
      reports about major ethnic groups in the Toronto schools assesses
      some of the English language skills of students; provides in-
      formation about the likelihood of immigrant students being in
      a five year program; and offers data about special English pro-
      grams for New Canadian students.

460   Rivers, Wilga M., et al., eds. Changing Patterns in Foreign Language
      Programs. Rowley, Mass.: Newbury House, 1972.
         A Report of the Illinois Conference on Foreign Languages in
      Junior and Community Colleges, 1972. The various reports, dis-
      cussions, and papers are concerned with teaching foreign langu-
      ages and English as a second language in junior and community
      colleges. The collection offers new and diversified approaches
      to teaching language that covers student surveys, the use of
      conversation, testing, and staff preparation. A selective bib-
      liography is included.

461   Robinett, Betty Wallace. "The Domains of TESOL." TESOL Quarterly,
      6, 3 (1972), 197-207.
         The writer, one of the leaders of the organization, discusses
      the purposes of TESOL, an organization concerned with "persons
      who speak languages other than English or dialects of English
      other than standard." TESOL therefore is concerned with those
      people whose learning English is cultural, those who have a
      practical purpose in learning English, those who want to join
      an English-speaking community, those in bilingual programs,
      and those who speak a dialect other than standard English.

462   Rowe, Pauline. Textbooks for English as a Second Language: An
      Annotated Bibliography. Los Angeles, Calif.: Los Angeles City
      Schools, 1971.
         An annotated list of teaching materials to be used in second-
      ary school classes where English is taught as a second language.
      Items include audio-visual aids; basic texts; supplementary
      skills development; and reading texts for beginning, intermed-
      iate, and advanced students. Included in the annotations are
      book organization, content, features, use, and ability level.

463 Sherif, June. Handbook of Foreign Language Occupations. New York: Regents Publishing Co., 1974.
A handbook on employment opportunities in the field of foreign language, containing information on the chances for work in certain fields, the requirements, exams and licenses required, working conditions, benefits, etc. The book is recommended for use by guidance counselors, students, teachers, and librarians. A bibliography includes directories, books, and federal publications relating to careers that require use of foreign languages.

464 Spencer, Mima., comp. Bilingual Education for Spanish-Speaking Children: An Abstract Bibliography. Urbana, Illinois: ERIC Clearinghouse on Early Childhood Education, 1974. ED 091075.
An annotated bibliography which contains 86 references listed in "Research in Education" and in "Current Index to Journals in Education." Among the various categories covered are materials, programs, issues, and techniques used in bilingual teaching.

465 Springer, Hisami K. 100 Books for Teachers of English as a Second Language: An Annotated Bibliography. Honolulu: Univ. of Hawaii, 1971. ED 070327.
An annotated bibliography of materials for English as s second language available at the University of Hawaii libraries. Sections of the bibliography cover methodology, testing, textbooks, preparation and analysis of materials, and information on teacher training.

466 Supreme Court of the United States, Law et al. v. Nichols et al. Washington, D. C.: Supreme Court of the United States, 1974. ED 090796.
A twelve-page report of the Supreme Court decision reversing the judgments of lower courts thus finding that the failure of the San Francisco school system to provide instruction in the English language to students of Chinese ancestry not speaking English was against the law.

467 The Teaching of English as a Second or Foreign Language, British Activities, 1967/68. London: English-Teaching Information Centre, 1968. ED 018789.
A report that covers new developments and expansions of projects in teaching English as a second language. It includes ESL courses, research projects in Britain, organizations and associations, international conferences, teaching materials, resources, and programs and other information. It was compiled for the Ninth International Conference on Second Language Problems held in Tunis in 1968.

468 TESOL NEWSLETTER, Washington, D. C.: Georgetown University, School of Languages and Linguistics.
The newsletter of TESOL (Teachers of English to Speakers of Other Languages). It lists new publications, the activities of groups in the United States and foreign countries having a

special interest in bilingual and English-as-a-second and English-as-a-foreign-language programs. One section is devoted to job opportunities. The newsletter is available through membership in TESOL only.

469 Thomas, Myra H., comp. <u>Books Related to Adult Basic Education and Teaching English to Speakers of Other Languages.</u> Washington, D. C.: Supt. of Documents, U. S. Gov't Printing Office, 1970.

This bibliography contains textbooks and professional resources in the Educational Materials Center. The list of sources (received between Sept, 1968 and May, 1970) for teaching adults reading, writing, and arithmetic skills range through grades seven and eight. Also included are materials on community living, citizenship, and those concerning teaching English to speakers of other languages.

470 Wardhaugh, Ronald. "TESOL: Our Common Cause." <u>TESOL Quarterly</u>, 6, 4 (1972), 291-303.

An honest, realistic, farsighted report on the current state and potentialities of TESOL with recommendations by the author who, recognizing the commonalities of language learning and other subject areas,suggests that TESOL seek contributions from the fields of linguistics, psychology, sociology, anthropology, and education. He contends that TESOL should utilize available talent and experience to draw "eclectically from many sources" in order to be a successful organization.

471 Wilson, Robert, et al. <u>Guide for Teaching English as a Second Language to Elementary School Pupils. Level I. Parts I & II. Teaching English Early.</u> Los Angeles, Calif.: Univ. of California, 1967. ED 025680, 81.

These guides offer detailed lessons for teachers working with non-English-speaking children in the primary grades. Each lesson follows a definite format that presents objectives, and lists tests, materials, procedures, and review lessons. Although the methods do not reflect recent trends in ESL theory, the guides can provide help in many areas to the inexperienced teacher when used as a reference.

Cross Reference

421	Spoken English
423	Bilingual
429	Curriculum
435	Adult
436	Methodology
441	Socio-Cultural
443	Audio-Visual
444	Bilingual
448	Bilingual
449	Methodology
452	Teaching Aids
455	Bilingual

```
458    Audio-Visual
459    Curriculum
462    Texts
464    Bilingual
469    Adult
```

SOCIO-CULTURAL

472   Abbey, Karin L. "Social Studies as Social Anthropology: A Model
       for ESL Curricula." TESOL Quarterly, 7, 3 (1973), 249-258.
            The author contends that it is important to teach social
       studies as social anthropology to students entering English
       medium schools speaking a language other than English. The
       cultures should not feature differences from Anglo-American
       culture but should show "that each human being though a part
       of a particular culture is a part of all mankind and an in-
       dividual as well." It is suggested that neither the differ-
       ences nor the similarities in the study of various cultures
       should be emphasized.

473   Abrahams, Roger D., and Rudolph C. Troike. Language and Cultural
       Diversity, Englewood Cliffs, New Jersey: Prentice-Hall, 1972.
            An anthology of essays aimed at teaching "present or pros-
       pective teachers how to recognize the linguistic and cultural
       differences of their students." Most of the essays are those
       written by people whose names are familiar in general and
       specific (grammar, dialect, culture) areas of language. The
       book is comprehensive, covering programs, bidialectalism,
       sociolinguistics, English language history, and minority groups.
       Although the reader might look for a specific direction as
       stated in the title, the essays provide the teacher with a
       wealth of material on language and culture and will probably
       affect teacher attitudes in recognizing linguistic differ-
       ences resulting from cultural diversity.

474   Adams, John V., and Wallace K. Ewing. "A Study of Student Atti-
       tude Toward English as a Second Language in Puerto Rico," 1971.
       (Unpub. report). ED 057695.
            An investigation of Puerto Rican students' attitudes toward
       learning English as a second language shows that there is an
       affirmative attitude in studying English. Information was
       gathered from students in grades five through eight that re-
       vealed student contact with English, amount of English used,
       and parental and student attitudes toward learning English.
       The inadequacy of the ESL program in the Puerto Rican town,
       it was assumed, was due to reasons other than student atti-
       tudes.

475   Allen, Walter Powell. A Cultural Checklist. Portland, Oregon:
       English Language Services, 1974.
            The main purpose of the checklist is to provide a guide for
       selecting English language reading materials that provide

a guide for selecting English language reading materials that provide foreign students with a background for understanding English. Believing that a non-native speaker should have experiences, reading or actual, in situations related to the second language, the author includes materials that intend to achieve this objective.

476   Annotations on Selected Aspects of the Culture of Puerto Rico and Its People. Albany, New York: New York State Education Dept., 1969. ED 059933.
      Since the teaching of English as a second language requires a knowledge of the culture of the students as well as a knowledge of the English language, this report, which presents material on the cultural and historical background of Puerto Rico, can be useful to the ESL teacher who works with Puerto Rican children. In addition to describing famous Puerto Ricans, the document contains information about the history, music, life and culture, and architecture of Puerto Rico.

477   Arthur, Bradford. "On the Art of Choosing Literature for Language Learners." Workpapers in English as a Second Language, 4 (1970), 6-101.
      The article points out some obvious aspects of teaching literature in an ESL classroom that are not always recognized by the teacher. Arthur reminds the teacher that in studying literature all aspects of the language must be dealt with at the same time and the student focuses on the story rather than the language. Literature, he states, can help students understand the culture related to the target language.

478   Bissett, Donald J., comp. "Books in the Classroom." Elementary English, 51, 2 (1974), 230-238.
      Reviews of 29 books that "may contribute in some way in various approaches to ethnic studies" and which could be used in ESL classes. Information includes author, publisher, number of pages, price, and recommended age range, both fiction and non-fiction. Ethnic groups included are Black Americans, Africans, Orientals, American Indians, Puerto Ricans, and others. Reviews are detailed, and the section devoted to the material includes illustrations.

479   Blatchford, Charles H. "Newspapers: Vehicles for Teaching ESOL with a Cultural Focus." TESOL Quarterly, 7, 2 (1973), 145-151.
      Although the newspaper is not easy to teach from, it can be used as a source for teaching about American culture if the teacher is selective in choosing material and provides guidance for the students. Such items as advice columns (Dear Abby), horoscopes, the front page, the classified section, and letters to the editor are suggested for study. The author believes that the newspaper could also aid in language study, but it mainly can inform, advise, and entertain the student from a cultural aspect.

480 Brandiwine, Aliza. "New York University Foreign Students' English, Achievement and Satisfaction." Diss. Yeshiva University, 1965.
An investigation of the relationship between English proficiency of foreign students at New York University in 1961 and their academic achievement, extent of cultural contact, and degree of social satisfaction. Objective language tests were administered to 384 foreign students along with cultural contact and social satisfaction of questionnaires. Results showed that foreign students exempt from taking the English Proficiency Test had higher grade point averages than those who took the test, and reported more cultural and social contact and satisfaction.

481 Braun, Carl, and Bernard Klassen. "A Transformational Analysis of Written Syntactic Structure of Children Representing Varying Ethno-Linguistic Communities." Research in the Teaching of English, 7, 3 (1973), 312-323.
An examination of written samples of children of different ethno-linguistic communities to find relative linguistic and dialectal variations. Other variables thought to influence language development were also examined including grade level, sex, and ability. The study involved 144 pupils from nine rural Manitoba schools representing communities that were distinct in linguistic-ethnic background. Results were not really definitive, but a "wide disparity" was found among the ethno-linguistic communities, and the researchers believe that the disparity was partly related to "the quantity and quality of adult spoken English communication in the home, community, and school environment...."

482 Brennan,Pamela, and Anna Acitelli Donoghue. "Biculturalism Through Experiential Language Learning." Paper given at Inter-American Seminar on Literacy in Social and Economic Development, Key Biscayne, Fla., 1972. ED 064603.
A description of a program for educationally disadvantaged Mexican-American adults in a program teaching English as a second language that gives practical experience to students by placing them in the community and by using materials that will enable them to become bicultural. Contrasts between the two cultures are studied so that students can better identify themselves in relation to both cultures.

483 Brooks, Charlotte E. "Motivating Students for Second Language and Second-Dialect Learning," 1969. (Paper). ED 030091.
Motivation is an important factor in second-language and dialect learning, and the author states that teachers must recognize that their students have already learned a first language that works well for them and that this language must be accepted. The student will be motivated after he and his language have been accepted by the teacher. After the learner finds that the dominant community and the teacher want to learn about his language and culture, he will be willing to use English or the standard dialect.

484   Brooks, Nelson. "Cultural Topics and Classroom Procedure: Two Checklists." Modern English Journal, 1, 1 (1970), 51-58.

This is a reproduction of two sections of the author's "Language and Language Learning" that offer reference material for the ESL/EFL teacher. In the first section is a comprehensive list of cultural topics that can be helpful in introducing students to everyday-life activities in English-speaking cultures. The second section offers the teacher a list of principles that he can use as guides in his teaching procedures.

485   Brooks, Nelson. "Teaching Culture in the Foreign Language Classroom." The Florida FL Reporter, 7, 1 (1969), 520-28.

Although culture, it is agreed, should be taught in a language course, there are different views concerning what culture is and how it can be utilized in the classroom. Brooks explains what culture is not and then identifies five meanings of culture with "patterns of living" as the most immediately useful in the classroom. He then recommends a combination of scientific and humanistic concepts of culture and shows they can be applied in class. His nine proposals at the end of the article are sensible and workable.

486   Brown, Dorothy S. "A Course for Foreign Students at a Small College." TESOL Quarterly, 8, 1 (1974), 73-77.

Berea College admits 25 to 35 foreign students each year and even though they have some proficiency in English, 10 to 20 of them usually need help in some area such as composition, reading, conversation, and aural comprehension. Therefore, the college puts these foreign students into one class, a course called American Culture and Language. The core of the course consists of weekly lectures by faculty members from different departments covering aspects of life in the United States. The course "serves as a buffer" during the students' first semester and aids their adjustment.

487   Chamot, Anna Uhl. "English as a Third Language: Its Acquisition by a Child Bilingual in French and Spanish." Diss. Univ. of Texas, 1972.

The dissertation describes the linguistic experience of a ten-year-old boy whose French and Spanish environments were changed to English environments with French spoken exclusively at home. No formal English instruction was given to the boy who made a natural transition to English. The main value of the study is the description of problems experienced by the child, the study's conclusions, and the suggestions about the learning process, all of which can be useful to teachers of ESL in elementary schools.

488   Cianciolo, Patricia Jean. "A Recommended Reading Diet for Children and Youth of Different Cultures." Elementary English, 48, 7 (1971), 779-787.

The author advises that when working with culturally different children, teachers should stress the "experience and human
value" that can be acquired. Since the world of children and
youth of different cultures is usually limited to segregated
groups, literature can be used to enculturate the reader. The
article mentions the titles of books that can be especially
useful in the enculturation process and presents a Bibliography of Children's Books that is recommended for use with
culturally different children.

489   Cobb, Martha K. "Multi-Ethnic Materials in Second Language Pro-
      grams Classrooms." TESOL Quarterly, 6, 4 (1972), 339-349.
          Readers are reminded that teachers in second language pro-
      gram classrooms must be aware of the cultural backgrounds of
      their students who need cultural reinforcement if they are to
      be psychologically motivated to learn another language. Speci-
      fic literary selections about Puerto Ricans, American Indians,
      Cubans, and other ethnic groups are recommended for use. Langu-
      age learning activities should be "relevant to cultural back-
      grounds." Since many teachers disregard cultural backgrounds
      of their students, the article is important to ESL teachers
      and quite convincing and helpful.

490   Condon, Elaine C. "Teaching the Cultural Context of ESL Classes."
      Paper given at Annual Convention of TESOL, San Juan, P. R., 1973.
          A paper that offers insights into an important, yet often
      neglected, area of ESL programs: the teaching of cultural
      patterns acceptable in American society. A knowledge of the
      bi-cultural patterns would enable students to choose between
      behaviors, and reactions. Space and time orientation--
      different in many countries--would be another area of study.

491   DeArmond, Louis, et al. Intercultural Education Series. Some
      Perspectives on Inter-America. Bryan Independent School District:
      Texas A. and M. Univ., 1968.
          A publication that provides information for understanding
      cultural events in Latin America, including the development of
      music, literature, and art. ESL teachers in both elementary
      and secondary grades can add to their awareness of Latin Amer-
      ican culture through this document that discusses the Latin
      American mind.

492   De Todo un Poco.Chicago: Chicago Public Schools, 1972. ED 066082.
          A helpful work to be used by teachers who want to develop
      cultural awareness in their ESL classrooms. It contains
      examples of the customs, art, traditions, and practices of
      various ethnic groups and teaching techniques to show how
      cultural differences cultivate everyone's life and enhance
      world-wide understanding. Many diversified topics are dis-
      cussed including foreign speakers in Chicago, facts on world
      geography, and cultural information about many countries.

493 Diaz, Luisa V. It Takes All Kinds of People. Miami, Fla.: Dade
County Public Schools, 1971. ED 062859.
Students in this study course are taught about cultural differences through reading, writing, and discussion in the English-
as-second-language program. An objective is to help them to
adjust to environmental changes at odds with their own culture
without impairing their cultural identity. Exercises dealing
with linguistic difficulties and a list of resource materials
are included.

494 Dubois, Betty Lou. "Cultural and Social Factors in the Assessment
of Language Capabilities." Elementary English, 51, 2 (1974),
257-261.
The writer stresses the need for a knowledge of the students'
language capabilities and the language background of the community when instituting a plan of language instruction, and then
discusses the importance of assessing language dominance and
dealing with individual problems after assessment. She refers
to actual studies that attempted to deal with problems of
language created by varieties of the same language, the dominance of one over another, and the cultural and social factors
involved.

495 Dulay, Heidi, C., and Helene Pepe. "The Influence of a Social
Setting on Second Language Learning," 1970. (Unpub. Paper).
ED 071472.
An educational experiment concerning second language acquisition that developed from the belief that low ethnocentrism,
positive attitudes toward the other cultural group, and an
integrative orientation toward language result in high motivation.   An attitudinal questionnaire concerning American
culture was given to Puerto Rican children in the experiment
and covered plans for living in the United States, attitudes
toward Americans, goals for children, and other pertinent
subjects.

496 English for the Children of Immigrants. New York: British Information
Services. ED 044674.
The topics discussed in this paper, though referring to the
immigrant child in Britain, contain information pertinent to
the teaching of English to any non-native speaker. Included
are a review of the size of immigrant communities in England
and Wales and the means for educating the non-English-speaking
children, the importance of language and the school in helping children adjust, and a description of the special project
on curriculum development sponsored by the British Schools
Council.

497 Epstein, Erwin H. Value Orientation and the English Language in
Puerto Rico--Attitudes Toward Second Language Learning Among
Ninth-Grade Pupils and Their Parents. Chicago: University of
Chicago, 1966.

This study was made to discover reactions to second-language learning of ninth grade Puerto Rican students in public and Catholic schools and to ascertain parental attitudes on the subject. Of primary interest was the question of whether or not those who were most interested in learning English were most likely to benefit from it. Results revealed, though, that little correlation was found between the place of residence and the attitude toward English, nor was there any real relationship between socio-economic status and the attitude.

498   Epstein, Erwin H., and Joseph J. Pizzillo, eds. A Human Relations Guide for Teachers; Linguistic Minorities in the Classroom. Madison, Wisconsin: Wisconsin State Dept. of Public Instruction, 1972. ED 066417.
       A collection of articles, suggested classroom activities, and various topics related to the teaching of groups from linguistic minorities designed to assist teachers and administrators in educating children of different cultural backgrounds, especially Mexican-Americans, Puerto Ricans, and American Indians. ESL teachers who may have strong linguistic preparation but little experience in teaching minority groups will find this a very helpful guide.

499   Fishman, Joshua A. "Attitudes and Beliefs About Spanish and English Among Puerto Ricans," in Viewpoints, Maurice L. Imhoof, ed. Bloomington, Indiana: Indiana Univ., 1971, 51-72.
       Fishman makes use of a study of New York City's Puerto Rican community to indicate how the importance of language consciousness has increased in the community of the kinds of Puerto Ricans residing in New York, the varieties of Spanish they speak, their competency in using Spanish, and the failure of English and "English America." The author insists that the Puerto Ricans--as well as other non-English-speaking groups-- must be given"an opportunity to be themselves."

500   Gardner, Robert C., and Wallace E. Lambert. Attitudes and Motivation in Second-Language Learning. Rowley, Mass.: Newbury House, 1972.
       The book deals with a twelve-year research program involving students from several states and the Philippines who were attempting to learn English or French. Researchers from McGill University and the University of Western Ontario theorized that a student who learns a second language successfully has to be prepared to embrace certain aspects of another linguistic and cultural group. It is written with clarity and offers some suggestions for further studies that might stimulate readers toward conducting their own investigations.

501   Gatbouton, Elizabeth C., and G. Richard Tucker. "Cultural Orientation and the Study of Foreign Literature." TESOL Quarterly, 5, 2 (1971), 137-143.
       The data in this study provide empirical support for the hypothesis that cultural background can affect the "understanding

or appreciation of American literature by non-native speakers." Misunderstandings resulted among Filipino high school students when reading American short stories because they read into them inappropriate values, attitudes, and judgments. Further research could aid the development of literature programs for non-native students reading American literature.

502 Gladstone, J. R. "Language and Culture," in Teaching English as a Second Language. Harold B. Allen and Russell N. Campbell, eds. New York: McGraw-Hill, 1972, 192-195.
    Materials in a language program should recognize "the relationship between culture and language." Language and culture cannot be separated. Cultural attitudes which a native speaker acquire are revealed in his speech patterns that sometimes are not understood by other speakers. The author maintains that there are both linguistic and cultural "blind spots," the former resulting from early language training, the latter from responses to environment.

503 Harmer, William R. "To What Extent Should Parents Be Involved in Language Programs for Linguistically Different Learners." Elementary English, 47 (November 1970), 940-943.
    A survey of literature related to parent involvement in language programs for children who were learning English as a second language indicates that there is little attention being given to the potentials of home involvement with school language programs. The author believes that "parent participation in instructional groups of other parents and teachers could be beneficial...." He states that if educators and parents can develop materials, methods, and equipment for easy use by interested family members, parental involvement could be successful.

504 Hermandez, Luis F. "Teaching English to the Culturally Disadvantaged Mexican-American Student." English Journal, 57, 1 (1968), 87-92, 123.
    A discussion of the problems facing the Mexican-American student learning English and some suggestions for making his language learning process an easier one. Hermandez clarifies the terms Mexican and Anglo and defines four different groups of Mexican-American students. He considers it imperative that the language curriculum--speaking, reading, usage, etc.--and the teacher should identify "with the individuality of each student in terms of Mexican culture."

505 Huntsman, Beverly. "Some Sogiological Factors in Bilingual Schooling." TESOL Quarterly, 6, 3 (1972), 255-260.
    Failure to succeed in learning a new language may be due to the students' poor attitudes. When students have an opportunity to "look at the language usage and attitudes of others" and see the role of language in their society, chances of succeeding are increased. In re-evaluating his methods, the teacher must

reconsider the corrective approach regarding Standard English, among other things.

506 Jacobson, Rodolfo. "Cultural Linguistic Pluralism and the Problem of Motivation." TESOL Quarterly, 5, 4 (1971), 265-284.
    A knowledge of Standard English is necessary for success in our society but its acquisition is ultimately a problem of motivation. If a person feels that America is a pluralistic society with a common form of English in addition to whatever language or dialect he is born into, he will be motivated to learn this shared dialect. It is suggested that American education be oriented toward functional bilingualism or bidialectalism to prepare students to utilize language according to the situation.

507 Jaramillo, Mari-Luci. "Cultural Differences in the ESOL Classroom." TESOL Quarterly, 7, 1 (1973).
    The author writes, "I would like to remind all ESOL teachers that our real job is making friends for our country by teaching students English and the way of life it represents." Teachers can learn about cultural differences by observing, reading, and getting information from informed people. Teachers can create conditions in which native and Anglo-American cultural examples can be practiced. Easing cultural conflict is an important duty of the ESOL teacher.

508 Jones, Earl, ed. Intercultural Education Series.Selected Latin American Literature for Youth. Bryan Independent School District: Texas A and M University, 1968.
    A collection of readings to help students become better acquainted with the literature of Latin America. The selections cover a wide range of topics: economic, social, and historical, and have been chosen mostly for pupils in the intermediate and secondary grades, Included are poems, songs, legends, short stories, and non-fiction, whose authors range from the unknown to those of literary fame.

509 Knapp, Donald. "Using Structure Drills to Teach Cultural Understanding." Journal of English as a Second Language, 4, 2 (1969), 43-48.
    Since foreign students learning English want to learn the English which will prepare them to use the language in everyday situations, the writer recommends that drill sentences should include foods with various meals, statements used in leaving the presence of others, etc. When cultural information is conveyed in the drills, the students will be more highly motivated.

510 Liedlich, Raymond D. Coming to Terms with Language. New York: John Wiley and Sons, 1973.
    A collection of 30 essays on language and communication dealing with practical applications and emphasizing social and cultural implications. Although all of the sections offer

interesting aspects of language study, those on Color Schemes: Language and Race; and The Last Word: Language and Culture are the most relevant for ESL teachers. Following each essay are questions for discussion and writing.

511 McCallum, George P., ed. Seven Plays from American Literature. Portland, Oregon: English Language Services, 1974.
Chosen for their portrayal of American life and values and dramatic interest, these plays, adapted from American short stories, are included in this text for intermediate to advanced level students. Each play takes ten to fifteen minutes to perform and is designed to be read and acted out. Seven tapes for use with the text contain professionally recorded versions of the plays for student listening practice.

512. Maxwell, Martha. J. "Foreign Students and American Academia Ritual." Journal of Reading, 17, 4 (1974), 301-305.
A forthright discussion of the general academic problems facing foreign students enrolled in universities in the United States. EFL/ESL teachers should recognize these problems. The author comments on the time that is required to read, think and write in English; the adjustment to various professors with different teaching methods; assignments, and tests; the difficulties encountered in large lecture classes and small seminars; cultural differences; and many other problems facing the foreign student.

513 Miller, Helen Nagtalon. "The Concept of 'Culture' in the Curriculum of Second Language Teaching." Diss. Ohio State Univ., 1972.
The study considers the problems concerning the teaching of culture in classrooms in which a second language is taught. The author finds that there are conceptual problems in understanding culture in second language teaching, that the concept of culture needs clarification, that textbooks and articles consider cultural concepts as evaluative rather than descriptive, and that decisions affecting the teaching of culture are value decisions.

514 Mowat, Susanne. Main Street School and Regional Reception Centres: A Comparison of Graduates. Toronto, Ontario: Toronto Board of Education, 1969. ED 069159.
A comparative study of two approaches to teaching English as a second language and providing cultural education for immigrant children arriving in Canada. One group of children was taught at the Main Street School, which is completely independent, and the other at the Regional Reception Centres operating in classrooms attached to regular schools. Results of the study were obtained from "graduates" of both programs and the regular school English teachers dealing with the "graduates."

515 Mowat, Susanne, and Christine St. Lawrence. New Canadian Activities: Summary of Teachers' Responses to a Questionnaire. Toronto, Ontario: Toronto Board of Education, 1969. ED 069160.

An open-ended questionnaire was sent to teachers of English as a second language about the education of immigrant children arriving in Canada. The results indicate that primary concern is with the educational attitudes, problems, and needs of the new Canadian child along with the role of the school in helping the entire family. Other topics include the differences in culture and the kinds of language programs to be offered.

516   Mullen, Dana. LEREC: Learning English as a Second Language through Recreation. Prince Albert: Saskatchewan New Start, 1972. ED 064993
        A novel method of making use of summer recreation projects in northern Canadian communities to develop the children's fluency in English. The report relates the LEREC (Learning English through Recreation) ideas by describing the recreational activities, naming the structural patterns and words for the activities, techniques to be used by recreation leaders, and the training needed by such leaders.

517   Nash, Rose. "The Place of the English Language in the U.S.S.R." Revista Inter-Americana Review, 1, 1 (1971). ED 053583.
        Some interesting comparisons are made in this report which discusses the teaching of English in the Soviet Union and in Puerto Rico. The former country utilizes well trained teachers, and good facilities, and emphasizes practical phonetics. Students are not afraid of losing their cultural heritage. In Puerto Rico, although facilities are good and there is contact with an English-speaking country, teachers are not well trained, and students lack the Russians' enthusiasm in studying English.

518   Osborn, Lynn R. "Language, Poverty, and the North American Indian," in Language and Poverty: Perspectives on a Theme, Frederick Williams ed. Chicago: Markham Publishing Co., 1970, 229-241.
        The results of several studies show that a lack of proficiency in the English language is a significant factor in the state of poverty of the Indian. The Indian child is able to perform within national norms in non-linguistic areas but, especially beginning in grade four, he falls behind his non-Indian classmates in general performance. The report clearly indicates that the Indian child needs more proficiency in English as a second language while retaining literacy in his own tongue.

519   Padron, Nora. What People Do--What People Did, English as a Second Language. ED 071496.
        A course description in this report contains learning activities, objectives, and grammatical patterns used in the program to help students function in other classes in the curriculum. Cultural aspects of the program deal with differences between North American and Spanish American cultural patterns. The use of the library to gather information is stressed, as it is for most programs of this kind.

520 Parker, Candy. School and Homes Getting to Know What Our School Is All About. English as a Second Language. Miami, Fla.: Dade County Public Schools, 1971.
Simple English is used in this course so that students will be able to understand school policies and rules and provide them with general information about their community through intensive listening, oral, and written practices. Students learn to ask and answer simple questions and develop simple and practical statements. The book contains drill material, instructional guides, and evaluative suggestions.

521 Parker, Sandra. Social Studies: School, Home, and Neighborhood, Getting to Know More People and Places. English as a Second Language. Miami, Fla.: Dade County Public Schools, 1971. ED 062233.
In order to help pupils speaking English as a second language function effectively in the community, the quinmester course was initiated. It intended to teach students to discuss in spoken and written form topics about transportation, family, friends, home, school, community, etc. Eight context areas with sub-divisions permit the teacher to concentrate on language specifics.

522 Pike, Eunice V. "Language Learning in Relation to Focus." Language Learning, 19/ 1, 2 (1969), 107-115.
If a student interacts with people, he is in focus; and when he is in focus, chances are that he will learn the language of these people at a faster rate than if he is not in focus. The author discusses many sociological factors bearing upon a student's second-language learning progress, based on her experiences in Mexico. Most of the advice is directed toward workers or students living in a country or community where it is necessary for them to learn the language quickly.

523 Plasencia, Piedad. Language and Culture, English as a Second Language. Miami, Fla.: Dade County Public Schools, 1972. ED 071499.
A course that combines grammatical function with the cultural topic of holidays, including the use of independent clauses, comparison of objectives and adverbs, and good voice inflection. Students are required to tell about important holidays in their written and oral work. Some time is spent on the development of certain library skills.

524 Richards, Jack C. "Some Social Aspects of Language Learning." TESOL Quarterly, 6, 3 (1972), 243-253.
The author believes that "the emphasis on the importance of standard English as a factor in school achievement and social mobility has been misinterpreted." After discussing the learning of English by immigrants, minority issues, and black English, he concludes that careful investigation is needed of the conditions for learning standard English. People cannot be expected to learn the language of a social group when they are denied the means for membership in that group.

525 Riggs, Virginia Fields. "Action Research in Oral English for the
Linguistically Different Secondary Student: Odessa, Texas."
M. A. Thesis, Univ. of Texas, 1971. ED 058763.

In order to help potential dropouts use English effectively
so that they could communicate in a dominant Anglo-American
culture, this program was established. It focused on nonstandard speakers of English in Texas classrooms and provided
linguistically different Negro and Mexican-American students
a chance to learn skills in standard oral English. The project at Ector High School is thoroughly reviewed, conclusions
are stated, and recommendations are made.

526 Robert, Holmes, Joy. "Culture Shock: Remedial Teaching and the Immigrant Child." London Educational Review (London), 2, 2 (1973),
72-79.

The principles of teaching immigrant children (West Indies)
in England could be applicable in any ESL situation. It was
found that teachers of immigrant children should understand the
children's background and language to motivate them to learn.
Jamaican Creole was introduced; and Jamaican attitudes to English and Creole, and interference by Creole with standard
English are dicussed. Teachers should also understand cultural
differences including the home, humor, discipline and the
parents' attitudes.

527 Rubel, Arthur J. "Some Cultural Anthropological Aspects of English
as a Second Language," 1966. (Symposium).

The author, after studying the social life of Americans of
Mexican descent in South Texas and Tucson,found that Mexican-
Americans had to develop traits of Anglo behavior to better
themselves. They accepted the need for acquiring English
language skills but not for adopting other Anglo cultural
traits. It was found that maintaining the Spanish language
and culture enabled the Mexican-Americans to maintain their
identity.

528 Ryan, Michael G. "Bilingual Attitudes Towards Authority: a
Canadian Study." Paper given at the Annual Meeting of the Speech
Communication Assn., Chicago, Illinois, 1972. ED 072480.

Teachers of English as a second language will be interested
to learn that the results of a study of attitudes of French-
English bilinguals lend partial support to the research
hypothesis that attitudes of bilinguals toward authority
differ from those of unilinguals. The use of standardized
questionnaires indicate that bilinguals would have different
attitudes toward authority regardless of language background.

529 Sabatino, David A., et al. "Perceptual, Language, and Academic
Achievement of English, Spanish, and Navajo Speaking Children
Referred for Special Classes." Journal of School Psychology,
10, 3 (1972), 39-46.

A study to determine perceptual language and academic achievement functions of English, Spanish, and Navajo children experiencing learning problems. Tests indicated that, taken as a group, the school learning problems experienced by the native Spanish or Navajo speaking children were the result of their limited linguistic proficiency in English, which was the language of instruction in their classrooms.

530 Scoon, Annabelle R. "Affective Influences on English Language Learning Among Indian Students." TESOL Quarterly, 5, 4 (1971), 285-291.
The problem of motivation in learning a second language is the topic here and although American Indian students are the focal point, many of the problems and suggestions are applicable to other ethnic groups. Because of white wrongs and prejudice against Indians, English language learning is thus impaired because of negative attitudes toward integrative motivation. The author maintains that when English language use improves "and attitudes toward the English-speaking world become clarified, Indian students' achievement scores will go up."

531 Spence, Allyn G., et al. "Home Language and Performance on Standardized Tests." Elementary School Journal, 70 (1971), 309-313.
The main purpose of the study was to investigate the relationship between language that Mexican-American parents of lower socioeconomic status speak to their children and these children's performances on standardized tests designed to measure intellectual abilities. Children in the first grade were classified as follows:1) parents speak to them only in Spanish or 2) parents speak to them in English and Spanish. A battery of tests indicated that Spanish-English groups scored significantly higher in intelligence but both groups were disadvantaged in academic readiness.

532 Spolsky, Bernard. "Attitudinal Aspects of Second Language Learning," 1969. (Paper). ED 031701.
The study described by the author indicates that attitude is an important element in learning English as a second language. In questionnaires administered to four groups of students representing 80 countries, the students revealed certain personal attitudes toward themselves, people using their language, and people using English. It was found that only 20% of the students could be considered motivated.

533 Tachibana, Ken. "Motivation: Fostering a Diligent and Positive Attitude Towards English Study." The Modern English Journal, 4, 3 (1973), 197-200.
This article discusses ways in which the ESL teacher can motivate students to learn English and maintain their interest in the language. The teacher should prepare a clear plan for each class, initiate more class activity, evaluate without using rote testing, and develop good student-teacher relations. A teacher

can also motivate students outside the classroom by conversing informally on the playground, becoming involved in student extra-curricular activities, and writing brief notes on assignments.

534   Watson, Guy A. "Training for Cross-Cultural Teaching." Audiovisual Instruction, 14, 1 (1969), 51-54.
      A report that really covers three areas: audio-visual, teacher training, and cultural orientation. The Southwestern Co-operative Educational Laboratory produced materials for infant and early primary teaching in Navajo, Spanish, and English. Twenty teachers received training in language and cultural orientation for two weeks and then were expected to train other teachers. Teachers lived in minority group homes for a time. The program aimed to acquaint teachers with the cultural background of the Navajos.

535   White, R. V. "Some Social Factors in Planning the ESL Syllabus." English Language Teaching, 27, 1 (1972), 8-15.
      One of the major problems in teaching English is to set up objectives, and the author believes that in teaching English as a second language, one has to recognize "the social factors affecting the use of language in the community." It is necessary to acquire and then apply the following information to set up an effective ESL syllabus in a country where English is not the native language: 1) the number of people using the language; 2) why it is used; 3) the forms of the language used; and 4) attitudes toward learning the language.

536   Wingfield, R. J. "English Idiom in a Second Language Teaching Situation." English Language Teaching, 22, 3 (1968), 231-234.
      The author maintains that the "culture-bound" idiom creates most difficulty in teaching idioms and advises teachers to "minimize their pupils' exposure to culture-bound idioms from non-local variants." He believes that ESL teachers should avoid using these kinds of idioms in the classroom, and that the various media to which students are exposed will eventually enable them to learn these idioms. Wingfield also discusses other classes of idioms here.

537   Wissot, Jay. "Some Effects of Teacher Attitudes and Current Methods Upon Second Language Learners." Paper given at Fifth Annual TESOL Convention, New Orleans, La., 1971. ED 052673.
      Negative attitudes of teachers of English as a second language toward the language and culture of their students result from lack of linguistic and cultural understanding. It may be possible at some time to measure the relationship between teacher behavior patterns and second language learning. More must be done to teach practical language usage rather than mere drill work.

538   Wolfram, Walt, et al. Overlapping Influence in the English of Second-
       Generation-Puerto Rican Teenagers in Harlem. Washington, D. C.:
       Center for Applied Linguistics, 1971. ED 060159.
           A thorough study of the influence of Black English and Puerto
       Rican Spanish on the speech of Puerto Ricans living next to the
       black community in Harlem. The book serves as a practical
       guide for teachers of language who want to learn the predominant
       features of the dialect. A description of the socio-cultural
       profile of the Puerto Rican community and its relation to the
       nearby black community is presented. Other material discusses
       the assimilation of linguistic features from Black English and
       Puerto Rican English, and generative-transformational grammar.

539   Young, Robert W. "Culture," in Language and Cultural Diversity in
       American Education, Roger D. Abrahams and Rudolph C. Troike, eds.
       Englewood Cliffs, New Jersey: Prentice-Hall, 1972, 35-47.
           The article describes culture as "more than a system of mater-
       ial and non-material elements that can be listed, catalogued and
       classified," and then discusses the Navajo and Anglo-American
       cultures, stressing the linguistic diversities based on cultural
       differences. The teacher with a wide background in culture and
       language can predict areas of "cultural conflict and linguistic
       interference" in language learning.

                              Cross Reference

                    473   Teacher Preparation
                    478   Reading
                    479   Teaching Aids
                    484   Teacher Preparation
                    487   Bilingual
                    495   Language Learning
                    499   Bilingual
                    504   Bilingual
                    505   Bilingual
                    508   Reading
                    523   Curriculum
                    525   Curriculum
                    528   Bilingual
                    531   Testing and Evaluation
                    532   Language Learning
                    533   Teacher Preparation
                    534   Audio-Visual, Teacher Preparation
                    537   Methodology

                              SPOKEN ENGLISH

540   Allen, Virginia F. "Teaching Intonation, from Theory to Practice."
       TESOL Quarterly, 5, 1 (1971), 73-81.
           Imitating sentences from textbook dialogues by ESL students
       doesn't always guarantee that they will absorb American English
       intonation, so the author recommends other methods that will be

more successful. When instruction draws attention to a very few major patterns, reveals differences between the punctuation and intonation systems, distinguishes between intonation used in isolated sentences and extensive discourse, and teaches the student to recognize the speaker's intention, students will be better able to understand intonation.

541   Alter, Jason B., Ray W. Collier, and Miho Tanaka Steinberg. <u>Utterance-Response Drills for Students of English as a Second Language.</u> Englewood Cliffs, N. J.: Prentice-Hall, 1966.
More than 200 drills appear in this text for intermediate and advanced students. The utterance-response practices simulate natural, true-to-life language and are accompanied by grammar summaries. The authors include a helpful introduction with suggestions for using the drills. The material covers determiners, modifiers, verbs, noun clauses, tense, modals and negative questions with utterances in black and responses in red. One of the strengths of the drills is the realistic context of the practices that discuss buying <u>Newsweek</u>, drinking beer, going to the beach, and washing a car.

542   Alvarez, Salvador. "The Influence of Phonological Characteristics Upon Orthography in Mexican-American Second Graders." Diss. Univ. of Texas, 1973.
The researcher studied the relationship of pronunciation to spelling in both English and Spanish for Mexican-American second graders, some of whom received monolingual instruction, while others received bilingual instruction. All students came from similar cultural and economic environments. Tests showed that pupils receiving bilingual instruction did significantly better in English phonology.

543   Amsden, Constance E. "A Study of the Syntax of the Oral English Used by Thirty Selected Mexican-American Children Three to Five Years Old in a Pre-School Setting." Diss. Claremont Graduate School and University Center, 1969.
A descriptive analysis of the oral English syntax of 30 Mexican-American children, ages three to five, to determine their syntactical patterns, identify the influences of oral Spanish on their English syntax, and develop hypotheses about oral language development of Mexican-American pre-schoolers. Tape recordings were made of children's spontaneous oral language during the pre-school day. It was found that the pre-schoolers used a forceful language with many imperatives and interjections but lacking in qualifiers and use of subordination. There was a generally low level of variety and complexity in their oral language.

544   Aronin, Eugene L., et al. "Teaching Oral Language to Young Mexican-Americans." <u>Elementary English</u>, 51, 2 (1974), 198-202.
For the young Mexican-American, acquiring proficiency in oral English as a second language is a difficult task. This article seeks to find reasons for the difficulties and solutions to the

problem by questioning the kinds of materials, subject matter, and curriculums as well as teacher attitudes. The authors present succinct summaries of reports that deal with the difficulties, offer oral language methods for teaching young Mexican-Americans, and present some curriculum suggestions.

545   Axelrod, Jerome. "Some Pronunciation and Linguistic Problems of Spanish Speaking Children in American Classrooms." Elementary English, 51, 2 (1974), 203-206.
A teacher must diagnose the particular language problem of the Spanish-speaking youngster before treating it. Some speech and phonetic techniques of remediation are singularly applicable to Spanish speakers. When the child mispronounces written words which are traced to errors in linguistics, he has to learn that English letters stand for many different sounds. When the child mispronounces written words which are pronunciation errors, the author recommends that the teacher must teach the youngster how to form the correct sounds physically.

546   Blackburn, Ruth M. "English for Foreign Students Goes Out on the Streets." TESOL Quarterly, 5, 3 (1971), 251-256.
The author believes that the best laboratory for the foreign students is in the community of native speakers of English and describes "field experiences" that her students write about in their compositions--three to five topics in one semester. It was found that, in addition to improving language skills, the program offered confidence in interviewing people and in developing their powers of observation. Speaking with people in the community also offers foreign students an opportunity to become acquainted with different varieties of English.

547   Bowen, J. Donald. "Contextualizing Pronunciation Practice in the ESOL Classroom." TESOL Quarterly, 6, 1 (1972), 83-94.
Since the teaching of pronunciation in ESOL classes has not attained the results of other features of English teaching, the author believes that it should not be taught as a separate skill but should be integrated in language courses. Among other things, he suggests that situations involving pronunciation training should be related to student experience, that drills should be minimized, and that some exercises should be practiced which focus on content rather than form.

548   Bowen, J. Donald. "A Multiple-Register Approach to Teaching English," in Readings on English as a Second Language, Kenneth Croft, ed. Cambridge, Mass.: Winthrop, 1972, 409-421.
An excellent article serving as an introduction to the importance of recognizing register in teaching English as a second language. Register is clearly defined and then discussed. Bowen classifies differences in the register system on three scales: 1) key, 2) mode, and 3) pitch. He then explains each classification. The material dealing with the need for flexibility and versatility and the difficulties of mastering the register system

is succinct and helpful. Bowen advises teachers to "begin from a literary composition and 'translate' to other registers."

549 Bowen, J. Donald. <u>Patterns of English Pronunciation</u>. Rowley, Mass.: Newbury House, 1974.
The primary aims of the text are to provide skills in developing the comprehension of informal American English and increasing accuracy and fluency of oral production. Designed for elementary or advanced students, the text introduces sounds, combines the sounds into patterns, and then synthesizes these patterns. Included are a variety of exercises for developing skills in pronunciation.

550 Brown, Thomas H., and Karl C. Sandberg. <u>Conversational English</u>. Waltham, Mass.: Blaisdell, 1969.
An intermediate textbook which provides aural-oral practice, mainly for college students who have difficulty conversing in English. Each of the twenty lessons begins with a dialogue commonly heard on college campuses. The major part of the book deals with patterns commonly used in conversation including tag questions, requests, questions, negative forms, etc. Taped recordings accompany the lessons.

551 Burkowsky, Mitchell R. <u>Teaching American Pronunciation to Foreign Students</u>. St. Louis, Missouri: Warren H. Green Co., 1969.
A simple and useful text for the ESL/EFL teacher who may have little training in phonetics or linguistics but who is teaching students with oral communications problems. The writer covers individual and group therapy, auditory training, and using the "tools" of instruction. Exercises are appropriate and relevant but not profuse. One chapter refers exclusively to supplementary sources of ideas and drill material. For the inexperienced teacher, this text can be an important aid.

552 Carr, Elizabeth B. "Teaching the <u>th</u> Sounds of English." <u>TESOL Quarterly</u>, 1, 1 (1967), 7-14.
Since the <u>th</u> sound occurs frequently in English but rarely in other languages, students need special help. Continued drill with the <u>th</u> as an isolated sound or even in a single word will not usually be helpful. The author shows how flash cards using the minimal-pair technique can be helpful, how phrases can be used in listening and repeating the sound, and how the tape recorder can be a helpful tool.

553 Coates, Thomas J., and Patricia M. Regdon. "THRICE: A Technique for Improving the American English Language Delivery of Non-Native Speakers." <u>TESOL Quarterly</u>, 8, 4 (1974), 363-373.
The THRICE technique can help the ESL student generally by helping him to recognize his own speaking errors and then correct them independently. The technique isolates the message-carrying sounds of English and teaches the student to produce appropriate utterances through self-conditioning methods.

Insights from ESOL teaching; speed therapy and drama instruction; and psychology are used to effect corrections. The author maintains that under the conditions described by him, "noticeable improvement...must be accomplished."

554   Croft, Kenneth. A Practice Book on English Stress and Intonation. Portland, Oregon: English Language Services, 1974.
Eighteen tape recordings supplement the text that provides study and drill on the patterns of English stress and intonation. There are 46 oral drills in the text that are presented with dot-and-line notation. The system resembles a music scale to mark the pitch levels of English, using data of varying sizes to mark the degree of stress syllables.

555   Cronnell, Bruce A. "Spelling sound Relations in ESL Instruction." Language Learning, 22, 1 (1972), 17-27.
This article focuses on the relationship between sound and spelling in English. Based on the large number of linguistic investigations, results have shown that systematic relationships between English orthography and English pronunciation do exist- "that there is a good fit between English spelling and English pronunciation." The author believes that such relationships can be used for both reading and spelling instruction, especially for the non-native speaker.

556   Crystal, D. "New Perspectives for Language Study. 2: Semiotics." English Language Teaching, 24, 3 (1970), 209-215.
The writer believes that semiotics, the bodily activity used by communities of various cultures in order to communicate, should be studied more closely especially since the bodily action may overule the linguistic material in a sentence. Variations in loudness, speed, pause rhythm, intonation, and stress appear as language signals, depending on the culture of the speaker, and must be considered as an important aspect of communication.

557   Davison, Walter. Sound to Speech: A Pronunciation Manual for English as a Foreign Language. Pittsburgh, Pa.: Pittsburgh University, 1973. ED 083840.
A manual that is designed to provide practice exercises in English segmental phonemes. The 39 lessons introduce sounds within words, emphasizing aural recognition and oral reproduction followed by the use of such words in phrases and sentences to help students understand meanings, develop language fluency, and appreciate language idiom. An index to sounds is included.

558   Dobson, Julia M. Effective Techniques for English Conversation Groups. Rowley, Mass.: Newbury House, 1972.
This text attempts to guide the student from rote drill to natural English conversation and includes questions and answers, dialogues, plays, speeches, field trips, and games. The author includes techniques that will stimulate conversation and then deals generally with the art of conversation.

559 Durel, Marie. Speak English: A Practical Course for Foreign Students.
New York: Barnes & Noble, 1972.
    The author considers this text to be a practical one, and in
    some sections it is practical when the structure of English is
    truly descriptive and when the material is especially relevant
    to the non-native speaker. The inclusion, however, of outdated
    "rules" (the subjunctive mood) limits its practicality. Some
    of the exercises are useful, when they deal with the language
    problems of the non-native speaker.

560 Funkel, Lawrence S., and Ruth Krawitz. Learning English as a Second
Language. Workbook--First Level. Dobbs Ferry, N. Y.: Oceana Pub.,
1970. ED 043034.
    Instructions for teachers are included at the bottom of each
    page of this workbook, which intends to help students improve
    speaking, reading,and writing skills. Classroom dialogues and
    other activities in the book are prepared for the maturity levels
    of the students. This workbook, the first in a series, stresses
    oral communications.

561 Finocchiaro, Mary. Let's Talk; A Book of Conversations. New York:
Simon and Schuster, 1970. ED 039518.
    A book of short conversational dialogues for students of
    English as a second language or as a second dialect at any level
    of instruction. The dialogues are 1) brief conversations of
    two or three utterances and graded for difficulty; 2) sustained
    dialogue in which speakers make more than one utterance; and
    3) a series of brief dialogues on one theme, growing progressively
    more complex. Everyday topics in the home, at school, and on
    the job are presented.

562 Gallagher, William. "English Conversation Through Classroom Dramatics."
TESL Reporter, 7, 4 (1974), 4.
    In order to develop greater fluency in English conversation,
    several students in the English Language Institute of the Church
    College of Hawaii participated in writing and producing class-
    room dramas based on typical student problems which were re-
    solved in the plays. Through the memorization of lines and the
    conversation necessary for the writing and the planning of re-
    lated activities, the students found the program beneficial.

563 Gilson, Jack, and Ray Past. "Listening and Response Theory: Implications for Linguistically Different Learners." Elementary English,
48, 8, 1060-1066.
    The thesis of the article is that training in listening and
    response can be valuable at any level of learning for the non-
    English speaking pupil. Fundamental skills can be developed by
    listening to and discovering the patterns of a language so that
    the pupil can eliminate later problems. The authors refer to
    several sources to support their contention. They add that the
    pupil's learning attitude is affected by his cultural surround-
    ings and those who use the language of that culture. A useful
    bibliography of 24 sources is included.

564 Gordon, Morton J. Speech Improvement, A Practical Guide for Native and Non-native Speakers of English. Englewood Cliffs, N. J.: Prentice-Hall, 1974.
A book that can provide necessary information about speech improvement for ESL teachers since it includes material on phonetics that can be helpful to inexperienced instructors who need to diagnose and help solve speech problems of their students. The text contains suggestions for using the exercises with a complete class and with individuals who have difficulty with English sounds. Only advanced ESL students could use the text.

565 Gregory, Omar Dean. "A Comparative Description of the Intonation of British and American English for Teachers of English as a Foreign Language." Diss. Columbia Univ., 1966.
A comparison of intonation contours of General American and RP British English and of their connotations for use by teachers of English as a foreign language. Their report includes a summary of the descriptions and studies of English intonation since 1900 and the steps followed in making the comparison. Differences were noted more often in degree of pitch rather than in direction of change, but there was more frequent use of the same contours than of different ones. Conclusions are tentative, and it is suggested that further study is needed.

566 Hacikyan, Agop, and Jack Cochrane. Teaching English Pronunciation; A Guide for French-Speaking Students. Quebec: Librairie Beauchemin Limitee, 1969. ED 034990.
The book deals with methodology rather than the technical study of the sound systems of French and English. Written specifically for the French-Canadian student of English, the book contains diagrams, pictures, and songs. It can be used on all levels and contains some bibliographical listings of references.

567 Halliday, M. A. K. A Course in Spoken English: Intonation. London: Oxford University Press, 1970.
This text consists of four chapters and is published along with a set of tape recordings that are considered to be good although there are discrepancies between the text and the tapes. The material covered is basic to developing proper intonation and serves best as background for the teacher with limited background.

568 Hornby, A. S., ed. "The Incidental Presentation of Teaching Items (1)." English Language Teaching, 21, 2 (1967), 178-180.
Hornby shows how items which are unsuitable for drills or those which have been insufficiently drilled may be taught and practiced incidentally. Some possibilities involve the use of questions by the teacher who uses intonation to depict various kinds of implications in his voice. The teacher can also discuss the proper use of verbs, pronouns, and pitch in using

tag-questions, serving as a model for his students. The value of this procedure is that it can be reinforced regularly and is used in real situations, not as part of a lesson.

569   Kaltinick, Arnold, and Clarice Wilks Kaltinick. "That Elusive Discussion Class: Some Suggestions for ESL Teachers." TESOL Quarterly, 8, 4 (1974), 339-346.

Discussion in an ESL class can bolster a student's confidence and help him to improve his language proficiency if the teacher uses appropriate techniques. A language learning experience will result if interesting topics and questions within the competence of the students are discussed. The authors maintain that the discussion will be effective if the teacher asks the right kinds of questions, acts as a "catalytic agent" and not an active participant, carefully corrects the students, and does not "overdirect" them.

570   Kvavik, Karen H. "Some Ideas for the Conversation Class." Hispania, 56, 4 (1973), 1054-1058.

A presentation of some ideas that will increase the effectiveness of the conversational class in practicing a foreign language The ESL/EFL instructor will be interested in many of the suggestions. The author recommends that there should be simultaneous conversations by small groups of two or three students with some preparation beforehand; the preparation of student speeches, dialogues, and class debates; and the allotment of days for conversational hours. She advises teachers to allow students to select their own topics.

571   Lado, Robert, et al. English Pattern Practices: Establishing the Pattern as Habits. Ann Arbor, Michigan: Univ. of Michigan Press, 1970.

A text that intends to help students of English as a second language practice English speech patterns and identify different kinds of patterns. Word and cartoon charts are included to help students test their knowledge of the vocabulary used in the lessons.

572   Leutenegger, Ralph R. The Sounds of American English: An Introduction to Phonetics. Fair Lawn, N. J.: Scott, Foresman, 1963.

A text that could be used with intermediate and advanced ESL students, containing apparatus in the form of simple drills, exercises, crossword puzzles, word games, charts, and illustrations. The author takes the reader step by step through the various sounds, covering the material comprehensively and in as elementary a manner as the subject permits.

573   Lorenz, Marian Brown. Patterns of American English: A Guide for Speakers of Other Languages. Dobbs Ferry, N. Y.: Oceana Publications, 1971.

A text designed primarily for adult students in colleges and adult education programs who need more practice in speaking

English while studying it as a second language. Although the book contains written assignments, the emphasis is on spoken standard American English. Mastery of verb tenses is featured but the text includes positions of adverbs, two-word verbs, modal auxiliaries, the passive voice, and other topics.

574   McCready, George. "Developing a Lesson Around a Dialogue," in _Readings in English as a Second Language_, Kenneth Croft, ed. Cambridge, Mass.: Winthrop Publishers, 1972, 106-114.
      McCready offers some helpful ideas about using the dialogue in class and shows how to construct a dialogue so that the dialogue sentences are related, meaningful, and natural. He lists five criteria for a good teaching dialogue and presents specific examples to illustrate its use in imitative-repetition drills, substitution drills, and simulated-conversation drills. Then he presents three basic steps from simulated to real communication. The dialogue also enables the student to use intonation, gestures and facial expressions properly.

575   Nilsen, Alleen Pace, and Don L. F. Nilsen. _Pronunciation Contrasts in English_. New York: Simon and Schuster, 1971.
      A practical and quite thorough text for teachers of English to non-native speakers that deals with pronunciation difficulties. It covers consonant and vowel contrasts and cluster contrasts and contains an explanation of the phonemic alphabet along with a glossary of linguistic terms. Charts, exercises, and diagrams (some facial) are included to help the teacher. An especially valuable aid for the teacher with little background in the subject.

576   Nine, Carmen Judith. "Linguistic and Methodological Concepts Underlying a Pronunciation Course in English for Spanish-Speaking Seventh Graders in Puerto Rico." Paper given at Third Annual TESOL Convention, Chicago, Illinois, 1969. ED 032516.
      A description of a course in remedial pronunciation which emphasizes concentration on hearing sounds, reproducing them, and then participating in drills in print. The course is geared to offset the fact that language learning gets more difficult as children get older and that there is interference from the vernacular.

577   Nine-Curt, Judith. "A Pronunciation Course on the Vowels of American English, with Audio-Visual Aids, for Native Speakers of Spanish." Diss. Columbia Univ., 1966.
      The purpose of The Pronunciation Course at the University of Puerto Rico is to provide freshmen with the tools to learn English grammar and acquire listening comprehension of oral American English. In conducting trial teachings at the University of Puerto Rico, the author made recommendations for changes in the Basic Course in English at the University which pointed out that grammar should be taught intensively in the first semester and reading in the second.

578   Paliquin, Michel, and Jack C. Richards. English Through Songs: A
       Songbook for English as a Second Language. Rowley, Mass.:
       Newbury House, 1972.
           A collection of songs and rhymes chosen for their use with
       children and adults during their first years of learning English.
       The songs, which are graded according to difficulty and are
       classed by content and interest, are designed for classroom
       teaching. A teacher's book demonstrates how to integrate the
       songs into the class work.

579   Paulston, Christina Bratt. "Linguistic and Communicative Competence."
       TESOL Quarterly, 8, 4 (1974), 347-362.
           The paper deals with the idea of communicative competence and
       the implications that can be drawn from it for language teach-
       ing. The author's sabbatical in her home town of Stockholm
       provided her with the impetus for the article. She states that
       "a systematic contrast of situational constraints on grammati-
       cal patterns" must be incorporated along with constraints on
       register variation. Greetings, introductions, farewells, non-
       verbal aspects of language, and a variety of social "formulas"
       should be taught to non-native speakers.

580   Phinney, Maxine Guin. English Conversation Practices. Ann Arbor:
       The Univ. of Michigan Press, 1968.
           A book that contains many worthwhile exercises and some
       creative conversational drills for use with advanced learners
       of English to help them increase their conversational skills.
       The teacher need not follow the text rigidly but should use
       the book as a source of exercises. The authors offer sugges-
       tions to teachers that are helpful and include exercises on
       role playing and some verbal games. This is an excellent
       supplement for the ESL class.

581   Prator, Clifford H. "How Well Should Our Students Pronounce?"
       MST English Quarterly, 20, 3 (1970), 41-44.
           A discussion of the accuracy of pronunciation and its
       importance--an essay that is relevant to any student learning
       English whose native tongue has a very different sound system.
       Prator shows that even slight pronunciation inaccuracies can
       affect meaning and that teachers who ignore these departures
       because they do not affect understanding assume that the
       learner can identify those speech errors that do and do not
       affect intelligibility.

582   Prator, Clifford H. "Language Teaching in the Philippines."
       MST English Quarterly, 2, 3 (1970), 1-19.
           Although the article refers directly to teaching English to
       Filipinos, the principles are applicable to other non-English
       speaking groups. Prator suggests that grammar rules should be
       learned from practical experience and not in discussion of
       them. In addition, since the sound systems between English
       and Filipino are so different, pronunciation is a major langu-
       age problem and Prator recommends that native speakers of

English should teach pronunciation since teachers serve as models. If native English speakers are not available as teachers, then prospective teachers should be required to take at least one speech course.

583 Ramirez, Jean A. "Hearing and Speaking Skills in Teaching English as a Second Language." Speech given at Fifth Annual TESOL Conference, New Orleans, La., 1971. ED 056581.
     The paper focuses on the roles of the student and the teacher regarding listening and speaking skills. The teacher serves as an example in speaking and must also listen for analysis just as the student must analyze. The implications of the paper indicate that ESL teachers must speak well, work individually with students, and know how to analyze the speech of students.

584 Rezazadeh, Gloria Iris. "A Comparative Analysis of the Structure of First Grade Children's Oral Speech in Spanish and English." Diss. Indiana Univ., 1967.
     A comparative analysis of the structure of first grade children's oral speech in Spanish and English as native speakers of these languages was made in order to provide a basis for improving the teaching of English as a second language to Puerto Rican children. The sample consisted of 100 English-speaking first-grade children and 50 Spanish-speaking children from Puerto Rico enrolled as first graders. Speech samples were analyzed, and the similar and different structural patterns in both languages were determined. Results indicated that there are different structural patterns that can be identified.

585 Richards, Regina. Programmed Phonemics. Rowley, Mass.: Newbury House, 1975.
     This is a self-teaching book for students who want to learn the basic units of phonetic American English. In addition to studying words, the student has an opportunity to verify the correct pronunciation of words in sentences. The book can be used as a classroom text as well as an individual self-teaching aid.

586 Rivers, Wilga M. "Talking off the Tops of Their Heads." TESOL Quarterly, 6, 1 (1972), 71-81.
     This article deals with the problem of preparing students to speak spontaneously in a foreign language. It is recommended that the student should be given situations that force him to use the foreign language as a complement to proficiency-acquiring activities. Twelve categories of activities are listed that can be helpful in getting students to use the foreign language spontaneously. Giving the student practice in using his ingenuity early in his language learning will help him "learn the control" essential for fluency.

587   Rojas, Pauline M. "Teaching English as a Second Language." MST
      English Quarterly, 20, 3 (1970), 199-205, 237.
            The article emphasizes the fact that specialists, not regular
      classroom teachers, should prepare the sequence of items that
      must be taught to pupils learning English as a second language
      and that pupils must listen and speak before they read and
      write. Rojas maintains that the Filipino student needs to
      learn thoroughly the basic speech patterns of English. In
      many cases, the Filipino student has been taught English in
      the same way in which the native speaker of English has been
      taught.

588   Santos, Percilia. From Brazilian Portuguese to American English:
      Pronunciation Problems and Drills. Tallahassee, Florida: Florida
      State University, 1973. ED 081255.
            As an aid to Brazilian Portuguese-speaking students learning
      to speak English, this paper offers a comparative analysis of
      the sounds of American English and Brazilian Portuguese. Prob-
      lem sounds are identified and methods of teaching are suggested.
      The author recommends that contrasting sounds should be taught
      together.

589   Schane, Sanford. "Linguistics, Spelling, and Pronunciation."
      TESOL Quarterly, 4, 2 (1970), 137-141.
            This article shows that English orthography is more regular
      than what it was thought to be and that a systematic treatment
      of spelling could offer a new approach for teaching correct
      pronunciation to non-English speakers. If a student learns the
      rules for predicting stress, alternations between long and short
      vowels, and consonant alternations, he will be able to use words
      in his spoken English that he may never have heard previously.

590   Schumann, John. "Communication Techniques." TESOL Quarterly, 6, 2
      (1972), 143-161.
            Realizing that communication practice, in addition to pattern
      practice, must be an integral part of the ESL program, the
      author describes four courses that intend to teach students to
      communicate. He then illustrates how each method can be used.
      The methods are 1) situational reinforcement; 2) audio-visual-
      structural-global; 3) microwave; and 4) verbal problem-solving.
      The author's examples are clear and offer new insights for the
      teacher.

591   Sibayan, Bonifacio P. Some Studies in Language Acquisition and on
      Varieties of English Pronunciation: Their Relevance in English
      Language Programs. Singapore: Oxford Univ. Press, 1970.
            The study gives attention to language learning and information
      concerning the variety of pronunciation of English taught in a
      country and the changes in the way language is taught in a coun-
      try. The teaching of English in the Philippines is different
      today than it was in the first half of the century. Three stud-
      ies that were made involved language developemnt, bilingualism,
      and the best variety of English pronunciation for use in the
      Philippines.

592   Stageberg, Norman C. "Structural Ambiguity and the Suprasegmentals."
      English Record, 21, 4 (1971), 64-68.
            At times in English as a second language, stress, juncture,
      and patterns of intonation are often neglected, thus affecting
      the student's ability to understand the language and express
      himself in it. The author advises teachers to offer their stu-
      dents exercises using patterns that utilize imitation and develop
      recognition of contrastive elements.

593   Thomas, Hadley A., and Harold B. Allen. Oral English. Oklahoma City,
      Oklahoma: The Economy Co., 1968.
            Containing a series of colored drawings whose identification
      requires the use of a variety of sounds, this book attempts to
      meet some basic objectives for children who do not know English.
      These objectives include helping the pupil communicate in the
      school environment; helping the pupil hear and pronounce English
      language sounds; helping the pupil learn language patterns and
      vocabulary found in the pre-primer and primer; and helping the
      pupil learn the English-speaking culture while maintaining an
      appreciation of his own.

594   A Total System Approach Attacking the Educational Problems of the
      Illiterate Spanish-Surnamed Adults Final Report. Albuquerque,
      New Mexico: Southwestern Cooperative Educational Lab., 1969.
      ED 060405.
            An interesting program designed to help Spanish-speaking
      adults who do not speak English. The basic oral English lessons
      include appealing and entertaining material with simplified
      exercises.

595   Valazquez, Mary D. Rivera de. "A Contrastive Phonological Analysis
      of Puerto Rican Spanish and American English with Application to the
      Teaching of English as a Second Language to Puerto Ricans." Diss.
      Indiana Univ., 1964.
            In order to identify similarities and differences in the
      phonological systems of Puerto Rican Spanish and American Eng-
      lish and therefore prepare English pronunciation lessons based
      on the results, the researcher conducted this study. Find-
      ings resulting from the comparison were 1) in those sounds
      resulting in a misunderstanding because of a different phoneme;
      and 2) in those sounds resulting from substituting one phoneme
      for another. The researcher offers suggestions for preparing
      pronunciation lessons based on the findings.

596   Valette, Rebecca M. "Developing and Evaluating Communication Skills
      in the Classroom." TESOL Quarterly, 7, 4 (1973), 407-424.
            The author emphasizes the necessity for teaching communica-
      tion skills in the foreign language classroom and suggests that
      a novice must get practice in listening comprehension, reading
      comprehension, and self-expression in speaking and writing and
      must be tested so that he can display competence in communi-
      cating. Only through proper evaluation can the teacher differ-
      entiate between the acquisition of language elements and the
      ability to communicate.

597 Wessels, Betsey Davis. The Development of Facility in Free Oral Expression. Master's Thesis, Univ. of Texas, 1971.
The purpose of the method of classroom language instruction for teachers of English as a second language formulated in this thesis is to facilitate student use of language skills from mere exercise to flexible oral expression. Within the study are guidelines for instruction and preparation of materials. An evaluation of activities by members of the model class is included.

598 White, Opal Thurow. "The Mexican-American Subculture: A Study in Teaching Contrastive Sounds in English and Spanish." Diss. Univ. of Oklahoma, 1972.
The most helpful section of this study for the ESL teacher is the presentation of a simplified version of English phonetics and contrastive areas in Spanish phonetics for use by prospective teachers with no Spanish language background and little knowledge of English phonetics. The study includes a discussion of the sound systems, phonemes, and intonation patterns of English and Spanish.

599 Wigfield, Jack. "Conversations and Dialogues." TESL Reporter, 8, 1 (1974), 6, 7, 11.
Dialogues can be very helpful to adults who are beginning to learn a new language, but they must be practical and not be merely pattern practice drills. Wigfield then offers samples of pre-drill dialogues that he calls "conversations" that create true communicative situations, and which become progressively more varied and complicated. These conversations are punctuated by words like "say," "hey," "you know," "Hi," etc.

600 Williams, George M., Jr. Some Errors in English by Spanish-speaking Puerto Rican Children. Cambridge, Mass.: Language Research Foundation, 1972. ED 061850.
A study of the kinds of errors found in the spontaneous speech of Puerto Rican children with intermediate ability in order to designate the areas in which training is needed. After discussing common pronunciation problems, the report deals with consonants, vowels, diphthongs, clusters, and various kinds of problems involving syntax.

601 Zerkel, Perry Alan. "Aural-Oral Skills and Different Models of Bilingual Education." Paper given at Sixth Annual TESOL Convention, Washington, D. C., 1972. ED 061792.
The author maintains that bilingual education involves linguistic, sociolinguistic and educational factors that must be recognized since language is only one element of a bilingual education program and the bilingual program should not be conceived as a purely linguistic one. The paper also seeks a re-definition of aural-oral skills.

Cross Reference

542	Bilingual
544	Curriculum
545	Methodology
550	Texts
552	Audio-Visual
553	Methodology
555	Reading
557	Texts
562	Teaching Aids
564	Texts
568	Methodology
569	Methodology
573	Adult
574	Methodology
577	Curriculum
578	Teaching Aids
582	Teacher Preparation
585	Texts
586	Methodology
589	Language Learning
591	Bilingual
592	Methodology
594	Adult
599	Methodology
600	Grammar
601	Bilingual

TEACHER PREPARATION

602 Adler, Elaine F. "Basic Concerns of Teaching English as a Second Language." Speech given at meeting of The Foreign Language Teachers Association (New Jersey Education Assn.), November, 1969.

As ESL consultant on the staff of the New Jersey State Department of Education, the writer offers some practical suggestions in the paper that are applicable to ESL programs in any state. She calls for more in-service training programs for teachers and recommends that undergraduates planning to teach in the field should take courses that include linguistics, methods of teaching ESL, and cultural anthropology. She advises communities setting up an ESL program to keep "school personnel, parents, and interested members of the community informed...."

603 Ainsworth, C. L., ed. Teachers and Counselors for Mexican-American Children. Austin, Texas: Southwest Educational Development Lab., 1969. ED 029728.

Much of the material in this report is devoted to the training of teachers of Mexican-American children who have limited language skills in Spanish as well as English. Teachers should know about the cultural backgrounds of Mexican Americans and recognize their values and aspirations. Teachers should also be well versed in linguistics. As usual, the report recommends that minority identity should be retained.

604   Alatis, James E. "Towards a LAPSE Theory of Teacher Preparation in
        English as a Second Language." English Language Teaching, 29, 1
        (1974), 8-18.
            The author organized the acronym LAPSE to stand for an area
        of concentration in the preparation of teachers: L - linguistics
        A - anthropology; P - psychology; S - sociology (or sociolinguis
        tics); and E - English and education. The paper is a report on
        the Model Teacher Preparation and Accreditation Program in ESOL
        and Bilingual Education at Georgetown University from July 1970
        to August 1971 in which Alatis discusses the courses and the
        teacher training methods in the program. He states that the
        vitality of TESOL will be increased by the interdisciplinary
        nature of language study.

605   Allen, Harold B. "Language Variation and Tesol." TESOL Quarterly,
        7, 1 (1973), 13-23.
            ESOL teachers should be well informed about regional variatic
        in language in order to expand their understanding of English
        and offer their students realistic drills involving English as
        it really is used. Textbook writers have not always recognized
        true regional variations. ESOL teachers must know when to cor-
        rect and when not to correct a variation. We should be aware
        of the work done in linguistic geography.

606   Bailey, Richard W., and Jay L. Robinson. Varieties of Present-Day
        English. New York: MacMillan, 1973.
            A book of readings that reflects the relationship between
        language and other fields: sociology, culture, and psychology.
        The opening heading is entitled "English in the Modern World"
        and includes essays on teaching culturally deprived children,
        bilingualism, Indian English, and Language imposition. These
        and other articles will help the ESL teacher develop a back-
        ground about "English in the world, because English is not
        just a national language."

607   Bartley, Diana E. Institute in Adult Basic Education: A Model Program
        1972. Final Report. Washington, D. C.: HEW, Division of Adult
        Basic Education, 1972.
            The 1972 Adult Basic Education Institute at the University of
        Wisconsin-Milwaukee developed a training and retraining program
        for teachers of English as a second dialect or as a foreign
        language to inner-city adults on the eighth-grade level or less.
        The program included micro-teaching, lecture -practicum sessions
        and workshops for the 48 participants. The report contains in-
        formation that describes the training and the evaluation of
        various segments of the program.

608   Bolinger, Dwight. Aspects of Language. New York: Harcourt, Brace,
        1968.
            A book that covers many different areas of language that in-
        clude sound, structure, dialect, morphology, and syntax. Two
        sections of this text are most helpful to the ESL teacher:

The Evolving Approaches to Language (Chapter 11) which discusses traditional grammar and linguistics, and Learning a
Second Language (293-300) which is really too brief but does
offer some worthwhile advice to the inexperienced teacher.
The book is always readable, even when it gets into technical areas of language.

609   Bowen, J. Donald. The UCLA-Philippine Language Program, 1957-1966.
Los Angeles: Univ. of Calif., 1968.
A detailed description of the growth and operation of a
language program in the Philippines beginning in 1957, with
the cooperation of the University of California, Los Angeles,
through the Rockefeller Foundation. Many difficulties were
encountered--a complex background of languages, a need for
improvement in language teaching, and a school system in the
process of rebuilding. The program was concerned with training second-language teachers in the Philippines and the
United States.

610   Bright, J. A., and G. P. McGregor. Teaching English as a Second
Language. London: Longman, 1970.
A valuable book for student teachers that is concerned with
ESL in the secondary school. The suggestions are very practical, and the book is generally very readable. Chapters deal
with reading, writing, speech, drama, poetry, and grammar.
The chapters on vocabulary, reading, and poetry are especially
good, since the authors present specific details about the
teaching in these areas rather than offer abstract educational
theories. The text should be available to all ESL student
teachers.

611   Building Bridges to Better Bilingual Education. Brooklyn, New York:
Board of Education, 1973. ED 081273.
A brief introduction to the program that was designed to
improve the language and general academic progress of Spanish-
speaking children in Title I whose achievement levels were
below average. A teacher training program which included
courses in bilingual instruction strategies, Puerto Rican
and Hispanic culture, and language proficiency in English
and Spanish was initiated to improve instruction.

612   Cadoux, Remunda. Final Report for the Summer Session of 1965 of
the Insitutute for Teachers of Foreign Languages and Institute
for Teachers of Children of Puerto Rican Origin. New York: City
University of New York, Hunter College, 1965. ED 010933.
The institute offered teachers an opportunity to upgrade
their teaching skills and to become familiar with new materials.
Special workshops were held for elementary and secondary
teachers of French and Spanish, and teachers had an opportunity to discuss theories of second language learning and
study contrastive analysis.

613   Calaug, Aida C. "A Proposed Program for the Preparation of Teachers of English as a Second Language in the Philippine Secondary Schools." Diss. Indiana Univ., 1971.

The methods used in developing this program would be relevant in training ESL teachers in most localities. Information was secured regarding English education in the United States, second language teacher training programs on the graduate level in the Philippines, theories and principles of linguistics, ESL program current at that time, and analyses of Filipino and English. As a result the program adopted a multidisciplinary approach to teaching, provided for more seminars and workshops for teachers, and closer cooperation between teacher training institutions and professional organizations.

614   Chastain, Kenneth. The Development of Modern Language Skills: Theory to Practice. Philadelphia: Center for Curriculum Development, 1971.

A text designed for teachers, containing approaches to language teaching from various perspectives that can be applied to teaching ESL. Although the book is written with clarity and is not difficult to understand, inexperienced ESL teachers will probably want more "how-to-do-it" information than the author is able to offer. The chapter on research serves as a good starting point for classroom teachers who may not be familiar with the investigations being made in the field.

615   Croft, Kenneth, ed. Readings on English as a Second Language: For Teachers and Teacher Trainees. Englewood Cliffs, N. J.: Prentice Hall, 1972.

An anthology of readings for ESL teachers that covers theories, experiences, and observations about second-language teaching. Topics include grammar, writing, speaking, vocabulary, testing, teaching aids, and trends; authors include Robinett, Prator, Twaddell, Spolsky, Saitz, and others. One of the important parts of the book is the introduction in which the editor acquaints the reader with the organization, publications, and teacher needs in teaching ESL. The majority of the readings offer practical help to teachers; the collection would be a good choice as a text in an ESL methods course.

616   Darian, Steven G. English as a Foreign Language. Norman, Oklahoma: University of Oklahoma Press, 1972.

A well-researched book that offers varied aspects of teaching English as a foreign/second language, featuring historical perspectives. The author gives the reader an overview of linguistics and language teaching before 1880 and its development in the United States, and then discusses present principles and methods of linguistic theory and language teaching. The appendices offer some pertinent information about programs and texts. A lengthy bibliography is included. Unfortunately, much of the material is not as current as the reader would like it to be.

617   Desilets, Germain-Nicolas. "Professional Preparation, In-Service
      Activities and Job Satisfaction of the Teachers of English as a
      Second Language at the Secondary Level in the Province of Quebec."
      Diss. Univ. of Michigan, 1970.
          An investigation to survey the professional status of second-
      ary school teachers of English as a second language in the
      Province of Quebec. An important question which the survey
      attempted to answer focused on the courses rated most important
      for preparing teachers of English as a second language. Based
      on replies taken from 385 questionnaires, the study revealed
      that courses rated most important were in English phonetics,
      educational psychology, and modern English grammar.

618   DiPietro, Robert J. Language Structures in Contrast. Rowley, Mass.:
      Newbury House, 1972.
          ESL teachers should find much helpful information in this
      book, which covers language design, the structure of the lexi-
      con, and phonology. The transformational approach is featured,
      but the author provides the reader with the linguistic back-
      ground necessary in using the educational approaches found in
      current foreign-language texts. Topics and problems for dis-
      cussion are presented after each chapter.

619   Ewing, Wallace K. "An In-Country Internship Program in the Teaching
      of English as a Second Language." Diss. Univ. of Illinois, 1971.
          A detailed report of the experiences and reactions of nine
      teachers of English as a second language (candidates for the
      M. A. in Teaching English as a Second Language) who were placed
      in fifteen Puerto Rican elementary and secondary schools. The
      teacher-trainees also enrolled in two "on-the-site" courses
      and became involved with the Puerto Rican community. Based on
      journals, term papers, and questions answered by the interns,
      the researcher evaluated the program. Generally, the effect
      of the program on the interns was good. A list of fourteen
      recommendations was made as a result of the study.

620   Ewing, Wallace K. "Internships and Teacher Training in ESL." TESOL
      Quarterly, 7, 2 (1973), 153-159.
          Teaching internships in ESL can be valuable to the student
      and the teaching profession, and this paper offers guidelines
      for establishing an internship program and suggestions for
      solving problems. The author describes two case histories of
      interns he observed in Puerto Rico, one successful, the other
      unsuccessful. The three "components" necessary for any TESL
      internship are the teaching experience, supervised teaching
      and seminars, and community involvement. The suggestions
      offered on the internship are very practical; directors of ESL
      internships should be familiar with them.

621   Finocchiaro, Mary. "The Crucial Variables in TESOLD: The Teacher."
      Speech given at Lackland Air Force Base, Defense Language Insti-
      tute. March, 1974. ED 091948.

The complexities of teaching English to Speakers of Other Languages and Dialects are reviewed here, and the author points out that even though teachers are confronted by different problems depending on the backgrounds of their students, all teacher and curricula share certain objectives and principles which reveal the need for specially designed linguistic and cultural instruction. The teacher is, however, the most important factor in the teaching process.

622   Finocchiaro, Mary. English as a Second Language: From Theory to Practice. New York: Regents Publishing Co., 1974.
        A revised and expanded edition of the author's popular text. The book contains some of the latest developments in a field that is still testing various theories. The book would serve well as a text for the training of teachers since it covers many aspects of language learning and the theories of second language teaching.

623   Finocchiaro, Mary. Teaching English as a Second Language. New York: Harper & Row, 1969. ED 036798.
        A revised edition of the author's 1958 publication. The book offers concrete suggestions to teachers and language students interested in learning about ESL in the classroom. The author discusses with clarity such things as the teaching of ESL, supervision, program evaluation, materials, and texts. The book is basic to a good ESL library.

624   Finocchiaro, Mary, and Michael Bonomo. The Foreign Language Learner: A Guide for Teachers. New York: Regents Publishing Co., 1974.
        A practical book for teachers working in the area of foreign and second language teaching that includes material not usually found in books of this kind, including curriculum planning, testing student achievement, ascertaining levels of achievement, and working with the community. In addition, the text contains actual teaching materials that are comprehensive and flexible.

625   Flood, Lily Wong. A Second Year Program in English as a Second Language Prepared for Para-Professional Teachers in Bilingual Pre-School Home Teaching Programs: Teacher's Manual. San Jose, Calif.: Santa Clara County Office of Education, 1970. ED 058781.
        A well organized teacher's manual that contains daily lesson plans for 22 weeks of class for a pre-school second-year program in English as a second language. The program, containing exercises, activities, subject matter, and goals, was developed to be used for two periods of English instruction a day.

626   Frey, Betty J. Basic Helps for Teaching English as a Second Language Tuscon, Arizona: Palo Verde Publishing, 1970.
        Personal teaching experiences provide examples for the procedures that the author recommends to teachers of English as a

second language in a book that offers practical help. The
appendices contain plenty of material for the teacher to use
although it is often unstructured and not sequential. The
text emphasizes spoken English and includes charts of sound
segments and various activities for practicing them. The book
is worthwhile for the ideas about ESL teaching that it presents.

627   Fries, Charles C. Teaching and Learning English as a Foreign Language.
      Ann Arbor: The University of Michigan Press, 1945.
          The first text to support the audio-lingual approach to
      second-language teaching. Although the theories of teaching
      ESL have undergone many changes since this was written, there
      is still much in it to retain. The book covers structure,
      sounds, culture, and some worthwhile advice about language
      teaching. Much of the book is really an appendix of materials
      used at the University of Michigan.

628   Frith, Mae B. "Developing a Course in TESL." Elementary English,
      50, 1 (1973), 111-113.
          The fact that the language needs of immigrant children from
      multi-lingual backgrounds on the island of Montreal were not
      recognized prompted the development of a course in the Teaching
      of English As a Second Language for graduating students from
      the Faculty of Education of McGill University in Montreal.
      The course focused on giving the students a background in lin-
      guistics, affording them an opportunity to tutor in nearby
      elementary schools, having them observe other tutors, and being
      observed by the author. The author states that the two main
      themes in TESL are linguistic and cultural.

629   Garvie, Edie. "Language Does Not 'Rub Off'." Times Educational
      Supplement, 2907 (1971), 4.
          The author writes about the problem of teaching English as
      a second language to immigrant children in infant schools in
      England. It was found that these non-English-speaking child-
      ren did not learn English merely by being exposed to it in the
      classroom and the playground. He states that teachers must be
      specially trained to teach these children and must have a know-
      ledge of language, culture, and language learning. The young
      immigrants have to learn to use English well and quickly if
      they are to compete with their British classmates.

630   Greenbaum, Sidney, and Randolph Quirk. A Concise Grammar of Contem-
      porary English. New York: Harcourt Brace Jovanovich, 1973.
          Two sections in this text are worthy of study by the ESL
      teacher: 1) Word-formation and 2) Stress, rhythm, and intona-
      tion. The former section (appendix I) includes helpful informa-
      tion about morphology, including the conversion of words from
      one part of speech to another through the use of suffixes. The
      latter section (appendix II) contains information about the
      spoken language that teachers certainly should be familiar with.

631 Griffin, Robert J. "Tenes Anyone?" American Foreign Language Teacher
3, 3 (1973), 27, 28.
Since there is a need for teachers who can instruct in a
second language and participate in bilingual education programs,
Griffin encourages foreign language teachers to become involved
in TENES (Teaching English to Non-English Speakers). He believes that, because of their training, foreign language teacher
would be competent as ESL teachers, but advises them to develop
or increase their background in English linguistics, methodology
and cultural anthropology.

632 Harrison, Helene W., and Damon Miller. Student Study Guide for Teaching English as a Second Language. San Antonio, Texas: Harlandale
Independent School District, 1972. ED 084904.
A study guide in teaching English as a second language for
teachers in bilingual education programs. The book contains 12
lesson plans which consider vowels, consonants, morphology,
intonation, syntax, and self-evaluation in addition to some
general methods for teaching English as a second language.

633 Hartig, Paul. "New Directions in the Training of Teachers of English
as a Foreign Language." English Language Teaching, 29, 1 (1974), 2-8
A discussion of teaching EFL with some implications for teach
ing ESL. The author maintains that English language in the worl
today will be taught as a means of communication and that the
practical acquisition of modern English as a spoken language wil
be emphasized. Future teachers will have to know the structural
analysis of the language under the heading of applied linguistic
and will be expected to be familiar with the problems of contemporary English (and American) civilization.

634 Heffernan-Cabrera, Patricia. A Handbook for Teachers of English to
Non-English Speaking Adults. ED 033335.
A practical handbook for teachers of English to adult speaker
of other languages containing helpful information on evaluating materials, developing techniques to meet student needs, and
recognizing variations in students of English as a second langu
age. A selected bibliography of TESOL materials is appended.

635 Hill, L. A., ed. Selected Articles on the Teaching of English as a
Foreign Language. London: Oxford University Press, 1967.
A group of selected articles (18) dealing with a variety of
problems that face a teacher of English as a second/foreign
language. Approximately half of the selections deal with technical aspects of the language: modifiers, clusters, tenses, noun
and form-classes, etc. The other half discusses teaching method
textbooks, examinations, and the use of audio-visual aids. The
articles have been wisely selected, for they are aimed at helping the ESL teacher, and each one of them contains practical
information.

636 Hudspeth, Robert N., and Donald F. Sturtevant, eds. The World of
Language: A Reader in Linguistics. New York: American Book Company,
1967.
This anthology covers a broad range of topics in the essays
written by Archibald Hill, Paul Roberts, L. M. Myers, W. Nelson
Francis, H. A. Gleason, and others, and deals with language
patterns, the system of punctuation, linguistics, characteristics of American English, etc. The text should be useful to
teachers receiving ESL training since it is so broad in scope.
The editors could make the book more useful to future teachers
by increasing the essays from its present number of twelve.

637 Jaramillo, Mari-Luci. "Bilingual Education: Ongoing Teacher Preparation." Today's Education, 64, 1 (1975), 74, 77.
The author discusses the need for teachers to prepare themselves to teach bilingual children and offers information about
courses and programs available to teachers. New Mexico High-
lands University offers both undergraduate and graduate majors
in bilingual elementary education. The University of New Mexico
prepares Spanish/English bilingual teachers in three semesters
concentrating on English, Spanish, and both languages and cultures together. The same institution is developing a bilingual
Navajo/English program off-campus on the Navajo Reservation.

638 Lee, Janice, and Jean Malmstrom. Teaching English Linguistically.
New York: Appleton-Century-Crofts, 1971.
Although this text is designed for the secondary school teacher
of English and not for the ESL teacher, much of the material that
it discusses is invaluable for the ESL teacher who needs a broader
background in linguistics and its pedagogical use. Chapters
cover such relevant topics as language learning, phonology,
grammar (mostly transformational), writing systems, dialectology,
and others. Each chapter is followed by a Bibliography for
teachers, which is annotated.

639 Lee, Richard R. "Performance Criteria for Teachers: Design of a Model
for Innovation." TESOL Quarterly, 7, 2 (1973), 137-144.
The article lists 30 objectives for teacher competencies in
the ESL classroom. Developed by the membership of the Florida
affiliate of TESOL, the objectives offer a worthwhile set of
tests for the teacher who is expected to demonstrate certain
academic skills. The author maintains that the objectives can
be used for in-service workshops, teacher evaluation and "for
performance-based certification requirements."

640 Logan, Gerald E. Individualized Foreign Language Learning: An Organic
Process. Rowley, Mass.: Newbury House, 197 .
The author succeeds in making this book a practical one, and
offers suggestions to the teacher in a sequential arrangement
about individualizing foreign language instruction. He discusses
the 12 most common problem areas in individualizing, and techniques to be used for varying programs, in addition to presenting

samples of tests, materials, conversations, and other essential ingredients.

641   Lugton, Robert C. Preparing the EFL Teacher: A Projection for the 70's Philadelphia: The Center for Curriculum Development, 1970.
       Four of the six articles in this anthology deal with subjects related to TEFL, and the other two discuss general topics. The articles offer some new insights into TEFL teaching and comment on applying linguistics to pedagogical lessons, the results of research in the EFL field, the effect of computation analysis for the teacher and student, and the problem of training ESL teachers in college. What is presented here is very worthwhile, but the collection needs more articles to cover the subject adequately.

642   Lugton, Robert C., and Charles H. Heinle, eds. Toward a Cognitive Approach to Second Language Acquisition. Philadelphia: Center for Curriculum Development, Inc., 1971.
       A collection of 13 articles mostly from different journals that feature essays on language teaching. Although there is some repetition, there is also enough variety to stimulate the reader. Among the topics considered in the anthology are the use of cartoons in language teaching, a discussion, and criticism of, early ESL teaching techniques, the dangers of adopting dogmas that can be restrictive, the importance of bridging old and new concepts, and other subjects. A knowledgeable teacher can adopt the more useful methods recommended and reject those that are more philosophical than practical.

643   Lumpkin, James. "How Does an 'In-Betweener' Teach ESL?" School Management, 16, 4 (1972), 32.
       Lumpkin explains how the Foster School in Baldwin Park, California, solved the problem of being "in-betweeners" (too poor to hire special teachers and too rich for federal aid) in helping non-English-speaking children learn English. The community used housewives who spoke both English and Spanish who worked with the author and others to learn how to use ESL materials and school equipment and learn effective teaching techniques. Lumpkin does not advise communities to substitute helpers for trained ESL teachers but, as an interim arrangement, the program succeeded.

644   McGregor, G. P. English in Africa: A Guide to the Teaching of English as a Second Language with Particular Reference to the Post-Primary School Stages. Paris, France. U. N. Educational, Scientific and Cultural Organization.
       A UNESCO source book on teaching English as a second language in order to provide better training to African educators in ESL teaching, especially at the secondary school level. Chapters cover such topics as writing, grammar, speech, study skills, drama, and poetry.

645   Marquardt, William F., et al. Selected Bibliography of References on
       Training of Teachers of English as a Second Language for Work Abroad.
       ED 017929.
       The bibliography consists of two parts. Part I contains
       articles and books that will interest teachers who want to train
       for English language teaching overseas. Part II lists articles
       and books that are useful for training teachers in English as
       a second language in specific areas such as Africa, Asia, the
       Middle East and other places.

646   Norris, William E. "Teacher Qualifications and Preparation: Guide-
       lines for TESOL/US." Speech given at Sixth Annual TESOL Convention,
       Washington, D. C., 1972.
       Since many states are now developing certification require-
       ments for teachers of English as a second language, this report
       will be of special interest to those involved in preparing stan-
       dards for these teachers. The main statement describes the
       function of the ESL teacher, discusses his professional and
       personal qualifications, and relates the important components
       of a teacher education program to prepare ESL teachers.

647   Otto, Dale Earl. "A Model for In-Service Workshops for Teachers of
       English as a Second Language." Diss. Univ. of Calif., Los Angeles,
       1971.
       The researcher developed a model for in-service workshops for
       ESL teachers because he believed that the workshop was the best
       in-service education medium for continued training of these
       teachers. The four components of the workshops were 1) goals
       and objectives; 2) workshop sessions and activities; 3) eval-
       uation; and 4) follow-up. The study includes applications of
       these four guidelines which were utilized in a three-day work-
       shop on the Navajo Indian Reservation where the researcher was
       a staff member and evaluator.

648   Past, Ray. Language as a Lively Art. Dubuque, Iowa: Wm. C. Brown,
       1970.
       Although the book is designed for the college underclassman
       who needs introduction to linguistics, it can be a helpful text
       to the prospective ESL teacher who needs to increase his know-
       ledge of language. The material is discussed in a casual style
       but it covers sound, morphology, semantics, syntax, and English
       usage in a professional and skillful manner. Each section is
       accompanied by Suggested Readings, and a Selected Bibliography
       appears at the end of the book.

649   Perren, G. E. Teachers of English as a Second Language. London:
       Cambridge Univ. Press, 1968.
       A book of nine chapters, each specially written for this text
       by British practitioners who discuss a particular aspect of the
       preparation of teachers. The chapters range from J. A. Bright's
       description of the training of ESL teachers in Africa to D. A.
       Smith's discussion of in-service training for teachers of Eng-
       lish in developing countries. Other topics covered are the

training of adults, advanced studies for teachers, language
practices, and methods of teacher training. The ESL teacher who
is interested in teaching overseas would find the book more helpful than his colleagues in the United States.

650 Phillips, Nina. Conversational English for the Non-English-Speaking
     Child. New York: Teachers College Press, Teachers College, Columbia
     Univ., 1968.
         A text that serves as a guide and reference book for teachers.
         It includes a variety of teaching materials such as picture
         games, instructional pictures, word lists, and others. Guide-
         lines are presented for teaching the disadvantaged child, and
         the reference section deals with the use of journals, language
         rating scales, evaluating pupil progress,and training programs
         for aides.

651 Pre-Service Training Model for TESOL/ARE Teachers and Teacher-Aides.
     Albuquerque, New Mexico: Southwestern Cooperative Educational Lab.,
     1969.
         The document is a result of a project for teachers and teacher
         aides teaching Mexican American adult students which recommends
         that training should be conducted for 30 hours over a 2-week
         period followed by weekly 2½-hour in-service meetings. It con-
         tains materials and suggestions covering the psychology of the
         adult learner, TESOL methodology, teacher motivation, and
         experience in the problems related to learning another language.

652 Rees, Alun L. W. "Training the EFL Teacher - An Illustrated Commen-
     tary." Lenguaje y Ciencias, 36 (1970). ED 044700.
         The author, commenting on the dissatisfaction with the train-
         ing of EFL teachers both in Britain and elsewhere, recommends
         a more practical approach to the training of teachers including
         training in class discipline, use of the blackboard, presenting
         oral work, making and using visual aids, selecting exercise
         books, etc. Teachers should have a chance to participate in
         seminars and discussion groups and should learn linguistics as
         related to its use in the classroom.

653 Reeves, Roy W., et al. Handbook for Teachers of English as a Second
     Language; Americanization-Literacy. Sacramento: California State
     Dept. of Education, 1969. ED 036784.
         A guide especially designed for teachers of English as a
         second language in programs directed toward Americanization
         and literacy. It includes a suggested curriculum concerning
         expected student achievement in sounds, vocabulary, structure,
         and language skills. The book is particularly helpful to
         teachers with little ESL background.

654 Reischauer, Edwin O. "The Teaching of English and Japan's Growing
     Role in the World." Modern English Journal, 1, 3 (1970), 137-146.
         Reischauer emphasizes the need for change in English langu-
         age teaching in Japan. He is critical of the textbooks and
         the materials now being used. He recommends that Japanese

teachers of English be retrained since many of them do not pronounce English correctly, and suggests that English should be
taught earlier than on the university level, where it is compul-
sory. He distinguishes between learning English as a foreign
language and learning it as a means of practical communication.

655 Rivers, Wilga M. _Speaking in Many Tongues_. Rowley, Mass.: Newbury
House, 1972.
Eleven articles by the author primarily for teachers of English as a second language, foreign languages, and those involved
in bilingual education. Some of the areas covered by the essays
are contrastive linguistics, motivation, cognitive psychology,
the foreign language department, teacher-student relations, and
language control.

656 Rivers, Wilga M. _Teaching Foreign-Language Skills_. Chicago and
London: The University of Chicago Press, 1968.
This is considered to be one of the best texts for use in a
methods course for ESL teachers or teachers who need some guidance in the pedagogy of teaching a second language. The author
covers the basic elements expected in a good text of this kind:
reading, writing, testing, grammar and grammar drills, sounds,
listening, speaking, etc. She contends that language can be
taught through the formation of habit and "the understanding of
a complex system with its infinite possibilities of expression."
The book is honestly written and practical for classroom use.

657 Robinett, Betty Wallace. "Teacher Training for English as a Second
Dialect and English as a Second Language." _Monograph Series on
Languages and Linguistics_, No. 22, James E. Alatis, ed., 1969.
The writer discusses the training of teachers of English as
a second language and teachers of English as a second dialect.
Both should have training in English phonology, morphology, syntax, language learning, and language systems. The ESD teacher,
although benefiting from many of the techniques in the ESL
classroom, must be trained in a program that implements "the
many sociolinguistic factors" which are peculiar to ESD teaching.

658 Smith, Philip D. _Toward a Practical Theory of Second Language
Instruction_. Philadelphia, Pennsylvania: The Center for Curriculum
Development, 1971.
Smith bases much of the text on the results of his experiences
with instructional programs for the Peace Corps and presents
practical approaches and varied materials that can be helpful
to ESL teachers. His prime approach of having the teacher inter-
act with the student with the former acting as participant rather
than "corrector" is a creditable one. The reader can find much
to disagree with about the writer's interpretations of second
language learning theories and his expectations for pupils, but
many of his suggestions can be adopted or are at least worthy
of trial.

659 Strevens, Pater. "Some Basic Principles of Teacher Training."
English Language Teaching, 29, 1 (1974), 19-27.

A discussion of the aims of EFL/ESL teacher-training programs and their principles. Variables which must be recognized include the trainee's personal attributes, the attributes of his pupils, the target situation for his training, and the conditions of training. Strevens deals with the selection of the trainee, his general professional training, and his special training as a teacher of a foreign or second language. Special training involves the acquisition of skills and information, and the development of theories. He suggests that teacher-training courses be re-assessed periodically.

660 Teaching English as a Second Language in the Middle Grades. Brooklyn, New York: New York City Board of Education, 1971. ED 091930.
A teacher's manual developed to acquaint New York City school teachers with the philosophy, methods, and materials of teaching English as a second language in the middle grades. It covers structure, oral pattern practice drills, the teaching of reading, basic language learning principles, and other topics. Also included are a bibliography, sound production exercises, and comparative analyses of English and other languages.

661 Timiraos, Carmen R. English as a Second Language Manual. Albuquerque: New Mexico: Southwestern Cooperative Educational Lab, 1970.
A teacher's manual in teaching English as a second language with emphasis on the audiolingual approach to teaching, attempting to motivate participants to adopt this method in their own teaching. The manual contains pre- and post-tests, sample drills, sample reading comprehensions, and examples of pronunciation tests.

662 Via, Richard. "TESL and Creative Drama." TESL Reporter, 5, 2 (1972), 1-3.
A report of a seminar for ESL teachers to enable them to learn how creativity can be used in the classroom. Those who participated in the five-week period studied non-competitive play as a learning technique, acted out short skits, and performed physical sensitivity exercises. The participants were later expected to act out a short story or poem by body movement and some words. At first, the teachers were hesitant in taking part in the activities but later reacted favorably to the activities.

663 Wardhaugh, Ronald. Topics in Applied Linguistics. Rowley, Mass.: Newbury House, 1974.
A helpful book written in non-technical language that can be used in an introductory course for teachers, especially those interested in teaching on the elementary level. The chapters on spelling, the teaching of reading, and those devoted to a discussion of generative grammar and cognitive psychology on second language teaching are especially relevant to the work of ESL teachers. Students without a background in linguistics will be able to use this text without difficulty.

664   West, Fred. _The Way of Language: An Introduction_. New York:
      Harcourt Brace, 1975.
              The new or inexperienced ESL teacher with a limited back-
      ground will find a diversity of material here that is closely
      related to second language teaching. Part II, Language:
      Structure and Meaning and Part III, Language and Man should
      be of special interest. Part II deals with phonology, morph-
      ology, grammar and syntax, and semantics. Part III includes
      material on culture and language, and language acquisition.
      Each chapter is accompanied by a bibliography; a 12-page
      glossary appears near the end of the book. A readable and
      compact text.

665   Wolk, Elsie. _Report of the Consortium of the NDEA Institutes in_
      English for Speakers of Other Languages. Brooklyn: New York City
      Board of Education, 1968. ED 030118.
              In 1968 a consortium program for Advanced Study in the Teach-
      ing of English to Speakers of Other Languages sponsored by the
      N. Y. Board of Education was held at four New York colleges to
      deal with significant problems in ESL teaching; training ESL
      teachers for various grade levels and informing them about
      research in the field and current techniques; and the involve-
      ment of parents and the community.

666   Womack, Thurston. "Preparing Teachers for TESOL--Where We've Been,
      Where We Are, and Maybe Where We Should Be Going." Paper given at
      Fifth Annual TESOL Convention, New Orleans, La., March, 1971.
      ED 051726.
              The paper describes and evaluates the M. A. program for pre-
      paring TESOL teachers at San Francisco State College. Although
      many different theories of teaching English as a second language
      had been changing and developing, the program at San Francisco
      State had changed little. Some adjustments had been made, how-
      ever, because of added experience of the staff, changes in the
      number of non-English speakers, and professional developments.

667   Wright, Audrey L. "Initial Techniques in Teaching English as a Second
      Language," in _Readings in English as a Second Language_, Kenneth
      Croft, ed. Cambridge, Mass.: Winthrop Publishers, 1972, 7-14.
              The suggestions that the author offers are rudimentary but
      important in helping students"to master a new set of communica-
      tion habits." She advises teachers to speak English in the
      classroom, let the students do most of the talking, introduce
      one new structure at a time, perform repetition with enthusiasm,
      assign an abundance of substitution drills, and encourage the
      students. Some of the suggestions are quite general, but the
      message is to the new teacher and the techniques are "initial."

668   Young, Robert W. _English as a Second Language for Navajos, an Over-_
      view of Certain Cultural and Linguistic Factors. Albuquerque, New
      Mexico: Bureau of Indian Affairs, 1968.
              The author recommends specialized training for teachers of
      English to Navajo children because of cultural and linguistic

differences. He points out that significant differences occur in the structure, grammar, and the phonology of the two languages. He then presents guidelines for developing materials, methodology, and teacher training programs for these teachers.

669   Zintz, Miles V. The Reading Process. Dubuque, Iowa: Wm. C. Brown, 1970.
      In Chapter 13 Zintz presents some very worthwhile introductory material on learning English as a second language and then discusses some methods used in teaching it. Although the material is not comprehensive, it does contain some of the important basic elements of ESL teaching and should convince the classroom teacher that second language learning and teaching call for the development of special skills for the student and teacher.

Cross Reference

608	Grammar
611	Bilingual
612	Language Learning
614	Methodology
625	Bilingual
626	Spoken English
629	Bilingual
630	Spoken English
632	Bilingual
637	Bilingual
639	Testing and Evaluation
648	Texts
650	Reference
651	Adult
653	Adult
654	Testing and Evaluation
656	Texts
662	Teaching Aids
663	Grammar
666	Testing and Evaluation
667	Curriculum

TEACHING AIDS

670   Allen, Robert L. "A Reassessment of the Role of the Language Laboratory." Journal of English as a Second Language, 3, 1 (1968), 49-58.
      The author points out that the help that can be obtained by a second-language learner from the language laboratory is limited He describes situations that call for a trained teacher to listen to the student's pronunciation and help the student correct it. Students need direct help with specific problems and many language lab monitors are not qualified to offer help. Allen believes that a good language lab will have tape recorders, tapes record players and records, and assistant teachers.

164

671   Allen, Walter Powell. More Easy Crossword Puzzles for People Learning English. Wilkins Court, Rockville, Maryland: English Language
Services, 1970. ED 043008.
This is the second series of "Easy Crossword Puzzles," both
of which are designed to make learning fun while studying English as a second or foreign language. In addition to helping
students develop their vocabulary, the puzzles intend to help
them become familiar with prefixes, suffixes, and everyday
grammatical elements.

672   Carter, Thomas P. "Crossword Puzzles in the Foreign Language Classroom." The Modern Language Journal, 58, 3 (1974), 112-115.
Some articles written by teachers of English as a second
language have reported some success in using crossword puzzles
in their classroom. The author also reports some success in
using these puzzles in teaching French as a foreign language
and offers some helpful suggestions. He states that, to maintain student enthusiasm, puzzles should be introduced once
every two or three weeks "to avoid overexposure," and recommends that classes should make up short puzzles of their own
using a flexible format, with students holding answers to the
spaces inventing clues for the answers.

673   Cartledge, H. A. "A Defense of Dictation." English Language Teaching, 22, 3 (1968), 226-231.
Cartledge offers some logical reasons for using dictation
in the ESL classroom, calling it a testing rather than a teaching exercise. It gives practice in oral comprehension and
"obliges students to contextualize and discriminate." He
explains the steps that an instructor should follow in the
dictation process and also suggests what activities should be
avoided (students should not correct one another's papers).
Dictation should not be used as an end-of-the-period activity.
The author says that dictation, properly taught, has been en-
dorsed by EFL learners.

674   Davis, G. Albyn. "Linguistics and Language Therapy: The Sentence
Construction Board." Journal of Speech and Hearing Disorders,
38, 2 (1973), 205-214.
Although this apparatus called the sentence construction
board was developed to teach language to deaf children, it
could easily be used in teaching English as a second language.
The board contains lights that are used as symbols for grammatical classes and, by using key words, the pupil can arrange
kernel sentences and develop transforms. The board could be
used in response to pictures. The board utilizes Fitzgerald's
method for teaching language to deaf children and the fundamentals of linguistics.

675   Deyes, A. F. "Learning from Dictation." English Language Teaching,
26, 2 (1972), 149-154.
The author believes that dictation properly prepared, presented, and evaluated can be valuable in the ESL classroom and
can be used "as a jumping-off point for other language exercises."

676   Dobson, Julia. "Try One of My Games," in Readings in English as a
       Second Language, Kenneth Croft, ed. Cambridge, Mass.: Winthrop
       Publishers, 1972, 361-377.
            The writer explains that games can be helpful in language
       learning as well as entertaining to the students in ESL/EFL
       classes, but language games should be evaluated according to
       some basic criteria. Then Dobson presents fifteen favorite
       games that fit the criteria she presents and offers advice in
       using the games according to class size and level and the pur-
       pose of the game. Some games follow familiar patterns: bingo,
       ghost, twenty questions, Simon Says, etc. The games are
       clearly and thoroughly explained and should be a part of the
       teacher's repertoire.

677   Fierro, Gustavo A. "A Study of the Role of Programmed Instruction
       in the Teaching of Foreign Language with Particular Reference to
       the Teaching of English as a Foreign Language." Diss. Georgetown
       Univ., 1973.
            An assessment of the relevance of programmed instruction to
       the task of teaching English to speakers of other languages.
       Advantages and disadvantages are discussed with attention focus-
       ing on relieving FL teachers of routine work, adjusting to the
       student's ability to learn, and applying various methods in
       using programmed instruction. Programmed instruction is recom-
       mended for helping ESL students reach a satisfactory command
       of English and for improving the training of EFL teachers, but
       it should not be the only means of instruction since contact
       with other human beings provides "motivations for human learning."

678   Fowles, Jib. "Ho Ho Ho: Cartoons in the Language Class." TESOL
       Quarterly, 4, 2 (1970), 155-159.
            The author explores the use of cartoons in the classroom as
       a means of introducing and teaching American culture. He main-
       tains that a study of one panel drawing--not political cartoons
       or cartoon strips--"can unearth much about the culture that
       relishes them." The three basic questions for discussing a
       cartoon in the classroom are 1) What is the factual situation?
       2) What is the incongruity that would make an American laugh?
       3) What is the cultural anxiety treated here which laughter
       helps to reduce?

679   Galarcep, Marietta Fernandez. "Puppets in Teaching English." English
       Language Teaching, 25, 2 (1971), 165-170.
            Puppets can be used as effective teaching tools as long as
       they are not over-used. The writer explains how to construct
       puppets from papier-mache and then discusses how they can be
       used. In most cases she offers specific examples of dialogue
       to teach greetings, the use of prepositions, and comparatives
       and superlatives. Puppets can also be used to dramatize dia-
       logues and be a part of classroom games and sketches.

166

680   Hines, Mary Elizabeth. _Skits in English_. New York: Regents Publishing Co., 1974.
Designed for use with students learning English as a Second Language to afford students an opportunity for role-playing in learning language under controlled conditions. Thirty-six graded skits are included covering different kinds of typical situations. Each skit is followed by exercises. After reading the skits, the teacher can write some of his own to suit the class.

681   King, P. B. "Translation in the English Language Course." _English Language Teaching Journal_, 28, 1 (1973), 53-59.
King believes that if we are "to equip the learner with the language skills relevant to his needs," then we should teach the ESL/EFL students the skill of translation. It is better that they know how to translate well since, according to King, they will attempt to use translation anyway. He maintains that if there is a practical need for the skill, then the instructor should try to meet the need.

682   Kreidler, Carol J. "Pictures for Practice," in _Readings on English as a Second Language_, Kenneth Croft, ed. Cambridge, Mass.: Winthrop Publishers, 1972, 378-387.
Demonstrations are offered here to show how pictures can be a help to the teacher of English as a second language, especially in drill-type and testing-type practices. In teaching pronunciation, for example, a picture of a ship and a sheep will illustrate the difference in the objects and thus a difference in pronunciation. Kreidler also shows how pictures can be used in teaching vocabulary and grammar. The suggestions are excellent--practical and logical.

683   LaFontaine, Herman. "Paraprofessionals: Their Role in ESOL and Bilingual Education." _TESOL Quarterly_, 5, 4 (1971), 309-314.
It is suggested here that para-professionals in ESOL and bilingual education programs can be invaluable to classroom teachers. Experience has shown that the team approach can be applied most appropriately when adults are properly trained and adequately supervised. The teacher and the assistant are in an excellent position "to help each other cross the bridge into the other's world."

684   Matthews-Bresky, R. J. H. "Translation as a Testing Device." _English Language Teaching_, 27, 1 (1972), 58-65.
Although the article does not recommend the use of translation as a means of teaching English, it does suggest that it can be a useful device for testing certain linguistic items. The author stresses the fact that certain conditions must be met in using this kind of test and offers examples when the test can be effective: 1) associating singular and plural relationships; 2) referring to word order and adverbial position; 3) selecting tenses; and 4) omitting commas. The author contends that translation is "a pedagogical tool that should not be totally disregarded."

685   Molina, Huberto. "Language Games and the Mexican-American Child
       Learning English." TESOL Quarterly, 5, 2 (1971), 145-148.
       The development of games is part of a tutorial component of
       the Language and Concept Skills for Spanish Speakers Program
       developed at Southwest Regional Laboratory for Educational Re-
       search and Development. The paper contains the 1969-1970
       results of field tryouts of the program. The mean raw score
       in vocabulary, following directions, and syntactical skills
       increased from 9.7 to 16.6 during the tryout. On the post-
       test, all children scored 67% or above, whereas only 4 of the
       17 children attained a score of 67 or higher on the pretest.
       To test the effect of the game component, future tests could
       be given to classes not utilizing the games.

686   Oller, John W., Jr. "Dictation as a Device for Testing Foreign-
       Language Proficiency." English Language Teaching, 25, 3 (1971),
       254-259.
       The results of this paper regarding the use of dictation as
       a technique for testing foreign-language proficiency tend to
       refute opposition to this form of EFL/ESL measurement. The
       data were gathered as part of an evaluation and revision of the
       English as a Second Language Placement Examination (ESPE) for
       the University of California at Los Angeles. The results
       warrant further investigation and experimentation in this area
       of testing and, as Oller states, "a decreasing dependence on
       the pronouncements of authorities."

687   Patterson, A. A. "English Oral Language." TESL Reporter, 4, 3
       (1971), 5-7.
       Physical activities can be helpful to students learning Eng-
       lish as a second language. After limiting the size of the area
       the pupils will work in, the teacher gives commands in the
       native language and then in English. Typical actions are walk-
       ing, crawling, and running which can then be combined with
       directions and more specific information. Directions in English
       given more quickly will then follow. Patterson includes a list
       of action words for the teacher.

688   Rees, Alun L. W. "The Display Board in Language Thinking." TESOL
       Quarterly, 4, 2 (1970), 161-164.
       Attention is drawn to the use of the bulletin board as one
       of the supplements "to the integration of second language
       learners in classes of native speakers." The display board
       (rather than bulletin board) can lead to conversation practice
       and develop a community spirit. Treated as a regular magazine
       with students as contributors, the board can increase motiva-
       tion to write, and to read various sources, including magazines,
       and copying material for board use.

689   Saitz, Robert L. "Gestures in the Language Classroom." English
       Language Teaching, 21, 1 (1966), 33-37.
       Saitz gets into the area of body language in this article and
       discusses the study of gestures in the language class as a means

of gaining student enthusiasm and interest that can carry over into the learning of linguistic patterns of the target language. He also shows how the teacher can introduce the use of gestures into the classroom by having students use them at appropriate times and also recognize those they need to know but need not produce.

690   Selected List of Instructional Materials for English as a Second Language: Adult Level. Arlington, Virginia: Center for Applied Linguistics, 1974.
This CAL Bibliography is comprised of three lists: Basic Education, English Language Development, and Professional or Pre-Professional. The Basic Education list includes consumer education, employment information, history, health, and other topics. The Professional and Pre-Professional category contains material on psychology, chemistry, economics, architecture, commercial correspondence, and other topics of special interest to adult learners.

691   Selected List of Instructional Materials for English as a Second Language: Audio-Visual Aids. Arlington, Virginia: Center for Applied Linguistics, 1974.
A CAL Bibliography containing audio-visual material considered useful to the ESL teacher at all levels. The list is divided into Pictures, Charts, Flash Cards, Flannel Aids, Games and Puzzles, Films, Filmstrips and Transparencies, Aural Aids, and Miscellaneous Aids. The last page of the Bibliography contains the addresses of publishers and distributors.

692   Selected List of Instructional Materials for English as a Second Language: College Level. Arlington, Virginia: Center for Applied Linguistics, 1974.
Another CAL Bibliography, this one containing material aimed at helping the ESL teacher on the college level. The sources cover divergent areas of study including advanced vocabulary, American folktales, sociology, politics, scientific English, physics, mathematics, economics, study skills, and others. The collection contains material ranging from reference guides to cassettes and tapes.

693   Selected List of Instructional Materials for English as a Second Language: Elementary Level. Arlington, Virginia: Center for Applied Linguistics, 1974.
One of the CAL Bibliographies listing materials for ESL teachers. The five-page collection includes helpful materials from textbooks to games. The variety of materials include songs, crossword puzzles, flashcards, handwriting aids, word study cards, filmstrips, movies, cassettes, records, workbooks, and many other teaching aids.

694 Selected List of Instructional Material for English as a Second Language: Reading. Arlington, Virginia: Center for Applied Linguistics, 1974.

The instructional materials in this CAL Bibliography on Reading is divided into the following categories: Elementary, Secondary, College and Professional, and Adult. Materials for the last three categories are plentiful, which is encouraging since teachers have often complained about a dearth of material on these levels. Materials include books on methodology and literature, including scientific literature.

695 Selected List of Instructional Materials for English as a Second Language: Secondary Level. Arlington, Virginia: Center for Applied Linguistics, 1974.

This Bibliography covers many different aspects of the ESL program at the secondary level including sources of material on reading, literature, conversation, writing, business English, American idioms, vocabulary development, and other topics. The sources range from workbooks to complete courses containing tapes, scripts, texts, and teachers' manuals.

696 Smithies, Michael. "Capitalizing on the Expendable: The Use of Pop Songs in the English Class." Bulletin of the English Language Center, 1, 2 (1971), 24-41.

An article that discusses the possibilities of language reinforcement through the use of pop songs. Smithies believes that the songs will offer examples of current usage and will also teach the foreign student something about the culture of the language. The writer uses a tune written by two members of the Beatles (Lennon and McCartney) to illustrate the use of these songs.

697 Taylor, C. V. "Why Throw Out Translation?" English Language Teaching, 27, 1 (1972), 56-58.

The author rejects the idea that all translation is bad and discusses three principles to guide teachers in using translation discriminately. The first principle states that the teacher's translation--if any is to be used--is preferable to the pupil's and that the teacher will understand that the "word-for-word" method is unsuitable. The second principle states that translation should be at "utterance level" to avoid the "single-word" level of translation. The third principle states that translation should be used only when communication breaks down.

698 Wissot, Jay. "The English-as-Second Language Trip: Its Structure and Value." TESOL Quarterly, 4, 2 (1970), 165-168.

The ESL trip can stimulate a student's recognition of his relationship to his second culture and can offer a foundation for many in-school and out-of-school experiences. The two main criteria for the field trip are 1) the relationship of the trip to the language development in the classroom and 2) the relevancy

of the trip to the age and social and economic needs of the
class. The trips provide "the possibility of really using a
new form of communication as a complement to the native language."

TESTING AND EVALUATION

699   Alkin, Marvin C., and Dale C. Woolley. A Framework for Evaluation
of TESOL Programs. Los Angeles: Univ. of California, 1970.
A model for evaluating TESOL programs that initially defines
evaluation, discusses the definition, describes the model and
then applies the framework for evaluation. One aspect of the
document defines the role of the "decision-maker" who, based on
"analyses,"recommends modification and retention of segments of
the program and also makes known "what works with which types
of children." Evaluation methods should be utilized early.

700   Allen, Harold B., comp. TENES: A Survey. Champaign, Illinois:
National Council of Teachers of English, 1966.
A report of TENES (Teaching English to Non-English Speakers)
that offers information gathered on the subject from April 1,
1964 to March 31, 1966, that covers teacher preparation and
qualifications, teaching situations, materials and aids, and
difficulties and needs. Recommendations appear in the Appendix, along with questionnaires used in the survey and a list
of tables and key findings. The recommendations are more
general than specific.

701   Anderson, J. "A Technique for Measuring Reading Comprehension and
Readability." English Language Teaching, 25, 2 (1971), 178-182.
Based on his experiences in teaching English in Papua and
New Guinea, Anderson presents some suggestions in using cloze
procedures. He advises that passages used in measuring the
reading difficulty of English for non-native speakers should
be long enough to allow about 50 deletions per passage; every
fifth word should be deleted; a missing word should be indicated by a blank of the same length as the deleted word; an
answer column should be available where subjects will record
their answers. The major problem is to match the difficulty
of reading material to the pupils' reading ability.

171

702   Beardsmore, H. Baetens, and A. Renkin. "A Test of Spoken English."
       IRAL, 9, 1 (1971), 1-11.
           A description and the results of the use of a test of spoken
       English given to students at the Institute of Phonetics of the
       University of Brussels. The idea is to create a fictitious
       dialogue with the student participating with a voice on a tape
       recorder to show how he can manipulate the spoken language
       actively. The content of the dialogue forces the student to
       use many different elements of the language. The reliability
       of the test was found to be very satisfactory and is easy to
       administer and correct.

703   Blanchard, Joseph D., and Annabelle R. Scoon. "The Relation of a
       Test of English as a Second Language to Measures of Intelligence,
       and Adjustment in a Sample of American Indian Students." Paper
       given at annual TESOL Convention, San Francisco, March, 1970.
       ED 039530.
           Tests given to 142 American Indian bilingual students at
       the Institute of American Indian Arts in Santa Fe, New Mexico,
       prompted testers to reach two important conclusions: 1) the
       TOEFL (Test of English as a Foreign Language) was found to be
       a valid measure of English language skill of American Indian
       students; 2) and the ITED (Iowa Test of Educational Develop-
       ment) measured language ability as did the TOEFL, although
       the former test may be too difficult.

704   Blatchford, Charles H. "A Theoretical Contribution to ESL Diagnos-
       tic Test Construction." Paper given at Fifth Annual TESOL Conven-
       tion, New Orleans, La., 1971.
           Some meaningful suggestions make up this discussion of
       diagnostic tests in English as a second language. The author
       believes that the various subscores of a test offer more
       information than the total scores and uncover specific needs
       or skills of the student. Scores of the complete tests should
       not be used for a comparison of the students, and the teacher
       should devote more time analyzing each student's test.

705   Bordie, John G. "Language Tests and Linguistically Different Learn-
       ers: The Sad State of the Art." Elementary English, 47, 6 (1970).
           A review of ESL tests in which the author finds deficiencies
       in the tests, even in measuring basic language skills of the
       linguistically different learner, and discusses how difficult it
       is to acquire a representative sample of a child's language,
       ascertain his difficulties, and then help him solve his prob-
       lems. The article discusses the Frostig-Developmental Test of
       Visual Perception and the Illinois Test of Psycholinguistic
       Ability and finds flaws in each of them. He maintains that
       oral language tests are, perhaps, the most difficult to devise.

706   Borrego, Eva R. "Teaching English as a Foreign Language to Children:
       First Three Grades." Diss. The Catholic Univ. of America, 1968.

A survey of the development of the teaching of English to Spanish-speaking children in the five Southwestern states in general and in Alamosa, Colorado, in particular. Information was obtained from "semi-documented personal experience" and by reading and research in philosophy, psychology, sociology, and educational psychology. It was concluded that teachers were generally unprepared, could not understand the needs of Spanish-speaking children, and did not realize that the children's native tongue must be retained in their culture.

707 Briere, Eugene J. English Language Testing Project for the Bureau of Indian Affairs, 1967. ED 034971.
A short pamphlet summarizing an English language testing project by the Univ. of Southern California to test American Indian children's performance in reading, vocabulary, and language. The tests should be helpful to people interested in measuring proficiency in English for other non-English-speaking groups.

708 Briere, Eugene J. "Testing ESL Skills Among American Indian Children," in Monograph Series on Language and Linguistics, No. 22, James E. Alatis, ed. Georgetown Univ., 1969.
This is a report of the language testing activities occurring with American Indian children to help place them at levels where they can function successfully. Pictures, repetition tests, and transformation tests were used with individual scoring procedures along with other testing devices. English speakers were administered the tests first to discover ambiguous items. The author discusses the purposes of the tests and the analyses of the data in some detail.

709 Briere, Eugene J., and Richard H. Brown. "Norming Tests of ESL among Amerindian Children." Revised version of paper given at Fifth Annual TESOL Convention, New Orleans, La., 1971.
Testing is an important yet difficult process in developing a program for the child in an ESL program. The paper describes the ways in which norms were developed for interpreting tests of proficiency in English for Amerindian children in grades 3 through 6 in the Bureau of Indian Affairs' schools. The objectives of the tests are to identify and place Amerindian children needing ESL training, provide teachers with linguistic information accordingly, and assess English programs.

710 Bryson, Juanita. Comparison of Bilingual Vs. Single Language Instruction in Concept Learning in Mexican-American Four Year Olds. Washington, D. C.: Office of Education, 1970.
A study of bilingual and unilingual instruction was made of 4-year-old students in the Mexican American Headstart program. Groups were taught 1) in Spanish only; 2) in English only; and 3) bilingually. Tests indicated that children in experimental groups scored higher than those in control groups. Generally, pupils instructed bilingually scored higher in tests.

711   Burgess, Thomas C., and Naguib Greis. "English Language Profic-
       iency and Academic Achievement among Students of English as a
       Second Language at the College Level," 1970. (Unpub. paper).
       ED 074812.
            This is a helpful paper for college teachers and administra-
       tors directly responsible for the education of foreign students
       in American colleges since it deals with the problem of select-
       ing a testing instrument that will best determine a foreign
       student's readiness for satisfactory performance in college,
       especially in courses requiring English reading and writing
       skills. Comparisons are made between various test results and
       performance in college courses.

712   Burke, Jack Dale. "The Predictive Validity of English Language
       Screening Instruments for Foreign Students Entering the Univer-
       sity of Southern California." Diss. Univ. of Southern California,
       1968.
            The study was concerned with determining the predictive
       validity of a battery of six ability and achievement tests given
       at the beginning of each semester over a period of three years
       to screen foreign students for English proficiency. Subjects
       were 178 foreign students. It was found that the California
       Reading Test, Speech Interview, and the Larry Ward English
       Examination for Foreign Students were the three most valid
       measures of predicting academic achievement among the six
       ability and achievement tests in the study.

713   Campbell, Russell N., and Harold V. King. An English Reading Test.
       Portland, Oregon: English Language Services, 1974.
            A 30-minute test of reading ability, with an interpreta-
       tion of scores, for students of English as a foreign language.
       One of the main uses of the test is to measure a student's
       ability to compete with native speakers at an American college
       or university. Results indicate that a score of 70 is essen-
       tial for recommendation to an American college.

714   Carroll, John B. "Fundamental Considerations in Testing for Eng-
       lish Language Proficiency of Foreign Students," in Teaching
       English as a Second Language, Harold B. Allen and Russell N. Camp-
       bell, eds. New York: McGraw-Hill, 1972, 313-321.
            A realistic discussion of testing the English language skills
       of foreign students that points out that a proficiency test
       should provide information about the student's performance in
       the fields he will be in after he is selected (engineering,
       liberal arts, etc.). The validity of a test is based on
       whether "it predicts success in the learning tasks and social
       situations to which the examinees will be exposed," and not
       on whether it is a good sample of the English language.

715   Chance, Larry Lynn. "The Development of an Objective Composition
       Test for Non-Native Speakers of English." Diss. Univ. of Kansas,
       1973.
            As a result of administering a specially constructed objec-
       tive composition test to 93 foreign students at the Intensive

English Center at the University of Kansas, the researcher was
able to establish certain conclusions after comparing the results with composition grades and scores of the Michigan Test
of English Proficiency. He concluded that 1) Skill in composition seems to be a function of total language proficiency;
2) The objective composition test measured grammatical correctness and vocabulary; 3) Objective composition tests can be used
diagnostically and correlate positively with composition grades.

716   Cooper, Robert L. "Testing," in Teaching English as a Second Language,
       Harold B. Allen and Russell N. Campbell, eds. New York: McGraw-Hill,
       1972, 330-346.
             After discussing the "users and uses" of second language tests,
       the author reviews the reasons for administering tests and states
       that a decision to use a test should be based on a comparison
       of the usefulness and cost of the test with information avail-
       able elsewhere. Also included in the report is information on
       determining the language skills to be tested, steps to be fol-
       lowed in constructing a standardized second-language test, and
       suggestions about interpreting test results.

717   Cordova, Joe E. English Proficiency and Behavioral Change in Spanish-
       Speaking Children. Pueblo: Southern Colorado State College, 1972.
       ED 066996.
             A description of an experiment with students selected from
       kindergarten, second, and fourth grades of elementary schools
       with principally a Chicano population. Although the control
       groups received no special instruction, experimental students
       were taught English as a second language by specially trained
       teachers. Students in both groups were tested before and after
       the experiment, the results of which are discussed along with
       suggestions.

718   Davis, Alva L. Diagnostic Test for Students of English as a Second
       Language. New York: McGraw-Hill, 1974.
             This test consists of 150 multiple-choice questions designed
       to examine students in English structure and idiomatic vocabu-
       lary in order to determine placement and the need for special
       instruction. Questions, which cover all areas of English usage,
       are answered on a one-page answer sheet. Instructions for ad-
       ministering and scoring the test are provided.

719   de Matos, F. Gomes. "Linguistic Claims in English Language Teaching."
       IRAL, 9, 3 (1971), 209-217.
             An examination of fourteen teacher's guides published in the
       United States, England, France, and Colombia since 1960 "to
       show the extent to which some principles of linguistic science
       exert an influence on teacher's manuals...." A claim was con-
       sidered to be an assertion of something as a fact. Some "tent-
       ative conclusions" of the study indicate that writers of teach-
       er's manuals in TEFL boast of the influence of linguistics
       (noticed particularly in American sources); linguistic principles

and concepts are often oversimplified; some authors overestimate the linguistic background of teachers; and manuals fortunately are reflecting the importance of psychology and including more descriptive information.

720   Edwards, Peter. An Evaluation of the English Enrichment Program for English Second-Language at Templeton Secondary School. Vancouver, British Columbia: Dept. of Planning and Evaluation, 1973.
Pre- and post-tests were given to students in an experimental and control group in a study to determine the effectiveness of the English Enrichment Program for students experiencing difficulty with the English language. The students, most of whom were from Hong Kong, were tested in listening, speaking, reading, and writing. Results showed that the experimental group performed significantly better than the control group in Oral and Written English.

721   Ehrlich, Alan, comp. Tests in Spanish and Other Languages and Non-verbal Tests for Children in Bilingual Programs: An Annotated B.E.A.R.U. Bibliography. New York: Hunter College, 1973. ED 074852.
Twenty-one verbal and non-verbal tests with annotations are listed in this bibliography. Tests are of intelligence, general ability, and language competency in English, Spanish, and French. A brief description is given for each test along with information about its grade range and the time required for its application. Additional sources of information on tests for bilingual programs are supplied.

722   An Evaluation of Improving the Teaching of English as a Second Language in Poverty Area Schools. New York: New York University, 1970. ED 058363.
An evaluation of the Linguistic Reader Projects (Merrill and Miami) and the Implementation of the English as a Second Language Program in Poverty-Area Schools in New York City. Emphasis was placed on the linguistic approach to the teaching of beginning reading. Workshops were provided for teachers in the project to concentrate on methods of the programs. Plans were also made to assign 35 specially trained teachers to area schools with the most serious needs.

723   An Evaluation of Teaching English as a Second Language in the Public Schools. New York: New York University, 1969. ED 058364.
The purpose of the evaluation was to ascertain the effectiveness of the materials, teaching, and learning situation of two programs sponsored by ESEA Title I involving students of English as a second language. No normalized testing measures were used because the learners were non-native speakers of English. Data were compiled by conducting personnel interviews, having teachers answer questionnaires, and analyzing program materials.

724 Golazeski, Clare T. <u>Language Interference and Visual Perception for Native and Puerto Rican Speakers of English in Second Grade.</u> Master of Education Thesis, Rutgers Univ., 1971. ED 051981.

Second grade pupils from Puerto Rico and New Jersey participated in a cross-cultural study to ascertain whether language interference would affect visual perception and whether boys or girls would be more noticeably affected. Results of tests indicated that there were no significant differences between the two groups or between the performance of boys and girls. Test materials and statistical results are provided.

725 Gregory-Panopoulos, John Fred. "An Experimental Application of 'Cloze' Procedure as a Diagnostic Test of Listening Comprehension Among Foreign Students." Diss. Univ. of Southern California, 1966.

A study that attempted to examine the reliability and validity of a cloze listening test in comparison with other tests of English ability. The Cloze Test of Listening Comprehension, the Brown-Carlsen Listening Comprehension Test and the California Reading Test were used, along with the USC English Placement Test, with two groups of foreign students. The Cloze test seemed to have some advantages in administering and scoring and was at least as valid as, and more reliable than, the Brown-Carlsen test.

726 Harris, David P. "Report on an Experimental Group-Administered Memory Span Test." <u>TESOL Quarterly</u>, 4, 3 (1970), 203-213.

Increasing interest has been shown in memory span tests as measures of achievement in language learning, especially as measures of foreign language proficiency. These tests are made up of sentences of increasing length and grammatical complexity. Through experimentation, the author found that a group-administered memory span test can be reliably scored; that it must be of sufficient length to get a broad range of scores; and that similar results will be obtained for content or grammatical accuracy. The author recommends the test for "evaluating achievement in a narrow range of language skills."

727 Harris, David P. <u>Testing English as a Second Language.</u> New York: MacMillan, 1969.

This book is designed mostly for ESL teachers working with young adults and is written clearly and simply. Harris covers the testing of vocabulary, reading comprehension, writing, oral proficiency, and other areas including test construction, administration, and interpretation. His discussions of interview-type tests disclose many helpful suggestions. The reader might be disappointed to find very little information about testing on the elementary school level and Harris's failure to include some of the results of testing experiments current at the time of the book's publication. The book, however, is a helpful one.

728 Harris, David P., and Leslie A. Palmer. <u>Comprehensive English Language Test.</u> New York: McGraw-Hill, 1970.

CELT attempts to measure the English language proficiency of intermediate and advanced ESL students by testing vocabulary, listening, and structure. Each test can be used separately if desired. Each part of the test can be administered in one class hour and can be graded by a scoring key.

729 Hoag, Sister Mary Immaculate. "Report on English Recognition Vocabulary of 100 Foreign Students Beginning Studies in an American College." Diss. Georgetown Univ., 1966.
The participants represented 18 different language backgrounds, were enrolled in 12 institutions of higher learning, and took a variety of courses. They were given a vocabulary test of 200 words randomly selected from Webster's Third New International Dictionary. Test results showed that the word range extended from 59.843 to 196.439. Results were also studied within certain subgroupings. The research disclosed that the three most influential factors on vocabulary were interest in language, reading in English, and knowledge of other languages.

730 Ilyin, Donna. Ilyin Oral Interview Test. Rowley, Mass.: Newbury House, 1972.
A test for use with ESL and EFL students given on a one-to-one basis with the examiner asking questions about pictures and the student responding with answers, questions, or statements. Comprehension and oral production only are tested. The test packet consists of an illustrated test book, a tester's manual of instructions, and a scoring pad with answer sheets.

731 Jameson, Gloria Ruth. "The Development of a Phonemic Analysis for an Oral English Proficiency Test for Spanish-Speaking School Beginners." Diss. Univ. of Texas, 1967.
This report should be helpful to any community offering an ESL program for Spanish-speaking children. An attempt was made to ascertain basic language problems and develop a test to rate the children's progress in oral English. The Phonemic Analysis Test of oral English ability was found to have a reliability of at least 85 per cent. The same children were graded by different teachers in order to increase validation of the phonological analysis.

732 Levine, Helene Faith. "Linguistic Changes in Spanish-Speakers Learning English." English Language Teaching, 25, 3 (1971), 288-296.
The writer discusses two techniques as effective means of measuring foreign-language learning: 1) delayed auditory feedback; and 2) cloze procedure. The former involves an "experimentally induced delay in the air conducted return of a speaker's vocal output to this ears." One significant finding indicated that although the subjects had improved their pronunciation, they seemed unsure of themselves, probably because they concentrated too much on pronunciation. Although pronunciation had improved, grammar had worsened during the course.

733 Lindfors, Judith Wells. "Two Approaches to the Evaluation of Early
Childhood Oral English Programs for Children Whose First Language
is Not English." Diss. Univ. of Texas, 1972.
The study was made in order to help educators select an early
childhood oral English program for students whose first language was not English. Two evaluation approaches are discussed
in the study. In the first approach, the evaluator examines a
program according to his own "intuitive, pragmatic criteria,"
whereas in the second approach the evaluator examines a program
according to "an explicit, previously established set of evaluative criteria." The relative merits of each evaluation approach
are discussed.

734 McGuire, Helen, and Susan Rao. English as a Second Language; Achievement Tests, Level 1. Milwaukee, Wisconsin: Milwaukee Public Schools,
1969. ED 083862.
One of the difficulties confronting the ESL teacher and admin-
istrator is that of achieving an accurate measurement of pupil
proficiency in learning the second language. This booklet tests
the pupil's proficiency in listening, speaking, reading, and
writing and helps the teacher to determine how long pupils should
stay at certain levels. Instructions for administering and scoring the tests are included.

735 Maynes, J. O., Jr. House Bill No. 1: Special English Classes Evaluations. Phoenix, Arizona: Arizona State Dept. of Education, 1971.
A summary of information taken from 19 school districts with
special English classes that attempted to give pupils audio-
lingual skills in English and their native language and help
them retain their own culture while being integrated into American life. Results of standardized tests showed significant
improvement in oral language. A standard testing method for all
school districts was recommended.

736 Michigan Oral Language Productive Test: Conceptual Oral Language Test.
Ann Arbor, Michigan: Michigan Migrant Primary Interdisciplinary
Project, 1969.
This test offers a new approach to testing. The COLT test
was devised in order to evaluate the pupil's ability "to solve
problems and think in terms of basic concepts in math, science,
and social studies." The pupil reveals his answers non-verbally,
by pointing to a picture; and verbally, by explaining his answer
in standard English. In this way the examiner's language differences do not affect the pupil's understanding, and the difference between the non-verbal and verbal score demonstrates
the pupil's deficiency in producing standard English.

737 Molina, Huberto. "Assessment in an Instructional Program Designed
for Spanish-Speaking Children Acquiring English Language Skills."
Paper given to California Assn. of Teachers of English to speakers
of Other Languages, San Francisco, 1974. ED 093910.

A description of the methods of assessment of each pupil's proficiency in using English vocabulary, pronunciation, and other language skills needed to communicate effectively by using the LCS Placement Aid and then a review of the methods of assigning pupils to various units to achieve objectives. The End of Program Test assesses the student's capability to retain the skills taught in the program.

738 Mosallai, Hooshang. "An Analytical Study of the Textbooks Used to Teach English in the High Schools of Iran." Diss. State Univ. of New York at Buffalo, 1967.
Although English is an important language study in Iranian high schools, none of the textbooks used to teach English as a foreign language had ever been thoroughly evaluated. Criteria were established in textbook evaluation that considered ideal textbook characteristics along with linguistic theories related to teaching English as a second language. Modern theories in psychology, sociology, and pedagogy were also considered. Deficiencies in the textbooks were in the lack of linguistic patterns and cultural information, and in lack of organization. The researcher concluded that none of the textbooks met all the criteria of excellence.

739 Nadler, Harvey. "Criteria for the Selection of ESOL Materials." Paper given at TESOL Convention, Chicago, Illinois, March, 1969.
Since there is an increasing number of ESL texts on the market, teachers often wonder which ones they should use. In this paper the author offers some criteria that can serve as guidelines for evaluating textbooks. Among the criteria that one should consider are the age and competency of students; the number of practice drills; the amount of time given to ESL classes; and the presentation of the various kinds of language skills relevant to second language learning.

740 Oller, John W., Jr. "Assessing Competence in ESL: Reading." TESOL Quarterly, 6, 4 (1972), 313-323.
The author believes that the ESL college student doesn't get enough practice in reading and what material he is given to read is far below college level material. He discusses the results of research with EMP (Eye Movement Photography) where he found that the real contrast between native and non-native performance is in the speed with which the students "process verbal information in short-term memory." His research indicates that there is a closer relationship between listening, speaking, reading, and writing skills "than has been assumed traditionally."

741 Oller, John W., Jr. "Dictation as a Test of ESL Proficiency," in Teaching English as a Second Language, Harold B. Allen and Russell N. Campbell, eds. New York: McGraw-Hill, 1972, 346-354.
Language teachers seem to favor dictation as a means of testing their students in English-as-a-second-language classes

although professionals in the area of language testing look unfavorably on this technique. The author reports on the results of two experimental studies which support "the use of dictation as a device for testing ESL proficiency." The author advises that the results of actual experiments in language testing should supersede the opinions of authorities.

742 Oller, John W., Jr., and Christine A. Conrad. "The Cloze Technique and ESL Proficiency." Language Learning, 21, 2 (1971), 183-195.
The authors concluded from their study that the cloze technique is applicable to the problems of ESL proficiency testing and that the method may be useful in placing non-native speakers and diagnosing their language programs. Their experiment involved students in beginning, intermediate, and advanced ESL classes along with two control groups of native (ENL) speakers. The cloze test correlated best with the dictation on the UCLA ESLPE 2c, and next best with the reading section. A bibliography appears at the end of the article.

743 Oskarsson, Mats. "Monolingual and Bilingual Vocabulary Learning: An Empirical Investigation." Paper given at IATEFL Conference, Budapest, 1974.
This investigation attempted to measure the effectiveness of monolingual and bilingual glossaries in teaching foreign language vocabulary to adults. Groups of students were taught new English words according to two approaches: 1) in half of the groups, word meanings were explained in the target language, English; 2) the other groups were taught word meanings by using the native language equivalents. Results showed that the bilingual approaches were more successful.

744 Paterno, A. "Foreign Language Testing." MST English Quarterly, 20, 3 (1970), 469-488.
Since Paterno believed that most of the tests available to him were developed for native speakers of English, he wrote this article to help teachers of ESL/EFL students prepare their own tests. He advises that teachers identify their teaching goals, determine what has to be measured, and suggests that items be measured separately. He offers examples of some tests developed by teachers to measure listening and reading comprehension, ability in speaking and writing, competency in pronunciation, and knowledge of grammar.

745 Pickett, G. D. "A Comparison of Translation and Blank-Filling as Testing Techniques." English Language Teaching, 23, 1 (1968), 21-26.
The subjects of this study were French-speaking Africans who were tested in an attempt to ascertain whether blank-filling or translation was the better way to test linguistic proficiency. Two tests were constructed which called for identical answers to the different types of tests. Using the average mark each pupil gained over a half-year's classroom work as a standard,

Pickett found that scores for the translation test were closer than those for the blank-filling test.

746   Poczik, Robert. English as a Second Language Tests. Albany, New York: New York State Dept. of Education, 1973. ED 086724.

For teachers and administrators who are involved in teaching English-as-a-second-language programs in adult education, these placement tests will be of great interest. The Oral Placement Test and the Oral Production Test Levels measure auditory comprehension, oral production, and conversational skills. The tests can help teachers place students at proper levels and ascertain the degree of mastery of special skills.

747   Politzer, Robert L. "Developmental Sentence Scoring as a Method of Measuring Second Language Acquisition." The Modern Language Journal, 58/ 5, 6 (1974), 245-250.

Developmental sentence scoring, a method of measuring a child' language and development, is discussed here along with the results of its use. Generally, the scoring is based on the child's utterance as it conforms to accepted adult speech and, in addition, whether or not it includes any of the eight grammar forms (main verb, negative, personal pronoun, etc.). After using the DSS-scale, the author concludes that it "is at least partially applicable to second-language learning processes of young children" since it is able to "pick up" second-language proficiency because it measures "increased syntactic complexity and greater correctness."

748   Politzer, Robert L., and Arnulfo G. Ramirez. An Error Analysis of the Spoken English of Mexican-American Pupils in a Bilingual School and a Monolingual School. Stanford, Calif.: Stanford University, 1973. ED 073879.

A sampling of 61 Mexican-American children attending a monolingual school and 59 Mexican-American children attending a bilingual school was shown a silent movie and then told the story on tapes. Deviations from standard English were then categorized into various kinds of errors. Results showed that deviations were due to interference of Spanish, improper application of standard English, and influence of nonstandard dialects.

749   Robinson, Peter. "Oral Expression Tests: 2." English Language Teaching, 25, 3 (1971), 260-266.

Regardless of the level of EFL/ESL teaching, the best way to measure the student's oral language proficiency is to place him in a situation where he must converse, and the oral expression test does this. The test should consist of an interview and discussion. The former involves simple conversational interrogations, while in the discussion, the subject talks about something that interests him. Robinson believes that evaluation criteria can be set up after enough samples of oral production have been taken and offers examples of evaluation problems taken from actual tests at Laval University in Quebec.

750   Robinson, Peter. "Testing the Second-Language Competence of Children and Adults." English Language Teaching, 27, 2 (1973), 190-199.
Language testing is considered to be an essential part of
teaching; evaluation of the student's progress is fundamental.
The author discusses several fundamental testing problems and
offers examples of each. The problems are form, error analysis,
norms, expressivity, representativity, and competence. The
discussion is important since the inexperienced teacher may
know little about second-language testing. For example, sub-
jective and objective tests are used to ascertain different
kinds of skills.

751   Seward, B. H. "Measuring Oral Production." English Language
Teaching Journal, 28, 1 (1973), 76-80.
Since testing speaking proficiency in foreign languages has
proved to be a dilemma, the author made a study to determine if
the results of objective paper-and-pencil tests of general language proficiency could measure students' speaking proficiency in
English as a foreign language. Using 94 subjects from the
classes of the English Language Institute of the American University in Cairo in his survey, the author found that "scores from
objective paper-and-pencil test batteries indirectly provide
much more effective and stable measurements of students' speaking proficiency than teacher evaluations."

752   Sharon, Amiel T. Test of English as a Foreign Language as a Modera-
tor of Graduate Record Examinations Scores in the Prediction of
Foreign Students' Grades in Graduate School. Princeton, New Jersey:
Educational Testing Service, 1971. ED 058304.
The hypothesis was that foreign graduate students scoring
high on the TOEFL (Test of English as a Foreign Language)
would be more predictable on the GRE (Graduate Record Exam)
than those with low scores. Results only partially supported
this hypothesis indicating that foreign students with low English verbal aptitude can succeed in American graduate schools.

753   Spolsky, Bernard, et al. "Three Functional Tests of Oral Proficiency."
TESOL Quarterly, 6, 3 (1972), 221-231.
A description of three experimental tests attempting to
measure communicative ability. One was developed to assign six-
and seven-year-old children to tracks in a New Mexico bilingual
school. Another attempted to validate teacher ratings in a
study of Navajo language maintenance. The third was an oral
placement test for adults for use in an ESL program. Each test
was "closely tied to the practical situation for which it was
prepared" and was intended for use by untrained testers. Results, though not definitive, were satisfying.

754   Stubbs, Joseph Bartow, and G. Richard Tucker. "The Cloze Test as a
Measure of English Proficiency." The Modern Language Journal, 58/
5, 6 (1974), 239-241.
The authors contend that the cloze tests are a very useful
evaluative tool as a measure of proficiency in English as a

183

second language and interpret the cloze test administered as part of the English Entrance Examination required at the American University of Beirut. The article describes the procedure, subjects, method of scoring, and results. Empirical data are provided concerning the use of the test, and the authors state that it can be valuable in measuring English-language proficiency and as a "diagnostic tool for the classroom teacher."

755   Testing Some English Language Skills: Rationale Development and Description. Toronto, Ontario: Toronto Board of Education, 1969. ED 069161.

In order to test English language skills of students learning English as a second language, materials were developed for use in the New Canadian Study (1967-68). A six-part "English Competence Test" was produced to test auditory perception and vocabulary. The report includes an objective evaluation of the test. The evaluation itself should be of interest to ESL teachers who are devising their own tests.

756   Upshur, John A. "Objective Evaluation of Oral Proficiency in the ESOL Classroom." TESOL Quarterly, 5, 1 (1971), 47-58.

Testing of oral proficiency is an important part of teaching English to speakers of other languages; the results of the tests can be helpful to both student and teacher. The author maintains that oral tests can always be improved if the teacher is willing to plan and prepare them well. The teacher must know the objectives of the course and the reasons for learning English; then he will be able to conduct a valid test. Games can help in the testing process.

757   Williams, Roger K. "Problems in Cloze Testing." TESL Reporter, 7, 4 (1974), 7-9.

Cloze tests can be "a useful supplement to vocabulary tests, tests of grammatical structures common to written English" and other elements, but the author points out that there are problems in devising cloze tests that measure reading skills. One problem is that cloze tests "only partially parallel the reading process" and scoring is therefore difficult. In addition, success in cloze tests is sometimes more a result of "intellectual functioning" and less a result of language efficiency. Furthermore, the ability to fill in blanks may depend on how familiar the student is with the subject matter.

Cross Reference

701   Reading
710   Bilingual
715   Writing
719   Texts
720   Methodology
729   Reading
731   Spoken English
732   Spoken English

733	Spoken English
735	Audio-Lingual
738	Texts
739	Texts
740	Reading
741	Teaching Aids
743	Adult
746	Spoken English
747	Language Learning
748	Spoken English
749	Spoken English
751	Spoken English
756	Spoken English

TEXTS

758   Alyeshmerni, Mansoor, and Paul Taubr. Working with Aspects of Language. New York: Harcourt, Brace and World, 1970.

For the prospective teacher who needs a general English language study background or a review before taking advanced courses to prepare for ESL teaching, this workbook is recommended. It is designed for use with Bolinger's Aspects of Language and contains exercises in phonology; morphology; grammar concepts; traditional, structural, and transformational grammar; sociolinguistics; principles of language change; and semantics.

759   Benjamin, Richard C., and Ralph F. Robinett. Michigan Oral Language Series (English as a Second Language or Second Dialect). New York: American Council on the Teaching of Foreign Languages, 1970.

A realistic approach to a regular early childhood curriculum and standard language skills consisting of short learning activities for pre-school and kindergarten children. The series was prepared especially for four-to six-year-old children of Mideast migrant workers with Spanish language backgrounds. The bilingual program expects to teach standard Spanish and English. The series consists of a set of guides on various aspects of the bilingual program for different levels. The program is somewhat formalized but could be especially useful to teachers with little ESL training.

760   Berger, Donald, and Paul Pimsleur. Encounters: A Basic Reader. New York: Harcourt Brace, 1974.

An elementary English reader that includes articles from American and Canadian newspapers and magazines most useful in developing basic language skills. Articles are adapted to a 1500-word vocabulary and graded according to length and difficulty. Each article is followed by exercises covering vocabulary, grammar, and comprehension. Articles cover a wide variety of topics including ecology, women's liberation, popular music and horoscopes.

761   Breckenridge, Robert G. Access to English as a Second Language.
       New York: McGraw-Hill, 1973.
              Two books, each one of which contains 17 lessons for stu-
       dents beginning their ESL studies in high school or later.
       Each lesson contains material covering vocabulary, structure,
       and pronunciation, and utilizes practice, review, pictures,
       transformations, and substitution drills. Texts include a
       workbook, reviews,a Teacher's Manual, and picture cue cards.

762   Butler, Diego. Exercises in English for the Spanish Speaker.
       New York: McGraw-Hill, 1972.
              A text/workbook for Spanish speakers of English offering a
       review of English grammar for the student who has had an intro-
       ductory ESL course. Material is related to its counterpart
       in Spanish with emphasis on contrasts. Lessons consist of a
       reading selection followed by exercises and drills. Additional
       information on rules and usage appears in the appendices.

763   Cargas, Harry J., and Edward T. Erazmus, eds. English as a Second
       Language: A Reader. Dubuque, Iowa: Wm. C. Brown, 1970.
              The anthology contains short essays and fiction by American
       authors from colonial times to the present. Each reading has
       a short introduction with historical background information and
       is followed by three essay topics, vocabulary builders, quizzes,
       and structure drills. The editors obviously intended the book
       as a means of introducing ESL students to American culture, but
       the selections are not particularly interesting and require a
       great deal of English language training of the reader. Much of
       the vocabulary is infrequently used. However, the text would
       be useful as a source of information by advanced foreign stu-
       dents in college.

764   Catto, Lucila S. de, et al. American English Series: English as a
       Second Language. Books 1-3. Lexington, Mass.: D. C. Heath,
       1965-69.
              A revision of the Fries American English Series begun in
       1952. Although the new series is structurally different, the
       material still emphasizes the importance of speech; the neces-
       sary order of listening, speaking, and reading; and the signi-
       ficance of descriptive linguistics. The teacher's guide is
       very helpful since each page of the student text appears in
       the guide along with suggestions and instructions. There is no
       doubt that the material in the series is well prepared, but
       there is little attention paid to new developments in second
       language teaching techniques.

765   Close, R. A. The New English Grammar. Cambridge, Mass.: Harvard
       University Press, 1968.
              The second volume of the text, this one dealing almost
       exclusively with the verb . The first volume was entitled
       English as a Foreign Language. As a supplementary and refer-
       ential aid in the ESL/EFL classroom, this text should be

useful. The explanations are clear, and the exercises cover the details of each lesson very well. Only students with at least an intermediate background could use the book. There is little that is "new" here (the title implies that there is) but much of the information is essential if a student wants to use English fluently.

766   Crymes, Ruth. A Textbook for Students of English as a Second Language. Honolulu: Hawaii Univ., 1970. ED 043856.
      This text was used in the English Language Institute of the University of Hawaii in 1969-70, and is geared for high intermediate and advanced students of English as a second language. Emphasis is on listening and speaking in informal situations, and in helping students develop skills in sentence embedding.

767   Crymes, Ruth, et al. Developing Fluency in English. Englewood Cliffs, N. J.: Prentice Hall, 1974.
      A text for advanced ESL students that provides them with apparatus for understanding and using English effectively, concentrating on reading, listening, speaking, writing, vocabulary, and grammar. The material is consistent with the language used by native speakers of English, and the subject matter in the reading selection is the kind that foreign students will find in their college courses. The vocabulary exercises are especially good--practical, varied, and closely related to the reading selections.

768   Dacanay, Fe Reisela M. "A Methodology for Constructing Beginning English Readers for Philippine Schools." Diss. Univ. of California, Los Angeles, 1969.
      A study designed to develop criteria for constructing beginning readers in English for Philippine school children. The report shows that linguists favor the "code approach" emphasizing spelling pattern - sound correlations for beginning reading and that they favor control of vocabulary and language structure in texts. Other recommendations emphasize the necessity of carefully arranged, sequential "tasks" within the student's comprehension level.

769   Dacanay, Fe Reisela M. Techniques and Procedures in Second Language Teaching. Dobbs Ferry, New York: Oceana Publications, 1967.
      Although this book was written primarily to help Filipino teachers of English, it contains practical suggestions for all ESL teachers by presenting drills, exercises, and tests in addition to material on teaching reading and writing for elementary, intermediate, and advanced students. The chapters on phonology and spelling are especially good, and the first two chapters show how newspaper articles, comic strips, stories and dialogues can be used in teaching the structures of English.

770   Danielson, Dorothy, and Rebecca Hayden. Using English: Your Second
       Language. Englewood Cliffs, N. J.: Prentice-Hall, 1973.
             A text that is designed for college students or adults who
       are at the intermediate or advanced stage of English language
       proficiency. The book is divided into units containing exam-
       ples, explanations, and drills. Exercises at the ends of
       units are not as relevant or valid as the material in the units.
       The material covered is important: wh-questions, tag questions,
       commands, auxiliaries, articles, clauses, comparisons, etc. The
       teacher, however, will have to be flexible in using the text
       in order to adapt it to the level of the students who might
       find the vocabulary difficult.

771   Day, James. An Advanced English Practice Course. London: Longmans,
       Green and Co., 1968.
             A book for advanced students who have studied English as a
       second or foreign language for up to six years. It intends to
       help students correct mistakes and refine their language, ex-
       pand their vocabulary, and evaluate the selections they are
       asked to read. In addition to the study of correct usage, the
       course offers students material intended to upgrade their use
       and understanding of English.

772   Dixson, Robert J. Complete Course in English. New York: Regents
       Publishing Co., 1974.
             A new edition of the book, with the expansion to a four-
       volume series. The first two books are intensive courses in
       basic English with lessons of increasing difficulty. Each
       lesson contains a variety of exercises. Books 3 and 4 place
       more emphasis on reading and conversation and includes New
       York City as the setting for the dialogues. Book 4 contains
       adaptations of stories of American authors. Cassettes and
       tapes are available.

773   Dixson, Robert J. Modern American English. New York: Regents
       Publishing Co., 1974.
             A series covering levels one through six with workbooks,
       posters, Teachers' Manuals, and tapes and cassettes. It is
       recommended for use in a high school or college curriculum
       having from four-to six-year levels. Included in the series
       are reading and oral practice, pattern practice, pronunciation,
       intonation, and general practices containing exercises, games,
       and other classroom activities.

774   Doty, Gladys G., and Janet Ross. Language and Life in the U. S. A.,
       Volume I - Communicating in English; Volume II - Reading English.
       Third Edition. New York: Harper and Row, 1973.
             This two-volume text has been split into two paperback
       volumes--a language text and a reader. The language text is
       oriented to the audio-lingual approach with pattern drills,
       plenty of exercises, and some activities which include games,
       a debate, and a play. The language text is not difficult for

teachers to use, but it does not reflect enough of the changes that have recently taken place in ESL theories. The volume of readings does attempt to cover a variety of topics but the readings are unexciting.

775 Estrada, Beatrice T., et al. Manual of Sentence Patterns for Teaching English as a Second Language. Gallup, New Mexico: Gallup-McKinley County Schools, 1966. ED 076079.
A guide that contains practical lessons for non-English-speaking students entering school. Selected vocabulary, patterns, and sounds are introduced and reviewed. Pattern sentences necessary for everyday living are included. Instructions for using the manual and related supplementary material are also included.

776 Ferguson, Nicolas. Teaching English as a Foreign Language: Theory and Practice. Chicago: Rand McNally, 1972.
An introductory methods text which presents classroom teaching techniques based on current theories in linguistics and psychology. The text includes a discussion of transformational-generative grammar, audio-visual methods, and language learner motivation in addition to a presentation of phonology, morphology, syntax and semantics. One chapter is devoted to help advanced students perfect their language skills.

777 Finocchiaro, Mary. Learning to Use English. New York: Regents Publishing Co., 1974.
A series, composed of two texts with one Teacher's Manual, for students of English as a second language on the upper elementary, high school, or college level. The texts cover a wide range of language skills with graded exercises for each lesson. Lessons progress through a four-phase sequence of listening, speaking, reading, and writing. The Teacher's Manual is designed for both experienced and inexperienced teachers.

778 Garst, Thomas Edward. The Third Miracle Series. New York: McGraw-Hill, 1971.
A series that features a varied approach to foreign language instruction including audio-visual, reading comprehension, and programmed teaching methods used in Spanish-English bilingual instruction. Emphasis is on correct discrimination, and fluency in speaking. For students beginning their ESL studies at upper secondary levels and above, the series should be helpful.

779 Goulet, Rosalina M., Lois McIntosh, and Teresita V. Ramos. Advancing in English. New York-Manila: American Book Co., 1970.
Although this book is primarily for young adults in Asia who are reaching the advanced level of learning English, it contains information that is of interest to ESL teachers in general. The book is divided into units containing questions, grammatical problems, oral practice, writing activities, and practice on

various aspects of phonology. The writers feature spoken language but spend some time on writing and sentence structure. The text focuses on practical and workable topics that teachers must deal with in their classrooms.

780   Hall, Eugene J. Grammar for Use. Silver Springs, Md.: Institute of Modern Languages, 1974.
       A textbook-workbook for advanced English-as-a-second language students with a descriptive approach to American English grammar. Each chapter contains questions on the grammar elements covered that intend to show students similarities and differences between English and their native language. Exercises follow each group of questions, and space is provided for writing.

781   Hall, Eugene J., and Earle W. Brockman, Jr., et al. English This Way. New York: MacMillan, 1965.
       A graded course using the audio-lingual method of language teaching prepared by English Language Services containing twelve books with a teacher's manual and key for Books 1-6 and 7-12. The texts contain many exercises that cover reading, writing, vocabulary, and oral work. Reading selections are followed by questions, and most of the drill work is designed to acquaint the non-native speaker with everyday English language. The texts are weak where they attempt to teach grammar instead of conversation.

782   Imhoof, Maurice Lee. "A Design for a Textbook to Teach Basic Language Concepts to Non-native Speakers of English." Diss. Columbia Univ., 1967.
       The immediate purpose of the project was to develop a text for an English teacher-training program in Afghanistan, but the design could be feasible for use in other regions which have similar cultural or educational backgrounds. Part One includes a description of the design for the text, the study itself, and the evaluation. Part Two includes the seven sample chapters of the textbook. The researcher concluded that teachers should develop more scientific attitudes toward language study and develop the ability to describe a language objectively.

783   Jacquette, Charles. English as a Second Language. Sahuarita, Arizona: Sahuarita High School District, 130, 1973. ED 084930.
       A textbook in English as a second language for use by Spanish-speaking high school students. The ten lessons are tightly controlled, each one containing the purpose, a pre-test, sources of information regarding the lesson, drill exercises, a final test and other activities. Although the text has self-instructional guides, teacher guidance is necessary.

784   Kernan, Doris. Steps to English. New York: McGraw-Hill, 1974.
       A four-book series covering listening, speaking, reading, and writing for beginning students, ages 6-11. Lessons are organized around vocabulary, structure, dialogues, reading,

pronunciation, and writing. An annotated Teacher's Edition
explains how to use the text along with a sample test for each
lesson.

785 Kurilecz, Margaret. Man and His World; A Structure Reader. New
York: Thomas Y. Crowell, 1969.
A reader for intermediate or advanced students of English as
a second language which may be used in secondary schools or on
the adult level. Emphasis is on reading, speaking, and writing,
with emphasis on vocabulary development as an aid to reading
comprehension. In order to appeal to students from different
cultures, the reading material features political, geographical,
and economic aspects of life.

786 Lado, Robert. The Lado English Series. New York: Simon and Schuster,
1970.
A program that attempts to help the student, in six graded
textbooks, to develop skills in speaking, listening, reading,
and writing. Each skill is dealt with separately. The course
is comprehensive, perhaps too broad in some aspects. It features structure and syntactical elements rather than practical
and communicative language practice. Although some of the
drills are very structured rather than realistic in content, a
selective teacher can use those that are helpful.

787 Lismore, Thomas. Welcome to English. New York: Regents Publishing
Co., 1974.
A revised edition of a course primarily designed for non-
English-speaking children in the lower elementary grades, containing 5 texts with colored illustrations. The series begins
with fundamentals and moves to more difficult areas. Lessons
are accompanied by conversational exercises. Each text may be
used alone. The books are physically attractive with large
type. Cassettes and reels are available for use with each book.

788 McGillivary, James H., and Audrey L.Wright. Let's Learn English:
Beginning Course. (Books 1 and 2). New York: American Book Co.,
1971.
This introductory set offers the usual approaches to the audio-
lingual method of teaching ESL in attractive books. The series
assumes no previous knowledge of English and the reading selections in Books 1 and 2 are restricted to a 500-word vocabulary.
This beginning course makes little attempt to teach reading but
includes a great many elementary exercises. The set has been
in use many years but does not reflect the most current ESL
theories.

789 Mackin, Ronald. Course in Spoken English. Portland, Oregon: English
Language Services, 1974.
A course intended for students who have already studied English but haven't achieved mastery of the spoken language. The
book contains ten units, each consisting of three different
kinds of material: language used in a situation; structural
drills; and tests.

790 Marquardt, William F., et al. <u>English Around the World</u>. Glenview, Illinois: Scott, Foresman and Co., 1970.
In this aural-oral program for non-English-speaking children in the primary grades, the pupils are taught English language skills and are also acquainted with customs from around the world. The program is highly detailed with teachers' guide-books, pupil skills books, posters, practice pad/test books, and record albums. The texts are brightly illustrated, truly international, unlike some ESL texts that are restricted to the culture of the native speaker or the second language area.

791 Monfries, Helen. <u>An Introduction to Critical Appreciation for Foreign Learners</u>. London: MacMillan, 1970.
An anthology of prose and verse designed for the advanced student of English. The selections are arranged in order of difficulty and theme. The collection attempts to acquaint the student with general approaches to literary criticism, familiarize them with the literary styles of British and American writings, and enable them to study the English langu-age. Questions accompany each selection. A glossary of use-ful terms is included in the text that includes selections of literary quality but is recommended only for students with a firm grasp of English.

792 Morelli, Leonard R., and Harvey Nadler, eds. <u>American English-An Integrated Series for International Students</u>. (Second Edition). Chicago: Rand McNally, 1971.
A complete elementary program covering all aspects of langu-age with materials that can be used in reading-vocabulary, grammar, and pronunciation classes and the language laboratory. Stories for the reading-vocabulary class are written around everyday situations, and the grammar materials embody the vocabulary items found in the stories. Pronunciation materials use the grammar and vocabulary of the stories and the labora-tory tapes review the materials used in class.

793 Neustadt, Bertha C. <u>Speaking About the U. S. A.</u> New York: Harper and Row, 1975.
A text specially designed to aid foreign students in under-standing written and spoken English while studying at American universities by helping them develop skills in taking notes, participating in discussions, and using the library. Current readings are included, each one dealing with one aspect of American society in order to motivate writing and discussion. Each chapter contains a glossary and listening and vocabulary exercises.

794 Pimsleur, Paul, and Donald Berger. <u>Encounters: A Basic Reader</u>. New York: Harcourt Brace, 1974.
A different kind of reader for the ESL student, containing 27 articles on contemporary subjects condensed from American magazines and newspapers. The articles are entertaining,

covering topics from Dear Abby to the story of Kentucky Fried
Chicken. Each article is followed by vocabulary exercises,
comprehension questions, and group and individual activities.
An imaginative teacher could use the text in many different
ways but only with advanced or high-intermediate learners.

795   Politzer, Robert L., and Freida Politzer. Teaching English as a
      Second Language. Lexington, Mass.: Xerox College Publishing, 1972.
            A text featuring basic language skills in English to students
      studying English as a foreign language on the adult, college,
      or high school level. A teacher using the text must be well
      prepared in the English sound system and in syntactical patterns.
      The introductory material serves as helpful background material
      for the teacher, and the bibliography at the end of the text is
      comprehensive.

796   Ross, Janet, and Gladys Doty. A Composition Text in English as a
      Foreign Language. New York: Harper and Row, 1965.
            This text is for advanced students of English as a foreign
      language, beginning with basic sentence patterns with subse-
      quent expansion and modification using the work of well known
      authors as models. The complete composition is discussed
      after work is done on paragraph development. The authors
      stress controlled writing, a procedure that has been found to
      be beneficial to non-native students of English.

797   Rutherford, Willaim E. Modern English: A Textbook for Foreign
      Students. New York: Harcourt, Brace and World, 1968.
            A text designed for foreign students studying at American
      universities; students using the text should be considered
      advanced in English preparation. The book consists of three
      major parts and is intended for use in a two-semester course.
      If the teacher is selective, he can find a great deal of in-
      formation in the text, but because the exercises are so diffi-
      cult and explanations take so much for granted, it is
      questionable for use by all students in an ESL classroom.

798   Saitz, Robert L., and Donna Carr, eds. Selected Readings in English:
      For Students of English as a Second Language. Cambridge, Mass.:
      Winthrop Publishers, 1972.
            Readings intended to reach the intermediate and advanced stu-
      dent of English as a second language who needs experience in
      reading and writing. The short stories and essays are examples
      of different writing styles. The selections are short, have
      high interest factors, and are accompanied by exercises.
      Selections include Saint-Exupery's The Little Prince, stories
      from Tom Sawyer and The Thurber Carnival and an interesting
      essay reprinted from Commonweal.

799   Samuelson, William. English as a Second Language-Phase One: Let's
      Converse. Englewood Cliffs, New Jersey: Prentice-Hall, 1974.
            The emphasis in this book is on speaking and is designed
      primarily for the adult college student non-native speaker or

the native speaker who needs remedial help in conversational speaking. The major topics in the text deal with such practical matters as buying school supplies, ordering materials, shopping for clothing, and getting a job. A Teacher's Manual is available for this text that covers one semester of work.

800   Sheeler, Willard D. Welcome to English. Portland, Oregon: English Language Services, 1974.
Consists of eight textbooks providing language in context presented in dialogues, monologues, conversation practices, and readings. The student participates as one of two speakers in a variety of drills and exercises. Emphasis is on natural speech in drills, exercises, and content. Review sections draw the material together and end with a fifty-item multiple choice test.

801   Slager, William R., and Elsie Wolk, et al. Core English One, Two, Three, and Four. New York: Ginn and Company, 1972.
A language arts program consisting of four kits for young non-English speaking pupils in the lower grades. Each kit has a teacher's manual containing the basic material of the program. In addition there are wall charts, picture cards, songs, games, puppets, and records. The manuals are very detailed with a workbook for each level. The wealth of material here and the highly organized approach provide the teacher with a kind of training course and offer a good linguistic groundwork.

802   Stoddard, John, and Frances Stoddard. The Teaching of English to Immigrant Children. London: The University of London Press, 1968.
This specialized text was based on the authors' experiences in teaching English to Indian and Pakistan immigrant children in England. The ESL teacher can borrow some excellent ideas in the chapters devoted to visual aids and activities which discuss the use of dramatization, models, pictures, stories, songs, playlets. The material in Chapter 7 on Reading offers some novel information about pre-reading preparation and phonic analysis. The "copying" approach to writing will also be of interest to ESL teachers.

803   Van Syoc, W. Bryce, and Florence S. Van Syoc. Let's Learn English. New York: American Book Co., 1971.
The advanced course of this series has a well organized reading and writing program and is highly recommended for nonnative speakers who have a background in English fundamentals but need more competence to function well as college students. The readings are appealing, and serve as good models for the exercises that follow.

804   Vinson, Jane. The Magic of English. New York: Harper and Row, 1969.
A program for non-English speakers in the elementary school based on the audio-lingual approach. Lessons are planned for

194

15- to 30-minute periods with groups of six to ten students. The book covers a wide area of subjects including colors, parts of the body, toys, counting, concepts of mathematics, foods, the community, etc. Enrichment lessons provide material about holidays, parades, the circus, and field trips. Instructions are helpful, especially to inexperienced teachers.

805 Ward, J. Millington. Practice in Structure and Usage. London: Longman, 1972.
This is a book of exercises in pronunciation, grammar, vocabulary, and idioms designed for use by students at the intermediate level of English as a second or foreign language. Each section of the text includes a passage that requires selection of certain English language elements (conjunctions, prepositions); answers to questions; pronunciation exercises; and exercises in English that are particularly difficult for foreign students.

806 Wardhaugh, Ronald. Introduction to Linguistics. New York: McGraw-Hill, 1972.
Although Wardhaugh emphasizes the generative-transformational theory, he champions no particular approach to language study since, as he says, "the discipline is in a state of flux." In addition to covering phonetics, phonology, morphology, patterns, transforms meaning, and other topics, the book includes a glossary of useful terms and a bibliography that many teachers will want to use. The material is readable and the explanations are clear. The text would be useful for the student who needs a basic background in linguistics before taking more advanced English language courses. A workbook is available.

807 Yorkey, Richard C. Study Skills for Students of English as a Second Language. New York: McGraw-Hill, 1974.
A text that offers instruction and practice in basic study skills for non-native speakers of English in high school and above. Some of the chapters deal with using an English dictionary, writing outlines, taking notes, using the library, and preparing for exams.

Cross Reference

758	Teacher Preparation
759	Bilingual
763	Reading
768	Reading
791	Reading
796	Writing
799	Spoken English
806	Grammar

808   Arapoff, Nancy. <u>Discover and Transform: A Method of Teaching Writing to Foreign Students</u>. Paper given at the Third Annual TESOL Convention, Chicago, Ill., 1969.

Many foreign students are studying in colleges in the United States where they have to compete with native speakers. The foreign students need more competence in writing and they must be taught the difference between spoken and written English. In the "discover and transform" method they compare two written models similar in content but different in form. By analyzing the models, the students discover the rules that operate to transform the first model into the second.

809   Arapoff, Nancy. <u>Writing Through Understanding</u>. New York: Holt, Rinehart and Winston, 1970.

A useful text for foreign students of English or speakers of nonstandard dialects that points out the similarities and differences between spoken and written English and explains how writing requires more clarity than speaking. The author presents various writing devices that help to achieve clarity. An Instructor's Manual is available.

810   Bander, Robert G. <u>American English Rhetoric: Writing from Spoken Models for Bilingual Students</u>. New York: Holt, Rinehart, and Winston, 1971.

A book recommended for use by foreign students with advanced English skills. It contains a variety of model paragraphs, each one followed by a writing discussion dealing with paragraph development and a grammar and punctuation discussion. Much of the material deals with parallel structure, subordination, variety of sentence structure and length, and the use of transitional devices.

811   Baskoff, Florence. <u>American English, An Integrated Series for International Students. Guided Composition Writing</u>. Philadelphia: Chilton Books, 1969.

Fifth in a series intended for teaching English to international students in the American Language Institute of New York University. Included are 30 models of compositions on various topics focusing on American culture. Each composition topic is accompanied by discussion questions and oral and written exercises. A special section is devoted to writing paragraphs, compositions, and letters.

812   Baskoff, Florence. <u>Guided Composition</u>, Philadelphia: Center for Curriculum Development, 1971.

This text is a useful one in helping non-English-speaking students develop writing skills. The author uses controlled composition to teach one thing at a time and offers the student practice in writing correct paragraphs by following carefully planned sequences. The text has 30 model compositions with exercises involving short answers, thus enabling students to refer to the models immediately to check on their responses. Also included are vocabulary exercises, some useful everyday expressions, and some rules for spelling, capitalization, punctuation, etc.

813   Bracy, Maryruth. "Controlled Writing vs. Free Composition." TESOL Quarterly, 5, 3 (1971), 239-246.
        The author offers suggestions for using the "free composition" approach in teaching composition to foreign students learning English. After reaching a certain stage in writing competency through controlled writing, the student is ready for free composition, but teachers have had difficulty in guiding the student writers, and the author spends some time on the problem of proper correction of composition work. For teachers of intermediate and advanced composition in ESL there are some useful techniques that will "bring structure and direction into the area of free composition."

814   Bracy, Maryruth, and Russell N. Campbell. Letters from Roger: Exercises in Communication. Englewood Cliffs, New Jersey: Prentice Hall, 1972.
        A book that offers an interesting approach to the study of English, and life in the United States for foreign students in the low-intermediate to advanced range who expect to be living in this country. The book features a variety of letters describing many aspects of American life. In addition, there are newspapers, magazines, essays, application blanks, and other materials. Various exercises, assignments, and questions are also included.

815   Chang, Winona Lee. "A Comparison of Certain Structures Written in English by Monolingual and Bilingual Sixth Graders." Diss. Boston Univ., 1971.
        The purpose of this study was to determine whether bilingual pupils twelve years of age with average- and above-average intelligence wrote English as their monolingual classmates of similar ability did. Two groups, one in Boston and one in Lewiston, Maine, were involved. The monolingual groups in Boston scored significantly higher in writing tests than their bilingual classmates. The Lewiston sample was really too small to warrant conclusions. Although the results might have been predicted, the bilinguals did demonstrate ability to write in English and, with special help, would probably be able to perform as well as their monolingual classmates.

816   Chaplen, Frank. Paragraph Writing. New York: Oxford University Press, 1970.
        A book for more advanced students of English as a second language focusing on writing clear and unified paragraphs. Many exercises intended to help students understand the basic elements of paragraph development are included. The text contains many

writing assignments covering various subjects, and are graded
according to difficulty. A teacher's edition includes a guide
for teaching and a key to the exercises.

817   Dykstra, Gerald. "Breaking Down Your Writing Goals," in Readings in
      English as a Second Language, Kenneth Croft, ed. Cambridge, Mass.:
      Winthrop Publishers, 1972, 214-223.
           Since the teaching of writing to high school students whose
      native language is not English is a difficult task, Dykstra's
      article can be very helpful, especially the four writing pro-
      grams that he includes that teachers can use as models. Before
      teaching writing, Dykstra states, the teacher must determine
      his goals and then work with "sub-goals," proceeding by small
      steps. His analogy between the development of writing skills
      and physical skills (knee bends) clearly shows the relation-
      ship between final goals and "sub-goals."

818   Dykstra, Gerald, and Christina Bratt Paulston. Controlled Composi-
      tion in English as a Second Language. New York: Regents Publishing
      Co., 1974.
           An advanced composition text with 65 model passages taken from
      American and British literature with instructional steps cover-
      ing language patterns and grammar. Emphasis is on mechanics,
      including sentence structure, use of idioms, spelling, grammar,
      and punctuation. The authors state that although the book is
      not intended to replace the grammar textbook, it can be used
      along with it.

819   Ekmekci, Ozden. Teaching Composition through Comprehension: A Survey
      of Teaching English Composition to Foreign Students and Its Applica-
      tion to the English Program at the Middle East Technical University
      of Turkey. Master's Thesis, Univ. of Texas, 1971. ED 060739.
           Teaching writing to students of English as a second language
      presents special problems to ESL teachers; therefore, the method
      described in this thesis is worthy of attention. It includes
      a survey of techniques for teaching English composition to
      foreign students along with particular methods for each kind of
      communication the student writes. Some lesson plans and a bib-
      liography are included.

820   El-Ezabi, Yehia Ali. "A Sector Analysis of Modern Writing Arabic
      with Implications for Teaching English to Arab Students." Diss.
      Columbia Univ., 1967.
           Some of the greatest difficulties met by Arab students
      studying English are caused by differences in word order be-
      tween English and Arabic; an analysis was therefore made of
      the syntax of written Arabic in order to identify such dif-
      ferences. The researcher found that there are both similar-
      ities and differences in both languages. Among the differ-
      ences is the lack of certain equivalent positions, the order
      of positions on certain levels, and differences in the kind
      of units that fill certain positions.

821 Friend, Jewell A. <u>Writing English as a Second Language</u>. New York: Scott Foresman, 1971.

A guide for non-native speakers of English that is designed to teach writing through organization and presentation of ideas. The book contains six units each one of which includes a discussion of sentence patterns and grammatical structures with examples and exercises. The text is very comprehensive in covering these structures and grammatical elements beginning with the types of sentences through the chronological process in writing.

822 Friend, Jewell A. "A Writing Program for Students of English as a Second Language, Based on a Critical Examination of Relevant Research and Theories in Linguistics, Psychology, and Composition." Diss. Southern Illinois Univ., 1970.

As a result of an examination of theories and research in linguistics, psychology, and English composition, Friend developed a writing program for students of English as a second language on the college level. The six units include lists of lexical items and syntactic structures; sample paragraphs; suggestions for teachers in using the sample paragraphs; exercises for discussion and writing; short anecdotes for discussion and writing; and an evaluation sheet for analyzing a composition.

823 Green, J. F. "Preparing an Advanced Composition Course." <u>English Language Teaching</u>, 21, 2 (1967), 141-150.

Since the foreign student in college needs skill in expository writing, this skill should be taught to him in his English classes. The importance of teaching the written language has too often been underestimated. Green explains compositions can be analyzed, and discusses the subject of classifying errors of grammar, style, and organization. He proposes using error analysis in preparing remedial exercises. This article stresses the need for designing a course in writing based on analysis. Courses will be more valid when this is done.

824 Hall, Eugene J. <u>Building English Sentences</u>. New York: Regents Publishing Co., 1974.

A series of ten workbooks designed to help students build sentences and understand those they read. Each book contains graded oral and written exercises and presents a different aspect of sentence production using one verb, using verbals, using adverbs and adverbial phrases, using auxiliary verbs, using three or more verbs, etc.

825 Heim, Alice Lederman. <u>The Use of English as a Second Language Techniques in Teaching Writing in Open Admission Colleges</u>. Diss. Univ. of Illinois, 1974.

A discussion of TESL materials and methodology, linguistic information, and helpful suggestions for teachers who wanted to help nonstandard dialect speakers to become more proficient in standard English dialect. A set of materials was developed for a college freshman composition course for students experiencing writing difficulties because they spoke a nonstandard dialect. Although the materials were not tested, indications were that TESL techniques could be useful.

826   Kaplan, Robert B. "Composition at the Advanced ESL Level: A Teacher's Guide to Connected Paragraph Construction for Advanced-Level Foreign Students." The English Record, 21, 4 (1971), 53-64.
        A proposed English language curriculum for foreign students in college who are at advanced levels but who need more training in writing style and semantics. Kaplan stresses expository writing, outlining, and the selection of topics. He advocates the use of a writing laboratory where students assist one another and collectively work within the classroom. An important article on teaching the advanced student.

827   Lawrence, Mary S. Writing as a Thinking Process. Ann Arbor, Michigan: Univ. of Michigan Press, 1972.
        A writing text for students of English as a second language who have intermediate and advanced ability, emphasizing writing as an activity that the student can learn so that he can write independently. Students are taught to transfer their knowledge of grammar and vocabulary to the writing process so that they can capitalize on their ability to think inductively and utilize the skills they learn.

828   Matthews, Patricia E., and Sabattat Tura. Practice, Plan and Write: Guided Composition for Students of English, 1, 2. New York: American Book Co., 1973.
        A text that provides English language patterns in a simple manner with supplementary examples and exercises that are practical. Students are "guided" toward composition by learning grammatical structures, basic sentence patterns, and paragraph development. Although highly controlled, the method can be helpful to advanced students who can insert their own words and phrases into the patterns they use to generate their own sentences.

829   Ng, Benton. "An Analysis of the Compositions of Bilingual Children in the Fifth Grade." Diss. Univ. of California, Berkeley, 1966.
        The experimenter analyzed compositions written by fifth grade bilingual children of Chinese ancestry in order to determine the relationship between the degree of their bilingual background with the structural patterns appearing in their written language. The Hoffman Bilingual Schedule was administered to 356 fifth grade children, to identify the upper and lower degree of bilingualism. Results included the following: subjects rated low manifested the most sensitivity to language conventions; the carry over of the unusual Chinese word order was frequent; members of the low group used more uncommon patterns and longer sentences, and showed a greater diversity in vocabulary.

830 Paulston, Christina Bratt. "Teaching Writing in the ESOL Classroom: Techniques of Controlled Composition." _TESOL Quarterly_, 6, 1 (1972), 33-59.

An article that comprehensively, and in detail, studies some of the fundamental ideas in teaching composition, referring to literature in the field, in order to offer methods of controlled composition to teachers in the ESOL classroom. Some techniques include the use of substitution tables; models with directions for rewriting and substitution; transformation; and modification conversions.

831 Povey, John F. "Cultural Self-Expression Through English in American Indian Schools." _Florida FL Reporter_, 7, 1 (1969), 131, 132, 164.

After discussing the differences between learning English as a foreign and a second language, the author discusses the "potential importance" of creative writing where English is taught to minority groups. He writes of an experimental project by Mrs. Terry Allen who, along with her husband, has written many books about the Navajo. Minority students who can write about themselves and their culture through the medium of the second language find that "English is no longer the exclusive property of the Anglos" and English ceases to be alien to them.

832 Rand, Earl. _Constructing Sentences_. New York: Holt, Rinehart, and Winston, 1969.

This is a book containing 112 tightly controlled transformational drills to be used to teach students to develop and understand sentences produced through co-ordination and subordination. The students will need a great deal of practice before they can learn to generate and read such sentences competently. The book, therefore, is recommended for intermediate and advanced foreign students of English and should be helpful to them once they get used to using the material.

833 Riemer, George. "Almost Everything I Know About Teaching Puerto Ricans I Owe To Vicks Vapo Rub." _The National Elementary Principal_, 50, 2 (1970), 73-77.

An amusing but instructive article in which the author describes his experiences in conducting a communication laboratory for primary grade children at St. Paul the Apostle School in New York City. He insists on using the i.t.a. since he believes that the i.t.a. is easier than the traditional alphabet and spelling for the Puerto Rican child "because every basic English sound has its own i.t.a. symbol." Using this method, teachers could see what children heard and determine which sounds and words needed special attention.

834 Robinson, Lois. _Guided Writing and Free Writing_. New York: Harper and Row, 1967.

A composition text for students of English as a second language designed to help them "correct informal English prose." Students are expected to focus on those grammatical elements

with which learners of English as a second language have difficulty. Each principle is introduced in a short grammatical
explanation followed by oral practices and then by written
exercises. Only advanced students will be able to handle the
material in the text which is quite comprehensive. The author
inserts items about American habits and history at certain
intervals in the exercises.

835　Sarantos, Robin L. Advanced Composition: English as a Second Language.
　　　Miami, Fla.: Dade County Public Schools, 1971. ED 063825.
　　　　　This course focuses on providing activities that will elimin-
　　　ate language interferences in the mother tongue in order to
　　　enable advanced students of English as a second language to
　　　write as skillfully as their North American classmates. Stu-
　　　dents sharpen their writing skills by preparing outlines of
　　　what they read and listen to, writing paragraphs developed in
　　　various ways, writing compositions, and developing a term
　　　paper.

836　Seward, Bernard Howard. "Teaching an Advanced Composition Lesson."
　　　TEFL, 6, 4 (1972), 1-2.
　　　　　The writer describes a procedure he recommends that will
　　　enable students in advanced composition classes to write better
　　　through class discussion, well developed topics, research, and
　　　student-teacher-developed guidelines. Using audio-visual aids
　　　or even field trips, the students select a topic of interest
　　　and pursue it after discussing it in class. A day-to-day
　　　process involves vocabulary use, delimited and specific topics,
　　　a rough draft, final draft, and follow-up lessons.

837　Smithies, Michael. "The Teaching of Writing." Bulletin of the
　　　English Language, 2, 1 (1972), 9-30.
　　　　　The author is critical of free composition, which often re-
　　　sults in a plethora of writing errors. He states that writing
　　　for EFL students must be guided and offers some specific re-
　　　commendations: controlled punctuation exercises; sentence
　　　completion drills; rearrangement of sentences into a logical
　　　order; and sentence substitution using a model. He also in-
　　　cludes material on letter writing and presents suggestions
　　　for marking the students' writing.

838　Wright, John T. "Writing Contextualized Drills." TEFL, 5, 2
　　　(1971), 4-5.
　　　　　Contrasts are made in this article between the substitution
　　　method of sentence formation and the"context-based drill."
　　　Since teachers instruct their students with the intention of
　　　having them use language for communication, students must know
　　　the contexts in which the language operates. The author re-
　　　commends that the students build a story that demonstrates the
　　　grammar problem. In this way they would get practice in using
　　　syntax and developing sentences that would do them more good
　　　than the usual kind of drill work.

Cross Reference

ADDENDUM

839   Allen, J. P. B., and Paul Van Buren, eds. Chomsky: Selected Readings.
London: Oxford University Press, 1971.
Although the book discusses transformational grammar, syntax,
phonology, and semantic theory, the ESL teacher will be particularly interested in Chomsky's discussions of Language Acquisition in Chapter 6. The material is not difficult and presents
Chomsky's theories on language acquisition in a clear and direct
manner. The final chapter on language teaching should also be
of interest to teachers.

840   Angelis, Paul Joseph. "Trends in the Application of Grading Procedures
in Texts of English as a Foreign Language." Diss. Georgetown Univ.,
1968.
An examination of the current status of grading as a language-
teaching principle and the trends in applying these procedures
to actual texts. Five different texts used in teaching English
as a foreign language were analyzed, each one of which represented a different method (transformational, audio-lingual, etc.).
The texts were compared on the basis of grouping and sequencing.
It was found that there was a close relationship between the
type of grading and the popularity of linguistic descriptions at
the time of publication. The researcher believed that improvement in the grading of EFL texts would be found in audio-lingual
and programmed methods.

841   Bellugi, Ursula. "Learning the Language," in Language Concepts and
Processes, Joseph A. DeVito, ed. Englewood Cliffs, New Jersey:
Prentice-Hall, 1973.
The author, along with Roger Brown and Colin Fraser, studied
the speech development of three children, two of whom were 27
months old; one was 18 months old. The first two were studied
for five years, the latter for only eighteen months. The article explains how the research was conducted and includes many
of the actual utterances of the children. The samples revealed
similar orders of development; it may be that "all languages
of the world share certain structural features" which "develop
as a result of relational abilities built into the human brain."

842   Decker, Donald M. "Drilling English Auxiliary Verbs in ESL Classes."
TESL Reporter, 13-15.
An article that offers some excellent examples of drills that
are recommended for use by ESL teachers in teaching auxiliary
verbs which are often difficult for a student to learn. Decker

discusses the frequently used auxiliary verbs "be" and "do" and eight modal auxiliaries. He covers auxiliaries used in answering questions affirmatively and negatively, in mixed questions, with pronouns, with common and proper nouns, and the auxiliary verb contractions. Suggestions are presented to make these drills challenging and yet enjoyable for the student.

843 Huffman, Maxine Fish. "The Preparation of a Science Reading Text and Program for Students of English as a Second or Foreign Language." Diss. Columbia Univ., 1966.
A controlled vocabulary and grammar were used to develop a beginning genetics reader for students of English as a foreign language, along with a programmed text. Both were used at the InterAmerican Institute of Science and Agriculture in Turrialba, Costa Rica, with students mostly at the intermediate stage of English. Students using the reader had access to review questions, and those using the program received answer sheets. Evaluation of the materials was based on the opinions of the students who were "liberal in their praise." The researcher believes that the materials are especially helpful in areas where people want scientific information.

844 Johnson, Francis C. "Macro and Micro Methodology in TESL." TESOL Quarterly, 6, 3 (1972), 237-242.
In discussing the two views of what happens in a classroom, one would consider as part of the macro view a plan operated through the students, teachers, materials, and the classroom in forming an efficient learning agency. The micro view considers the material, manner of presentation, and learner responses. Macro methodology is concerned with overall learning--the interaction of learner, teacher, and materials. Micro methodology is concerned with the way each element is presented. Both methods are important.

845 Kagan, Jerome, and Ernest Havemann. Psychology: An Introduction. New York: Harcourt Brace Javanovich, 1972, Chapter 5, 156-161.
The fifth chapter in this text includes elementary but important information about language learning that is current and described with clarity. The section on Acquiring the Rules discusses "telegraphic" and"holophrastic" speech, and the section on Theories of Language Learning discusses the learning process, including the theory "that the use of language and its rules may be a species-specific behavior." In the same chapter, the authors consider the development of word concepts.

846 Malmstrom, Jean, and Constance Weaver. Transgrammar: English Structure, Style, and Dialects. Glenview, Illinois: Scott, Foresman, 1973.
A book that offers the reader clear explanations and relevant related exercises about the grammatical theories and practical applications of the structure of American English.

The authors discuss transformational theory and the importance of knowing this approach to language study while they present definitions and relate structure to style. The book contains excerpts from different kinds of literature that the authors use to show directly how the literature is structured.

847   Malititz, Frances Willard von. <u>Living and Learning in Two Languages.</u> New York: McGraw-Hill, 1975.

    A resource book on bilingual-bicultural education that should be of interest to ESL teachers, administrators, and others who have an interest in bilingual education. The book lists bilingual regulations and policies in all of the states, and descriptions of the manner in which other countries deal with language minorities. Also included is a chapter on language teaching in Puerto Rico, one on bilingual-bicultural education for native American Indians, and a listing of bilingual-bicultural centers in the United States.

848   Martin, Charles B., and Curt M. Rulon. <u>The English Language Yesterday and Today.</u> Boston, Mass.: Allyn and Bacon, 1973.

    Chapter IV of this book, which discusses English Grammar Today; A Transformation-Generative Approach, offers the ESL teacher some excellent information on transformational grammar and syntax. The authors use specific examples and include relevant exercises. The chapter on English Phonology Today: A Feature Approach is also especially good since it so graphically presents an introduction to the sounds of American English. Other chapters on dialect and usage should also be of interest.

849   Norris, William E. <u>Teaching English as a Second Language: A Survey of 1969, a Projection for 1970.</u> Washington, D. C.: Center for Applied Linguistics. ED 044699.

    A survey of what was done in TESL as revealed in the literature, research, and various other sources in order to ascertain trends, significant subjects, and needs. It is designed to apprise language students of areas in which developments have been made and in which more attention should be focused. A reference list including 86 items is included.

850   Samuelson, William. <u>English as Second Language Phase Two: Let's Read.</u> Englewood Cliffs, New Jersey: Prentice-Hall, 1975.

    This edition of Samuelson's work, designed for a one-semester course, introduces reading skills for the college student learning English and intends to increase the student's comprehension skills so that he can read independently. In this text, the author introduces narration, exposition, and description, with much of the reading material focusing on American life.

851   Saville, Muriel R. "Curriculum for Teachers of English in Kindergarten for Navajo Children." Washington, D. C.: Center for Applied Linguistics, 1969. ED 030122.

    In September, 1969, a curriculum designed to teach Navajo as the primary language and English as a second language was in development. A guide listed sounds of English to be studied, basic sentence patterns, vocabulary, and available texts. The major basis of the language lessons was the use of contrastive analysis.

852 Thomas, Owen. _Transformational Grammar and the Teacher of English._ New York: Holt, Rinehart and Winston, 1965.
This text can be a helpful one to teachers of English as a second language who need some background in transformational grammar. Thomas, calling himself "a pedagogue and not a linguist," presents his material with clarity and covers the basic elements of transformational grammar. Each chapter has a summary or discussion and exercises.